Scenic Driving

CALIFORNIA

By
Stewart M. Green

FALCON®
HELENA, MONTANA

A FALCON GUIDE ®

Falcon® is continually expanding its list of recreational guidebooks. All books include detailed descriptions, accurate maps, and all the information necessary for enjoyable trips. You can order extra copies of this book and get information and prices for other Falcon® guidebooks by writing Falcon, P.O. Box 1718, Helena, MT 59624 or by calling toll-free 1-800-582-2665. Also, please ask for a free copy of our current catalog. To contact us via e-mail, visit our homepage at www.falconguide.com.

© 1993 by Falcon® Publishing, Inc.
Helena, Montana

5 6 7 8 9 0 MG 03 02 01 00 99 98

Printed in the United States of America

Front and back cover photos: by Kathleen Norris Cook.
All photos are by Stewart M. Green

Library of Congress Cataloging-in-Publication Data
Green, Stewart M.
    [California scenic drives]
    Scenic driving California / by Stewart M. Green.
       p. cm.
    Originally published: California scenic drives. c1993.
    Includes index.
    ISBN 1-56044-450-9
    1. California—Tours. 2. Automobile travel—California—
Guidebooks. I. Title.
F859.3.G74 1997
917.9404'53—dc21   97-5566
                                                 CIP

 Text pages printed on recycled paper.

CAUTION

Outdoor recreational activities are by their very nature potentially hazardous. All participants in such activities must assume the responsibility for their own actions and safety. The information contained in this guidebook cannot replace sound judgment and good decision–making skills, which help reduce risk exposure, nor does the scope of this book allow for disclosure of all the potential hazards and risks involved in such activities.

Learn as much as possible about the outdoor recreational activities you participate in, prepare for the unexpected, and be cautious. The reward will be a safer and more enjoyable experience.

ACKNOWLEDGMENTS

Scenic Driving California was, beyond a doubt, a most excellent adventure. My goal was to find, travel, photograph, and write about California's most beautiful highways. The only downside was having to limit the book, in the end, to only twenty-four drives. I started with a list of forty-five and slowly pared it down until I found the ones I liked the best. The others will have to wait for a future volume.

My thanks to Falcon Press and publisher Bill Schneider, senior editor Chris Cauble, and new guidebook editor Randall Green for publishing this book and the opportunity to contribute to their excellent book list. I am grateful to the numerous state and federal employees in California who generously dispensed information, answered questions, and reviewed portions of the manuscript for accuracy, including Jim Warner with Kings Canyon National Park, Ginger Burley of Yosemite National Park, Arthur C. Webster III at Joshua Tree National Park, Elizabeth Knight of Lassen Volcanic National Park, Chris Roundtree with Lava Beds National Monument, Mark C. Jorgenssen at Anza-Borrego Desert State Park, and Donn Headley of Angeles National Forest. Thanks also to Mark Green of Sonoma, California, and Allstate Insurance who quickly processed my claim after a midnight burglary at a national forest campground outside Lake Tahoe. A special thanks to Nancy, Ian, and Brett Spencer-Green. They shared the starlight, the desert heat, the fog-shrouded forests, as well as traffic jams, a Sunday drive around Fresno in search of a new tire, and the rest of the nonsense found during eight weeks on the road.

The Bixby Bridge spans a precipitous gorge between rugged headlands along the Big Sur Coast.

CONTENTS

The Scenic Drives

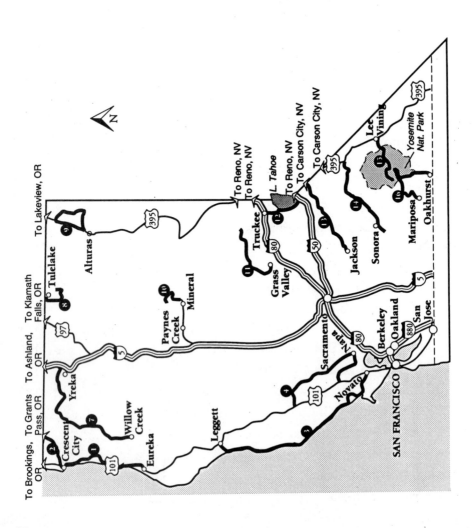

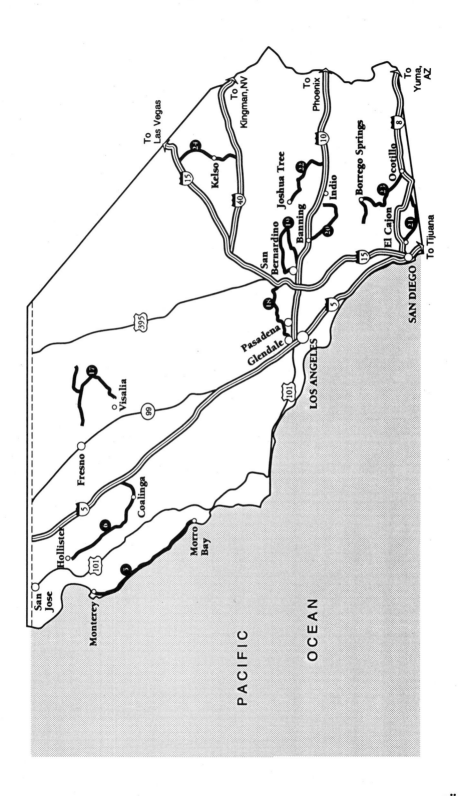

Half Dome lies beyond Olmsted Point on the Tioga Pass Road.

INTRODUCTION

California stretches along the edge of North America, perched on the watery rim of the vast Pacific Ocean. California, in a sense, is an island surrounded by both water and desert, an insular land shaped by the earth's most basic forces and populated by an astonishing diversity of plants, animals, and people. Its primeval landscape, suffused with golden light, dictates, defines, and measures us against its ancient rhythms.

California—the promised land, the land at the end of the rainbow. That's what early American settlers thought after crossing the bleak continent, wading its snows and enduring its heat, and finally reaching this fertile country with its plentiful rain, pleasant climate, and abundant resources. As long as the promised "lands beyond sundown" lay open to exploration and exploitation, Americans walked across the hard miles to this new country and the new hope it offered. It's still like that almost 150 years after the peak of the famed California Trail. People still find the most populous of the states an irresistible golden magnet. Californians, as one wag put it, are people born somewhere else and then came to their senses.

California is a land of startling variety. Its landscape offers every geographic shape and form and every climate. Precipitous peaks, chiseled by glaciers, lift snowcapped summits into the matchless turquoise sky. Abrupt desert mountains, baked in a crucible of brilliant sunlight, form obtuse angles with creosote-studded bajadas. Vegetable fields, fruit orchards, and vineyards weave a green tapestry across broad valleys. Snow, hundreds of inches deep, blankets California's highest ranges; sere desert basins lie almost untouched by rain; and dense fog shrouds the redwood-lined coast.

The state, with 158,693 square miles, is roughly divided into four main geographic provinces—the Coast Ranges, the Central Valley, the Sierra Nevada and Cascade Mountains, and the Basin and Range desert regions. Climate and topography lend each area a unique flora and fauna.

The Coast Ranges can be further divided into separate ranges. The Klamath Mountains spread across rough, forested country up to 8,000 feet high in northeastern California. The Coast Ranges themselves stretch from near Crescent City to San Luis Obispo, a maze of mountains that includes the famed redwood forests, the Napa wine country, and the Santa Cruz, Diablo, and Santa Lucia ranges above the Big Sur Coast. These ranges all lie along the heralded San Andreas Rift, an active fault zone that stretches some 650 miles from the Mexican border to Cape Mendocino. The Transverse Ranges, some of the only east-west trending mountain ranges in the United States, lie north of the Los Angeles Basin, while the Peninsular Ranges march southward from the basin to the border with Baja California.

The Central Valley is drained by the Sacramento and San Joaquin rivers and forms a broad, level plain for 500 miles from Bakersfield to Redding. This area was once rich in wildlife and wetlands but is now America's garden, growing almost every type of crop. Vast fields and orchards, watered by melting snow in the mountains, create a patchwork quilt broken only by arrow-straight roads, silver silos, and country towns.

The Sierra Nevada and Cascade Mountains form a twisting spine down eastern California. The Cascades, beginning with Lassen Peak and extending into Oregon and Washington, are punctuated by symmetrical, volcanic peaks. Mount Shasta with its snowy summit lifting to 14,162 feet is itself a sleeping giant. This dormant volcano could awaken any day and spread fiery destruction across its flanks. The Sierra Nevada, "snowy range" in Spanish, raise a 400-mile-long towering wall of lofty peaks excavated by millions of years of glaciation. The range high point is 14,494-foot Mount Whitney, which is the nation's highest point outside Alaska. Nearby lies Death Valley, North America's lowest point at 282 feet below sea level. The Sierra also houses some of California's stunning natural wonders—granite-walled Yosemite Valley, the massive sequoia trees at Sequoia National Park, the precipitous gorge at Kings Canyon National Park, and shimmering Lake Tahoe.

The Basin and Range province isolates California from the rest of the nation. It's northern section is characterized by thick volcanic plateaus formed when lava, measured in cubic miles, spread across the land's surface. Two of North America's great deserts—the Sonoran Desert and the Mojave Desert—meet and mingle in southern California. Rough mountain ranges separated by wide basins scatter across this arid region of scanty rainfall and fierce temperature ranges.

California is an amazing place for the naturalist. It's topographic diversity shelters a startling variety of plants and animals in almost every type of ecosystem found on earth, from off-shore canyons and tide pools to mixed conifer forests and delicate alpine tundra. The state harbors some 5,200 plant species, with over thirty percent endemic to California, meaning they live here and here alone. The state is called the California Floristic Province by ecologists. It is the home for the bristlecone pine, the world's oldest living thing, the sequoia, the world's largest living thing, and the coast redwood, the world's tallest living thing. Sixteen oak species live here, with eleven exclusive to California. Pine trees are represented by twenty-one distinct species, with eight endemic to the state.

The state's wildlife is equally diverse. But wholesale habitat destruction caused by its ever-growing population and the accompanying development threatens California's wildlife and wildlands. California's known vertebrate species total 748. Almost forty percent of its freshwater fish, thirty percent of its amphibians, and ten percent of its mammals are endemic. Animals include the ubiquitous black bear, fleet-footed pronghorn antelope, bighorn sheep, several rattlesnake species, California gray whale, sea otter, desert tortoise, and mountain lion. The grizzly bear, featured on the state flag, and the jaguar are both extinct here. More than 550 bird species have been identified in California. Vast flocks of migratory birds pass through on the

A wall of ferns adorns lush Fern Canyon in Prairie Creek Redwoods State Park along U.S. 101, the Redwood Highway.

Pacific Flyway; the majestic, endangered California condor, now survives only because of a successful captive breeding program.

California presents a spectacular assortment of natural wonders, scenic attractions, historic points of interest, and recreational opportunities. Its numerous national park lands include: Yosemite, Sequoia, Kings Canyon, Lassen Volcanic, Death Valley, Joshua Tree, and Redwood national parks; Muir Woods national monument; Point Reyes National Seashore; and Golden Gate National Recreation Area. Nineteen national forests scatter across the state, attracting recreationists to 2,500 lakes, more than 13,000 miles of trails, and 1,800 miles of Wild and Scenic Rivers. The Pacific Crest

National Recreation Trail, beginning on the Mexican border, wends its way north to Oregon across numerous mountain ranges. The bucolic Sonoma and Napa valleys invite travelers to sample wines from one of the world's premier grape-growing regions. The state's 1,264-mile-long Pacific coastline offers sweeping sand beaches and rocky, windswept headlands. The East Mojave National Scenic Area, administered by the Bureau of Land Management, is a stunning 1.5-million-acre desert marvel.

Scenic Driving California explores and discovers the best of California. The twenty-four drives, following more than 2,000 miles of highway and back road, showcase the wonder and mystery of California to both traveler and resident alike. The drives sample the state's beauty spots, scenic wonders, and hidden jewels. They thread across the state, introducing highway travelers to the diversity that is California. Along the drives, highway recreationists find: secluded glens, soaring redwoods, plunging waterfalls, ghost towns, abandoned gold mines, lava flows, damp caves, active volcanic areas, windswept shores battered by Pacific breakers, shimmering alpine lakes, wagon ruts from pioneer trails, and elegant stands of Joshua trees. The scenic drives also stray far from the urban path into the still-wild heart of California.

These twenty-four drives are only the beginning of California's scenic drives. These are admittedly some of the Golden State's best and most beautiful highways, but others lie beyond, inviting travelers to discover their wonders with new appreciation and understanding. It is simply impossible to detail all the scenic drives found in California. After traveling these gems, travelers will want to explore Ebbetts Pass over the Sierras, the fabulous back roads over the Coast Ranges both north and south of San Francisco, the Trinity Heritage Scenic Byway west of Redding, the Sierra Vista Scenic Byway in Sequoia National Forest, the Sunrise Scenic Byway east of San Diego, the Bureau of Land Management's Back Country Byway's lacing the East Mojave National Scenic Area, the various state highways crossing Death Valley National Park, and U.S. 395 along the Sierra Nevada's abrupt eastern escarpment.

Be prepared for every emergency and inclement weather while traveling California's scenic drives. Many of the roads twist and curve across steep mountainsides. Maintain a safe speed, use pullouts to allow other traffic to pass, stay in your own lane, and watch for blind corners. Weather can quickly change and drastically alter driving conditions. Drive carefully on rain-soaked roads, and, in winter, use proper snow tires and carry chains, extra clothes, and a shovel. Dense fog along the coastal drives often creates visibility problems. Slow down and keep alert. Watch for heavy traffic in urban areas and allow ample time to travel through cities. Most of the drives feature frequent viewpoints and scenic pull-offs for sight-seeing. It's a good idea to top off the gas tank before embarking on any of these trips. Be prepared for hot weather in the state's desert areas. Be sure your car is in proper working order and carry plenty of water.

Travelers and campers are, unfortunately, potential crime victims. Stow

A Swainson's hawk perches on a fence post along the Rim of the World Drive.

Kelp, pepples, and sand form a still life along the Sonoma Coast and California 1.

all valuables out of sight in a parked car. Better yet, take them with you when leaving a vehicle. Campers should be wary of auto break-ins at popular overnight destinations. Keep all valuables, including money, cameras, and video equipment with you in your tent at night. Bears are a serious problem at many campgrounds. Keep all food stowed and covered in your car. Bears recognize ice chests as food sources and will break windows to get at them.

The scenic drives cross both public and private land. Respect private property rights by not trespassing. Remember federal laws protect both archeological and historic sites, including Indian ruins and artifacts, petrified bone and fossils, and historic structures. Camp only in designated sites to minimize impact, put out all campfires, and carry your trash out.

California—there's magic and beauty in that word. Out there is the impermanent land, always changing yet always vigorous and alive. Drive its scenic roads and you will find a land of awesome proportions, a land of dreams. Uncover its human history, find its animals and birds, rejoice in its forests. The open road is out there, unfolding across soaring mountain ranges, threading through craggy canyons, and traversing wide open spaces. The road swoops up to meet the sky and lifts our spirits. Every road we travel is a promise, a ribbon of asphalt that leads somewhere, anywhere. On this road we follow, we discover, explore, and share the mystery.

MAP LEGEND

Scenic Drive		Interstate	
Interstate		U.S. Highway	
Other Roads		State Highway	(375)
Hiking Trail		Forest Road	4296
River or Stream		Pass or Saddle	) (
Waterfalls		Mountains	
Point of Interest	■	Hills	
Tunnel		State Boundary	
Picnic Area		Forest Service Land	
Campground	▲	State and National Parks, Indian Reservations	
Lake or Ocean			
Dry Lake			

Redwoods and ferns in Del Norte Coast Redwoods State Park along U.S. 101, the Redwood Highway.

General description: This seventy-eight-mile section of U.S. Highway 101 parallels the rugged Pacific coast, passing redwood groves and a rugged wave-carved shoreline of beaches, cliffs, and sea stacks.

Special attractions: Redwood National Park, Del Norte Coast Redwoods State Park, Prairie Creek Redwoods State Park, Humboldt Lagoons State Park, Patrick's Point State Park, Trinidad State Beach, Little River Beach, Humboldt Bay National Wildlife Refuge, Eureka, Fort Humboldt State Historic Park, Crescent City, wildlife, hiking, camping, backpacking, fishing, picnicking, world's tallest tree, redwood forests.

Location: Northwestern California. The drive runs along the coast from Eureka to Crescent City, twenty miles south of the Oregon border.

Drive route name and number: U.S. 101, Redwood Highway.

Travel season: Year-round. Fog often envelopes the road in summer, while heavy winter rains make hazardous driving conditions.

Camping: Elk Prairie Campground in Prairie Creek Redwoods State Park offers seventy-five sites and water, tables, and showers. The park also has Gold Bluff Beach, a twenty-seven site primitive campground on the beach. Jedediah Smith Redwoods State Park, just east of Crescent City, has 107 sites. There are 123 campsites at Patrick's Point State Park and 145 sites at Del Norte Coast Redwoods State Park's Mill Creek Campground. There are small primitive campgrounds in Redwoods National Park. Ask at the visitor centers for information. Several campgrounds scatter through Six Rivers National Forest, most on the three-forked Smith River, as well as numerous private RV campgrounds. Reservations through MISTIX at (800) 444-PARK are advised, particularly in summer.

Services: All services are found in Eureka, Arcata, McKinleyville, Trinidad, and Crescent City. Limited services are in other towns along the road including Orick and Klamath.

Nearby attractions: Smith River Scenic Byway, Jedediah Smith Redwoods State Park, Six Rivers National Forest, Oregon coast, Klamath River scenic drive, King Range National Conservation Area, Humboldt Redwoods State Park, Avenue of the Giants, Grizzly Creek Redwoods State Park.

For more information: Redwood National Park, 1111 Second St., Crescent City 95531, (707) 464-6101. Del Norte Coast Redwoods State Park, 4241 Kings Valley, Crescent City 95531, (707) 464-9533. Prairie Creek Redwoods State Park, Orick, CA 95555, (707) 464-9533. Eureka Chamber of Commerce, 2112 Broadway, Eureka, CA 95501, (707) 442-3738. Crescent City-Del Norte County Chamber of Commerce, 1001 Front St., Crescent City, CA 95531, (707) 464-3174.

The drive: The Redwood Empire stretches almost 500 miles from south of Monterey to a small pocket in southwestern Oregon along California's coastal ranges. This immense span of land, wreathed in summer fog and pounded by winter storms, is home to *Sequoia sempervirens*, the coast redwood. The Redwood Highway, U.S. 101, traverses seventy-eight miles of the empire's best redwood country between Eureka and Crescent City in northwestern California. This long strip of land is northern California's frontier with the ocean and boasts an almost unsurpassed natural beauty with craggy headlands jutting boldly into frothy surf, majestic stands of pristine redwood trees, broad bays and estuaries that teem with wildlife, and glistening sweeps of sand that form the tenuous boundary between land and sea. The land along the drive is truly unique, one of California's greatest and most memorable scenic attractions.

California's north coast is a land of heavy rain. As much as 100 inches falls on parts of the Redwood Coast, making lush forests and thick meadowlands. Most of the rain falls in winter when Pacific storms lash against the coastal mountains. Temperatures are also cool. January's average high in both Eureka and Crescent City is fifty-three degrees. Summer hardly warms up, with average July temperatures in Eureka only a paltry sixty degrees; and temperatures in Crescent City climb to a sixty-nine degree average. Eureka is the usual winner of the coolest city year-round in the continental United States, with little variation between summer and winter. Expect thick fog in summer along the coast and in the redwood forests. Sometimes it burns off by mid-day, but the mist usually hangs around all day. Biologists estimate as much as twelve percent of the moisture redwoods need is derived from the moist summer fogs. A good raincoat and hat are needed for both hikers and beachcombers.

The drive begins in Eureka, the largest city on California's northern coast. Eureka is now a charming, historic town that started as a prosperous seaport for the Trinity mining boom to the east. San Francisco land speculators and merchants saw beckoning opportunity on the north coast in 1850, and several different companies raced northward to grab land and potential profits. Irishman James Ryan's group claimed the east shore of Humboldt Bay, a long inland bay named for famed naturalist Baron Alexander von Humboldt, and established a new town dubbed Eureka. Eureka is a Greek phrase meaning "I have found it!" Within three years, Eureka housed a population of 3,000. After the mining boom busted, the port became a major logging center. The harvested wood was, of course, redwood. By 1855, nine mills operated around Humboldt Bay.

The city today has a population of 27,000 and offers many restored houses, including the elegant Gothic Carson Mansion, an Old Town area, and numerous sights and services. Eureka also has several fine museums such as the Humboldt Bay Maritime Museum and the Clarke Museum with its excellent collection of North American Indian basketry. Fort Humboldt State Historic Park preserves the site of an 1850s military garrison that established order between settlers and Indians. Captain Ulysses S. Grant, later Civil War

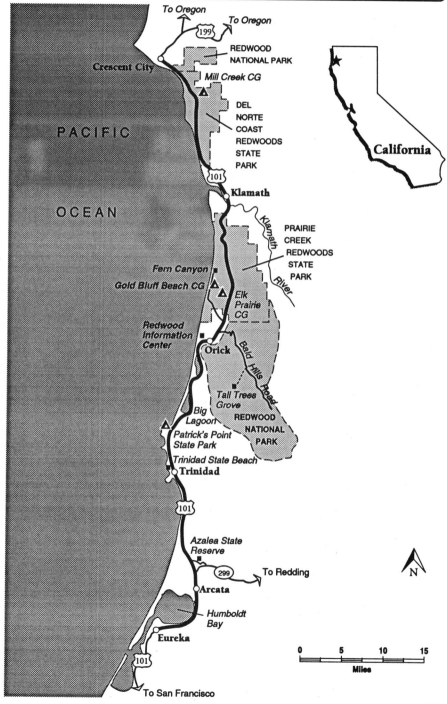

hero and President, was stationed here before being drummed out of the service for drunkenness in 1854. On leaving Eureka, Grant prophesied to his friend Post Surgeon Jonathon Clark, "My day will come, they will hear from me yet." Eureka's Old Town is worth a stroll. This "skid row" collection of brothels, sailor's taverns, card houses, and flophouses have been renovated into a trendy area with art galleries, cafes, and shops. Skid row itself is a North Coast logging expression. Logs were laid crossways on steep slopes or marshes and logs pulled by oxen teams were skidded along the improvised road to railheads and mills.

The scenic drive, following four-lane U.S. Highway 101, leaves Eureka and swings around broad Humboldt Bay. The bay is California's second largest and is enclosed on the west by long sand spits with a narrow, treacherous channel that has grounded many ships. The bay was first discovered by Russian-American Fur Company traders in 1806. The bay's east part, called Arcata Bay, is part of Humboldt Bay National Wildlife Refuge. This fertile wetland of tidal flats and marsh is a resting stopover for birds on the Pacific Flyway. The bay supports more than 250 bird species and seventy-five fish species. Arcata lies eight miles north of Eureka on the Arcata Bottoms floodplain. The town, second largest in Humboldt County, is home to Humboldt State University and the Humboldt Crabs baseball team. Arcata offers a pleasant downtown plaza, 20-acre Redwood Park, and the nearby 213-acre Lanphere-Christensen Dunes Preserve on the Samoa Peninsula. Here, dune plant communities from both the south and north coasts overlap in a unique transition zone.

From Arcata the highway runs north across low farmland and through McKinleyville, a small town renamed in 1901 for assassinated President William McKinley. The area's industry includes bulb and tree farms, cheese, dairies, and truck farming. The thirty-acre Azalea State Reserve lies east of the road on the Mad River. The site is spectacular in May when the aromatic pink western azaleas bloom. Beyond McKinleyville, the highway hugs the coast, passing Clam Beach County Park and Little River State Beach. The state beach offers picnicking, surf fishing, and clamming; the county park has a campground.

Trinidad sits a few miles north at Trinidad Head, a large promontory that juts into the ocean. This headland was discovered and christened Trinidad by Spanish explorer Don Bruno Hecata on June 11, 1775. A large pine cross erected on the site marked the territory as a Spanish possession. The wooden cross was replaced by a stone one in 1913. Trinidad, like Eureka, grew out of the mining boom in the nearby mountains, serving as a supply and whaling port and later as a shipping center for lumber bound for world markets. Trinidad State Beach, just north of town, offers good beachcombing for driftwood and moonstones.

Patrick's Point State Park is another headland north of Trinidad. The 630-acre park is covered with grassy meadows sprinkled by spring wildflowers and a fringe of forest that includes Sitka spruce, Port Orford cedar, red alder, and hemlock. Sand beaches and abrupt cliffs and promontories chiseled by

Roosevelt elk, an endangered species, roam the forests and meadows at Prairie Creek Redwoods State Park along U.S. 101, the Redwood Highway.

the relentless surf compose the park's landscape. The area's rich game, vegetation, and sea life attracted the Yurok Indians who lived here seasonally. They ate sea lions as well as plentiful mussels, leaving huge shell middens at their campsites. Three park campgrounds—Agate Beach, Abalone, and Penn Creek—offer 123 sites with water, restrooms, and showers. Several good hiking trails lace the promontory. Two-mile Rim Trail, following an old Indian path from Agate Beach to Palmer's Point, is one of the best. The park is also one of the best whale-watching spots on the Redwood Coast. The gray whales follow a 12,000-mile, eight-month migration from Arctic feeding grounds to winter calving lagoons off Baja California. From November to January and from March through May are the best times for whale watching. Binoculars are helpful in spotting the whales.

Past Patrick's Point, the highway curves around several huge inland lagoons—Big, Stone, and Freshwater lagoons. These comprise Humboldt Lagoons State Park, a large area of both salt and freshwater marshes and dense woods that shelter numerous migrating birds on the Pacific Flyway such as ducks, herons, egrets, and pelicans. Long sand spits front the ocean on the west, and densely forested mountains rise steeply over the wetlands.

The park offers boating, fishing for trout, salmon, and steelhead, and primitive camping.

At the north end of Freshwater Lagoon, the highway bends inland along Redwood Creek. Here among the sand dunes sits the Redwood Information Center. It is the southern gateway to Redwood National Park, a unique 106,000-acre national park jointly managed by the National Park Service and California State Parks. The park scatters along the coast from here to Crescent City like a string of pearls. Eastward stretches the Redwood Creek section with its tall trees, and northward lies Prairie Creek Redwoods State Park, Del Norte Coast Redwoods State Park, and Jedediah Smith Redwoods State Park. Logging over the last century decimated eighty-five percent of California's coastal old-growth redwoods, leaving huge stumps where massive giants once stood. Redwood National Park, incorporating the three state parks, preserves some of the best forest left, including the world's tallest living thing. The park was declared a World Heritage Site for its unique forests in 1982. Redwood Information Center is a good place to stop for information on camping and hiking, and to view exhibits detailing the park's unusual natural history, coastline, and history.

Past the center, the road enters Orick. This small town nestles in a broad pastoral valley flanked by redwood-studded mountains. Dairy farms and small ranches are scattered along the highway. The Yurok Indians inhabited the area seasonally, and the town's name is derived from their word "Ore'q" meaning "mouth of the river." The town offers all services to travelers including gas, lodging, restaurants, and RV parks.

The Bald Hills Road takes off east from the highway just north of Orick. This narrow road, with grades as steep as fifteen percent, twists into the Bald Hills above Redwood Creek. Just up the road is the one-mile Lady Bird Johnson Grove self-guided nature trail. Ten miles up the road, the Tall Trees Trail, which is accessible from the road by shuttle bus, drops steeply down to Redwood Creek and the world's tallest tree. This spire-like redwood towers 367.8 feet above its massive base. It was discovered by National Geographic naturalist Paul Zahl in 1964. The tree, along with many other 300-footers, grows on a moist gravel bench above a Redwood Creek meander. The discovery of the tree on privately owned timberland helped ensure the establishment of the national park in 1968. Prior to that, environmental organizations including the Sierra Club and Save-the-Redwoods League had urged the protection of California's remaining big trees. But much of the land that was purchased for the park was already clear-cut and in dire need of rehabilitation.

The drive runs north up Prairie Creek from Orick and quickly reaches Prairie Creek Redwoods State Park, a spectacular 14,000-acre sanctuary of pristine redwood forests. Eight miles of U.S. 101 wend through the park, past silent groves that reach skyward. A four-lane, twelve-mile-long bypass skirts the east boundary of the park for those in a hurry. The park features several dirt side roads that make fabulous excursions. Cal Barrel Road runs three miles through mature redwood forest. The Coastal Drive turns west at the north end of the park and runs down through redwoods to an unimpeded view of Gold Bluff Beach and the Pacific Ocean, before turning north to Highway 101 on the south side of the Klamath River. The Davison Road is a favorite; it begins three miles south of the park boundary and uncoils four miles through second-growth forest to Gold Bluff Beach. It then runs north below the bluff alongside the crashing surf for another four miles to the secluded trailhead for Fern Canyon.

Fern Canyon is simply one of the most beautiful spots imaginable. A short trail leaves the parking lot, crisscrosses Home Creek, and enters Fern Canyon, a fifty-foot deep gorge etched into soft sandstone. Above the pebbled canyon floor, five-finger ferns and other species blanket the walls with a verdant, hanging garden. Quiet reigns in this green kingdom, broken only by occasional bird songs, wind rippling the lofty treetops, and the distant roar of waves breaking on the strand. Redwoods, Sitka spruce, and Douglas fir loom over the canyon, blocking sunlight on rare clear days. An excellent twenty-five-site campground sits on the dunes a couple miles south of Fern Canyon.

The park's other campground, Elk Prairie, offers seventy-five sites and sits among giant redwoods just off U.S. 101 six miles north of Orick. Nearby is the park's "prairie," a large open meadow. Elk Prairie and Gold Bluffs Beach are home to the park's two herds of endangered Roosevelt elk. These elk are members of the deer family and are larger than their Rocky Mountain cousins. An adult Roosevelt bull weighs 1,000 pounds and boasts a spectacular rack of antlers 3 feet high. Despite their docile appearance, remember these are wild animals and are particularly aggressive during the fall rut. A long pull-off lane on the drive allows visitors to safely park off the highway and view the grazing elk. Other animals found in the redwood forest include black bear, rabbit, squirrel, mountain lion, bobcat, coyote, and fox. More than 250 species of birds have been identified in the park's wide variety of habitats. Notable birds are the infamous spotted owl and marbled murrelet, both dependent on old-growth forests.

More than seventy-five miles of hiking trails thread the park, making it a walker's paradise. Stop along the drive in either Prairie Creek or Del Norte Coast state parks and hike into the redwood forest. It's an unforgettable experience. Standing there among the silent trees is to stand in the forest primeval. The redwoods soar overhead, caring nothing for their great antiquity and offering a serene aloofness to our own scattered lives. The oldest of the trees have witnessed as many as fifty human generations that have come and gone. The great woods were slender saplings at the time of Christ's birth and forest giants when Columbus arrived on North American shores. No wonder that author John Steinbeck called redwoods "ambassadors from another time." These impressive trees, growing on California's coastal ranges within thirty miles of the Pacific shore, tower over 350 feet, weigh more than 2 million pounds, live as long as 2,000 years, and supply enough wood to build several houses. Yet these gentle forest titans grow from seeds hardly larger than a pinhead; the seeds come from a cone that is smaller

Fog shrouds tall redwood trees in Del Norte Coast Redwoods State Park along U.S. 101, the Redwood Highway.

than most western evergreens produce, less than an inch long.

The coast redwood once spread over much of the Northern Hemisphere, growing in diverse locales including Alaska, Siberia, Greenland, Europe, and North Dakota. Subsequent changes in climate and topography reduced those great redwood forests to their present small range on California's foggy coast. Their closest relatives are the giant sequoia atop the crest of the Sierra Nevada and the rare dawn redwood found only in a secluded Chinese valley and a transplanted stand in Jedediah Smith Redwoods State Park.

The highway drops down from Prairie Creek and crosses the mouth of the 263-mile-long Klamath River, the state's second largest river. The Klamath is famed for its huge runs of Chinook salmon and steelhead that migrate upriver in autumn to spawn and die. The town of Klamath, built on the river's north shore, was erased on the terrifying night of December 22, 1964, when the river rose to unprecedented levels after weeks of heavy rain and snow saturated the coastal ranges. Klamath is now a popular stop for fishermen and offers all services; be sure and sample its famous smoked salmon jerky. Nearby sits the Trees of Mystery, a hokey tourist attraction made famous by Ripley's *Believe It Or Not!*. Farther north lies Requa, a small town that was once a thriving mining and lumber camp and earlier a Yurok Indian village. A county road runs west from the scenic drive through Requa to Klamath Overlook with a great view of the mighty river emptying into the ocean. The Coastal Trail travels north along the coast from here to Crescent City.

The highway continues north from Klamath and after a few more miles reemerges on the coast at False Klamath Cove. It then enters 6,400-acre Del Norte Coast Redwoods State Park, another division of Redwood National Park. This road section is lined with towering redwoods, butting against the asphalt like wooden pillars. An excellent hike travels two miles along Damnation Creek Trail, an old Yurok Indian trail, from the highway to the seashore, losing 1,000 feet along the way. Splendid old redwoods loom over the path, their spire-like tops hidden by swirling mist. Lush undergrowth of sword ferns and rhododendrons carpet the forest floor. The park's 145-site campground, in second-growth redwood forest logged in the 1920s, sits east of the drive on Mill Creek.

At the north end of the state park, U.S. 101 curves northwest and enters Crescent City, another old seaport founded in 1853. The town was almost destroyed by a huge tidal wave or tsunami from a 1964 Alaska earthquake. Jedediah Smith Redwoods State Park, another gorgeous part of Redwoods National Park, lies just east of town on U.S. 199. The Smith River scenic drive continues up route 199 to the Oregon border. U.S. 101 runs north nineteen miles from Crescent City past Lake Earl State Park and Easter lily fields to Pelican State Beach and the Oregon border.

2 U.S. 199
Smith River Scenic Drive

General description: This thirty-three-mile scenic drive traverses the spectacular Smith River Canyon as it winds eastward from Crescent City on the Pacific coast to the Oregon border.

Special attractions: Jedediah Smith Redwoods State Park, Redwood National Park, Six Rivers National Forest, redwood forests, salmon and steelhead fishing, hiking, camping, swimming, rafting, picnicking, scenic views, diverse floral community.

Location: Extreme northwestern California. The drive begins at the junction of U.S. 101 and U.S. 199 just north of Crescent City and travels up 199 to the Collier Tunnel just south of the Oregon border. U.S. 199 continues north to Grants Pass, Oregon.

Drive route number: U.S. Highway 199.

Travel season: Year-round. Heavy rain and possible snow in the higher road elevations can make hazardous driving conditions.

Camping: Three Six Rivers National Forest campgrounds—nineteen-site Grassy Flat, forty-two-site Panther Flat, and seventeen-site Patrick Creek—scatter along the drive. Jedediah Smith State Park offers 108 campsites with tables, restrooms, and nearby showers.

Services: All services are found at Crescent City including gas, food, lodging, restaurants, and RV parks. Limited services are at Gasquet on the drive.

Nearby attractions: Redwood National Park, Pacific coast, Siskiyou Wilderness Area, Oregon Caves National Monument, Del Norte Coast Redwoods State Park, Battery Point Lighthouse Museum and Del Norte County Historical Society Museum (Crescent City), Prairie Creek Redwoods State Park, Klamath River scenic drive.

For more information: Jedediah Smith Redwoods State Park, 4241 Kings Valley Road, Crescent City, CA 95531, (707) 464-9533. Six Rivers National Forest, 507 F Street, Eureka, CA 95501, (707) 442-1721. Crescent City-Del Norte County Chamber of Commerce, 1001 Front Street, Crescent City, CA (707) 464-3174.

The drive: There's magic in rivers. Sit beside a river and it unlocks some of the land's deepest secrets. Listen to its flow, watch its waters glisten in the sunlight, hear the stories it tells of far-off winter snows, cascading waterfalls, tumbling rapids, and water-worn cobbles. The Smith River, tinted emerald by its riverbed rocks, unravels a tale in its tumbling currents of ancient, untrammeled wildness, of tall trees standing quietly like sentinels along its banks in cathedral groves, of the furtive comings and goings of Indians and the mountain man for which it was named. The Smith River scenic drive follows U.S. 199 as it weaves along the river for thirty-three miles through what is simply some of the best and most beautiful country in all of California. This is the kind of place that takes hold of you and won't let go. It imprints itself on your memory and becomes a resting place in hectic times.

The three-forked Smith River arises high atop the Siskiyou Mountains and boasts the distinction of being California's last undammed river system with 315 miles of wild and scenic waterway. The coastal mountains dissected by the river basin are not particularly rocky and high, none reach over 7,000 feet, but they form a rugged tangle of forested ridges that march from the Siskiyou crest almost to the river's floodplain on the Pacific coast. The drive follows the Middle Fork of the Smith River and traverses the Smith River National Recreation Area. The 305,337-acre area is managed by the U.S. Forest Service to protect the region's unique scenery, pristine rivers and creeks, wildlife, fisheries, rich ecological diversity, and historical sites.

Summer weather is generally ideal along the Smith River, although fog and cool temperatures are often found along the coast. Expect highs between seventy and eighty-five degrees, with rising temperatures as you drive inland. Summer rain is generally infrequent and short-lived. Winters are cool and rainy, with daily high temperatures in the forties and fifties. It can be colder with occasional snow in the higher elevations at the Collins Tunnel. Be prepared for heavy rain from October through April. The average annual rainfall at Gasquet is 94 inches, and the coastal area here receives as much as 120 inches.

The drive is a National Forest Scenic Byway that begins just north of Crescent City where U.S. 101 intersects U.S. 199. Turn east on 199. Crescent

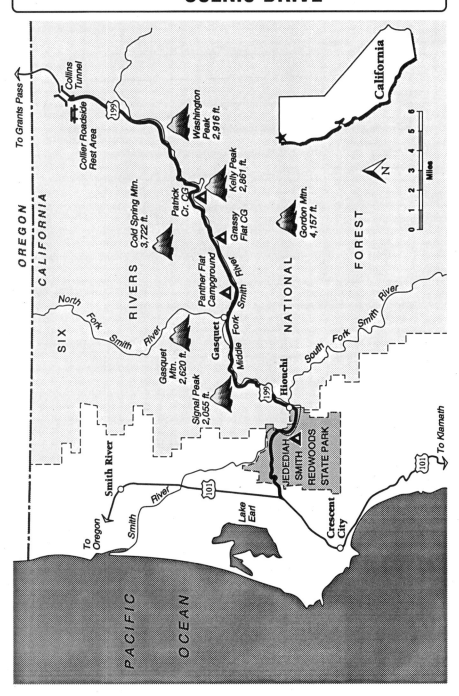

The Smith River plunges through a rocky canyon below the Smith River scenic drive.

City, famed for its Easter lily farms, was laid out in 1852 along a crescent-shaped harbor. The town offers a rough, weather-worn look with its cool, foggy days and sea breezes. A tsunami or tidal wave in 1964, spawned by a great Alaskan earthquake, almost leveled the town. The Battery Point Lighthouse Museum is an interesting stop on the city's waterfront. All services, including gas, food, lodging, and restaurants, are found in Crescent City.

The drive, after exiting U.S. 101, quickly climbs into rounded hills and twists into a deep, silent forest of towering redwoods in Jedediah Smith Redwoods State Park. The 9,200-acre park is California's northernmost redwood park land. It is named for pioneer trailblazer, mountain man, and fur trader Jedediah Smith. Smith was the first white man to travel overland from the Mississippi River to the Pacific coast, discovering South Pass in Wyoming along the way. This low Rocky Mountain divide later opened the western gates to a flood of emigrants who journeyed across the California and Oregon trails in the 1840s and 1850s. In 1828, Smith was expelled from California, then Mexican territory, and set northward with a small party and more than 300 horses and mules to the Hudson Bay outposts in Oregon. The party often made less than a mile a day through the rugged coastal mountains. Indians harassed them constantly, thinking the horses were a new type of elk. Eventually, Smith's party reached the beach and rested for several days on the site of today's Crescent City before pushing on to Oregon where Umpqua Indians massacred all but Smith and three men. Smith died three years later at the hands of Comanches on the Santa Fe Trail at the age of thirty-three.

The first four miles of the drive are breathtaking. Tall coast redwoods, *Sequoia sempervirens*, rear up along the narrow, winding road and a dense undergrowth of ferns, rhododendrons, and azaleas carpet the forest floor. The park was established in 1932 and contains forty-six memorial redwood groves. The park's largest tree in Stout Memorial Grove soars 340 feet high with a 20-foot-thick trunk. The coast redwood, except for a fourteen-mile incursion into Oregon, is exclusively a California tree. The redwoods are the world's tallest living things, thriving in a moist, cool, 500-mile-long fog belt from just south of Monterey Peninsula to southern Oregon. They prefer this strip of lowland mountains between the stinging sea breezes and the warmer inland ranges that mimics the mild weather of their heyday millions of years ago in the Tertiary epoch when they spread over much of western North America, China, Europe, and even the Arctic. The redwood is not a drought-tolerant species; it needs the fog moisture during California's dry summer months. Fog along the northern coast contributes as much as twelve inches of the region's annual precipitation.

The redwoods here at Jedediah Smith State Park flourish along damp riverside terraces above the Smith River, growing in almost pure stands with only shade-tolerant shrubs and trees carpeting their feet. A good stop along the drive is the mile-long Simpson Reed Discovery Trail in the roadside Simpson Reed Grove. The path leaves a parking area and winds among the forest giants, passing fallen trunks, dense fern thickets, sprawling vine maples, western hemlocks, huckleberries, and clover-like redwood sorrel.

The drive continues through the redwoods and after four miles crosses the Smith River, its placid waters skimming over gravel bars. A side road, California Highway 197, turns north here and follows the river north to U.S. 101. A side trip well worth taking is the meandering Howland Hill Road, a redwood-lined lane that follows Mill Creek southwest to Howland Summit and Crescent City. The road begins in Hiouchi. The state park's main facilities nestle along the river almost a mile east of the highway bridge. The park offers 108 campsites with restrooms and nearby showers, along with a slew of outdoor opportunities, including hiking on the park's seventeen trails, swimming, and fishing. The park also harbors a stand of rare dawn redwoods, a tree thought to be extinct until discovered in a remote Chinese valley in 1948. A Humboldt State University professor brought these trees from China as seedlings.

The drive heads east up the Smith River's Middle Fork from the state park's eastern boundary. A Redwood National Park information center sits just beyond the turnoff for the park campground. A short distance beyond, as the road and river bend northeast, Forest Road 427 heads up the river's South Fork. This sparkling stream is in a deep, wooded canyon. Just past Hiouchi, the drive enters Smith River National Recreation Area and Six Rivers National Forest. The river is considered the crown jewel in the nation's Wild and Scenic River System. After entering the national forest, the drive climbs away from the open valley and enters the Smith River's slashing canyon. The winding highway clings shelf-like to steep mountain slopes, while the river cuts through a narrow, rock-lined gorge below. After a few miles, the canyon broadens below 2,620-foot Gasquet Mountain and enters the country town of Gasquet at the confluence of the Smith River's North and Middle forks. Gasquet offers most visitor services, and a roadside ranger station provides information on the area's hiking trails, wilderness areas, campgrounds, and fisheries. Panther Flat, the largest forest campground on the river with forty-two sites, lies just beyond Gasquet.

Past Gasquet, both the climate and vegetation begin changing. The weather warms and dries as the highway ascends the canyon floor and the surrounding plant communities correspondingly change. The lush vegetation of the fog belt is left behind, but an equally diverse population of plants clot the steep-sided mountains. Impressive old-growth stands of Douglas fir mingle with Port Orford cedar (a representative of the Pacific Northwest rainforest) on moist slopes, while incense cedar, madrone, tan oak, pines, poison oak, and white fir form a dense mixed woodland. The Smith River area boasts of seven separate plant communities. The land's remote and rugged character makes excellent wildlife habitat with more than 300 wildlife species, including endangered bald eagles and peregrine falcons that nest in the area. Mountain lion, black bear, bobcat, mink, gray fox, raccoon, skunk, and blacktail deer roam the forest. River life includes otter, mergansers, ducks, osprey, kingfisher, a variety of snakes, and, of course, the steelhead and salmon for which the river is justly famed. Steelhead is an ocean-going rainbow trout. They grow in the twenty-pound range in the Smith River and

A hiker treads among tall ferns and soaring redwoods in Jedediah Smith Redwoods State Park along the Smith River drive.

run from December into March. Salmon run September to December. A fishing license is required, and the limit is two fish.

The Smith River country also offers superb hiking trails. The sixteen-mile South Kelsey Historical Trail, a National Recreation Trail, is one of the best. The path follows an 1851 army supply route from Crescent City to the site of old Fort Jones. The first seven miles march along the river's South Fork before climbing onto timbered ridges in the Siskiyou Wilderness Area and the lofty summit of 5,775-foot Baldy Peak. Spectacular views abound. Other good hikes include the 0.75-mile Myrtle Creek Trail, the 3.75-mile Craigs Creek Trail, and the Doe Flat Trail. Ask at the Gasquet ranger station for maps and information. The river also gives great rafting adventures. The twelve-mile section above Gasquet is a good run, while the placid waters through Jedediah Smith State Park are ideal canoeing waters. The South Fork provides thrilling kayaking on tough rapids hemmed in by rocky cliffs.

Past Panther Flat, the canyon again narrows down. Numerous pull-offs allow river access for fishing and swimming. The drive passes nineteen-site Grassy Flat Campground, and a few miles farther lies seventeen-site Patrick Creek Campground. The highway slims down and twists up the rocky river canyon. Steep side canyons with moss-covered trees and cliffs, dense undergrowth, and occasional cascading waterfalls line the walls above the river. The Smith River spills over boulder-choked rapids and gathers in deep, aquamarine-colored pools in the mountain shadows below the drive.

The canyon and road widen at Washington Flat and bend northward past 4,778-foot Wounded Knee Mountain and 3,702-foot Monkey Ridge. The highway, now three lanes, soon leaves the Smith River, which arcs southeast to its headwaters on 5,708-foot Rocky Knob atop the Siskiyou range crest. The road follows Griffin Creek upwards to the scenic drive's end at Collier Tunnel and 2,200-foot-high Collier Roadside Rest Area among high, rounded ridges. The rest area makes a good turn-around spot. Retrace the drive back down to Crescent City or continue on through the tunnel, drop down Kettle Creek to Oregon, and follow U.S. 199 to Grants Pass.

---

3 CALIFORNIA 1
The Mendocino-Sonoma Coast Scenic Drive

General description: This 209-mile-long drive borders the Pacific coast north of San Francisco. The highway passes historic sites, redwood forests, abrupt headlands, sandy beaches, windswept coves, and numerous recreation areas.

Special attractions: Muir Woods National Monument, Point Reyes National Seashore, Golden Gate National Recreation Area, San Andreas Rift

Zone, Sonoma Coast State Beach, Goat Rock, Fort Ross State Historic Park, Salt Point State Park, Kruse Rhododendron State Reserve, Point Arena Lighthouse, Manchester State Beach, Van Damme State Park, Mendocino Headlands State Park, Mendocino, Fort Bragg, Westport Union Landing State Beach, camping, hiking, redwoods, beaches, rock climbing, scenic views.
Location: West-central California. The drive runs north on California 1 from U.S. 101 in Marin City just north of San Francisco to U.S. 101 north of Willitts.
Drive route number and name: California Highway 1, The Shoreline Highway.
Travel season: Year-round. Summer mornings are often foggy. Winters are wet, windy, and cool. Watch for slick pavement.
Camping: A sixteen-site campground lies at Mount Tamalpais State Park just off the drive. Four hike-in campgrounds are at Point Reyes National Seashore. Permits are required. Several campgrounds scatter along the Sonoma County shoreline. Salt Point State Park offers 178 sites; Stillwater Cove Regional Park has twenty-three sites; Bodega Dunes has ninety-eight sites; Wrights Beach has thirty sites; Westshore Regional Park has forty-seven sites; Doran Regional Park offers 138 sites; Gualala Point Regional Park has twenty-six sites. The Mendocino County campgrounds include 150-site Westport Union Landing State Beach, 140-site MacKerricher State Park, twenty-eight-site Russian Gulch State Park, seventy-one-site Van Damme State Park, and forty-three-site Manchester State Beach. Reservations at the state park units are necessary in summer through MISTIX at (800) 444-7275.
Services: All services are found along the drive at Marin City, Bodega Bay, Jenner, Gualala, Manchester, Mendocino, and Fort Bragg. Other services are found at numerous other small towns along the highway.
Nearby attractions: San Francisco, Golden Gate Bridge, Sonoma, Napa Valley, Clear Lake, Standish-Hickey State Recreation Area, Smithe Redwoods State Reserve, Richardson Grove State Park, Avenue of the Giants, Jackson State Forest, Santa Rosa, Guerneville, Russian River, Armstrong Redwoods State Reserve, China Camp State Park, Mount Tamalpais State Park.
For more information: Fort Bragg-Mendocino Coast Chamber of Commerce, 332 N. Main Street, P.O. Box 1141, Fort Bragg, CA 95437, (707) 461-6300, (800) 726-2780. Bodega Bay Chamber of Commerce, 555 Hwy. 1, P.O. Box 146, Bodega Bay, CA 94923, (707) 875-3422. Point Reyes National Seashore, Point Reyes, CA 94956, (415) 663-8522.

The drive: This 209-mile-long scenic drive follows Highway 1 up California's spectacular Pacific coast from the Marin Peninsula north of the Golden Gate Bridge to U.S. 101 south of Eureka. The highway traverses steep, wave-carved headlands, quiet sandy coves, grassy terraces punctuated by grazing cattle, towering redwood trees in moist canyons, long sweeping beaches, and dense woodlands of oak and pine. The shoreline, called the Sonoma-Mendocino Coast for its two counties, is a wildly beautiful meeting of sea and land. Much of the area is protected by numerous state beaches and parks,

Muir Woods National Monument, Golden Gate National Recreation Area, and Point Reyes National Seashore.

The Sonoma-Mendocino Coast lies in California's fog belt. Thick fog, particularly in summer, hangs over the shoreline and backs up against the coastal mountains. The fog is the result of moist air blowing over cold offshore currents. Fog forms when the air condenses into tiny water droplets. Inland, even just a few miles, the fog dissipates as the sun warms the air. Point Reyes is considered one of California's foggiest and windiest spots. Some coastal areas, notably the Point Arena headland, are "banana belts" that are warm and virtually fog free because of protective mountains and ocean currents. Expect cool temperatures, with summer highs ranging from sixty to seventy degrees, and breezy afternoons. September and most of October brings glorious, balmy days. September days average sixty-five degrees with temperatures occasionally climbing into the eighties. Clear skies dominate with fog occurring on only one out of every eight days, generally. Winters are cool and rainy. Most of the coast's annual precipitation comes from wet Pacific storms. December and January both average seven inches of rainfall along the Mendocino coast. Temperatures are moderate, falling between forty and sixty degrees. Expect heavy rain, slick roads, and stiff winds during stormy weather. A raincoat over a sweater usually provides plenty of protection for winter hikers, beachcombers, and whale-watchers. Wet weather continues into spring, but greenery adorns the grasslands and forests.

The drive begins in Marin City just north of San Francisco and the Golden Gate Bridge. Exit off U.S. 101 and head west on California Highway 1, the Shoreline Highway. After a couple miles, the highway leaves the town behind and passes along a rounded ridge lined with eucalyptus and oak trees. The road quickly narrows and begins winding across the hillsides—a character it assumes for the next 200 miles. Vehicles over thirty-five feet in length are prohibited. The traveler will not encounter another traffic light until Fort Bragg, which is more than 160 miles up the coast. Just over three miles from the drive's start, the highway intersects the Panoramic Highway. The Panoramic Highway climbs north into Mount Tamalpais State Park and the Muir Woods Road. Mount Tamalpais park is one of the Bay area's most beloved natural areas. The state park offers pastoral beauty with 200 miles of hiking trails, camping, and picnicking. The view from atop 2,600-foot Mount Tamalpais encompasses the entire bay region.

The Muir Woods Road spirals down to Muir Woods National Monument, a small 560-acre national park that preserves the last virgin stand of coast redwoods in the San Francisco Bay area. The forest was spared from logging when Congressman William Kent bought it in 1905; he later donated the land to the federal government. After President Theodore Roosevelt established the national monument in 1908, Kent urged the new park be named for famed California naturalist and writer John Muir. Muir later told Kent "This is the best tree-lover's monument that could possibly be found in all the forests of the world." The tall trees nestle in Redwood Canyon, lifting their

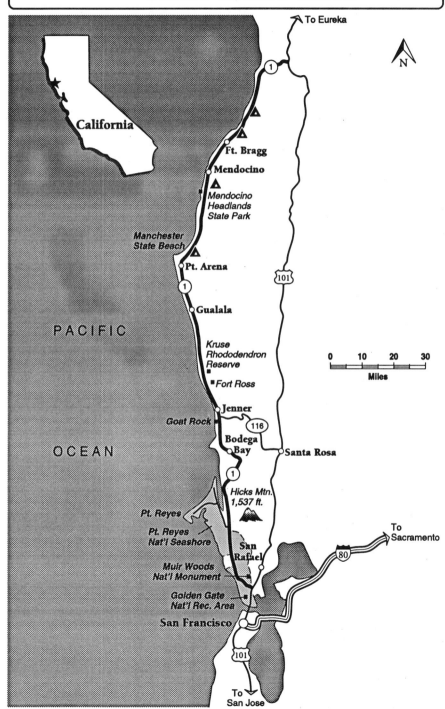

To Eureka

N

California

PACIFIC

Ft. Bragg

Mendocino

Mendocino
Headlands
State Park

Manchester
State Beach

Pt. Arena

Gualala

Kruse
Rhododendron
Reserve

Fort Ross

Jenner

Goat Rock

Bodega
Bay

OCEAN

Hicks Mtn.
1,537 ft.

Pt. Reyes

Pt. Reyes
Nat'l Seashore

San
Rafael

Muir Woods
Nat'l Monument

Golden Gate
Nat'l Rec. Area

San Francisco

To
San Jose

1

101

116

Santa Rosa

80

To
Sacramento

101

0 10 20 30
Miles

towering crowns high above the damp forest floor. Ferns, including the sword fern, ladyfern, California polypody, and bracken fern, moss, and redwood sorrel blankets the forest undergrowth, while red alders line trickling Redwood Creek. Six miles of trails explore the park. Most popular is a short loop that follows the creek up to the Cathedral Grove. The tallest tree here measures 252 feet high. A visitor center, snack bar, and gift shop lie at the trail's start. The monument is very popular, making parking in its small lots a perennial problem.

Return to Highway 1 by following the Muir Woods Road west down Redwood Creek for three miles. Muir Beach lies in a curved, south-facing cove south of the road intersection. The drive twists toward the northwest like an asphalt ribbon above tawny bluffs, rugged sea stacks, and crashing surf before dipping into shallow canyons and emerging onto bold headlands with expansive views. Muir Beach Overlook offers one of the best views on clear days. The Farallon Islands, one of the largest seabird nesting areas in American waters, jut like haystacks above the ocean horizon to the southwest. Closer at hand is the Point Bonita Lighthouse and the entrance to the fabled Golden Gate, named by explorer John C. Fremont in 1846. The coastal region from the Golden Gate to Point Reyes is managed by the National Park Service as Golden Gate National Recreation Area.

The highway straightens out when it reaches Stinson Beach, an old resort town. The large beach stretches alongside the road, attracting swimmers and sunbathers. Nearby Bolinas Lagoon is protected from ocean waves by a thin sand spit. At low tide, it is a tidal mud flat inhabited by numerous birds and waterfowl. A great blue heron and snowy egret rookery lies in a shallow canyon at the Audubon Canyon Ranch just east of the lagoon. From March to July, visitors can hike into the canyon and view the bird's nests high atop the Schwartz Grove redwoods. The Panoramic Highway, one of California's best back road scenic roads, begins in Stinson Beach and climbs east into Mount Tamalpais State Park.

The highway joins up with the San Andreas Fault zone at Stinson Beach and follows it north up Olena Valley and Tomales Bay. The famed fault separates the North American crustal plate from the Pacific plate and stretches some 650 miles from northern Mexico to Cape Mendocino where it plunges into the ocean. The two plates have been slowly creeping past each other for the last thirty million years at an annual rate of about two inches. Underlying rocks, contorted and broken by faulting, are easily eroded forming the broad valley the drive traverses. The coast range east of here is composed of sandstone and chert. The granite rocks on the low hills to the west were moved 350 miles from the south by the fault. During the great 1906 San Francisco earthquake, horizontal movement along the fault here was twenty feet. The San Andreas Rift Zone contains numerous large and small faults. As the two plates grind against each other, pressure builds to a breaking point and the faults jump and release the pressure.

The turn to Point Reyes National Seashore sits just north of Olena. Down the narrow lane lies the park headquarters and an excellent visitor center.

The Pacific Ocean washes against rugged headlands and sandy beaches on California Highway 1's Mendocino Coast.

Spectacular 70,000-acre Point Reyes National Seashore, administered by the National Park Service, preserves a magnificent slice of California coastline. The region is geographically part of the coastal ranges with brushy, chaparral-coated hillsides, grasslands that waver under ocean breezes, pine and fir-choked ridges and vales. A wild twenty-mile-long beach is pounded by Pacific breakers and scoured by gales. The triangular peninsula, a scrap of Sierra granite hauled north by the fault, was named El Punta de Los Reyes by Spanish explorer Don Sebastian Vizcaino on January 6, 1603. That day was Epiphany, the twelfth day of Christmas and the Feast of the Three Kings. Sir Francis Drake beached his ship, *The Golden Hinde*, a few years earlier in 1579 to make needed ship repairs for his round-the-world voyage. After five weeks Drake dubbed the land New Albion, claimed it for England by placing "a plate of brasse, fast nailed to a great and firme post," and sailed west into the sunset.

Point Reyes is a great place to explore. A couple roads pierce the peninsula's interior and allow trail access to numerous points of interest. Two trails begin near the Bear Valley Visitor Center—the 0.7-mile Earthquake Trail along the San Andreas Fault and the Woodpecker Nature Trail. Nearby is Kule Loklo, a replica of a Coast Miwok Indian village. The Miwoks were a hunting and gathering tribe that harvested this rich land for centuries before the Spanish and English arrived. Popular trails include the Sky Trail and the Coast Trail. The Sky Trail leads to the summit of 1,407-foot Mount Wittenberg, the park's high point. Diverse ecosystems inhabited by varied plant communities and animals await the walker along the Coast Trail. The park, lying on the Pacific Flyway, boasts 361 bird species, including eight hawk species, herons, egrets, numerous ducks, and woodpeckers. Exotic deer, such as the fallow and axis deer, have flourished here since the 1940s. A Tule elk refuge sits on Tomales Point. Sea lions colonize the rocky shore at Point Reyes itself. A nearby overlook gives a good view of the large seals. Point Reyes is also an excellent and popular whale-watching spot. More than 100 California gray whales a day are usually sighted during the peak migration in January. Four walk-in campgrounds scatter across the park.

From Point Reyes, the drive runs north along the east shore of Tomales Bay, a long sea-arm that separates Point Reyes peninsula from the mainland. The San Andreas Fault plunges underwater and runs along the bay's floor. The rounded hills of Bolinas Ridge, broken by grass and trees, stair step eastward from the drive. The highway bends inland near the bay's north end, crosses rolling hills and enters Sonoma County and the Sonoma Coast.

The countryside slowly changes after leaving Point Reyes. Gone are the dense forests and tall coastal peaks. In their place is a bucolic landscape, with low grassy hills seamed by creeks and rivers. After entering Sonoma County, the drive turns abruptly west and drops back down to the shore at Bodega Bay. Bodega Bay is a charming seaside town that served as the backdrop for Alfred Hitchcock's classic 1962 film *The Birds*. The harbor here is enclosed by a sand spit. Bodega Head was named in 1775 for Don Juan Francisco de la Bodega y Cuadra, a lieutenant aboard the Spanish ship *Sonora*.

The next ten miles from Bodega Bay to Jenner and the Russian River is

A climber scales Sunset Rock at Goat Rock State Beach along California Highway 1, the Sonoma Coast.

lovely country. The highway rolls over grass-covered terraces backed by tawny hillsides. Coves and sandy beaches, broken by cliffs and bluffs, line the shoreline below the drive. A succession of state-owned beaches, dubbed the Sonoma Coast State Beaches, scatter along the highway. Bulky Bodega Head is a piece of granite dragged north on the San Andreas Fault. It offers good hiking trails. Salmon Creek, Portuguese, Gleasons, Duncan's Landing, Wright, Shell, and Goat Rock state beaches lie just off the drive. Numerous pullouts allow beach access. Wright's Beach has a thirty-site campground and Bodega Dunes offers ninety-eight sites with showers and restrooms. Goat Rock State Beach is a dramatic meeting of land and ocean, and a side road runs along a ridge to the craggy rock. In winter, towering whitecaps crash against the cliffs. It's illegal to climb around on the rock; treacherous waves and currents have drowned many people here. Safe rock climbing is found on nearby Sunset Rock, a small crag perched on a grass table below the entrance road to Goat Road. None of the state beaches along the highway are good for swimming. Dangerous undertows, riptides, sleeper waves, and cold water conspire against the swimmer. Most visitors indulge in surf fishing, picnicking, walking, and beachcombing in the rocky tide pools.

California Highway 1 joins route 116 on the Russian River just east of Jenner. Route 116 makes a good inland excursion. The highway winds along the deep Russian River, its banks flanked with willows, eucalyptus, cypress, and mixed conifers. At Guerneville the route leaves the river and plunges through dark woods to Santa Rosa and U.S. 101.

The drive travels north from Jenner and the Russian River, and, after crossing Russian Gulch, begins spiraling and edging across steep slopes almost 1,000 feet above the cobbled beach. This road section is one of the most dramatic on the northern coast. It lies adjacent to the off-shore San Andreas Fault. Breathtaking views are found from airy pullouts. This is open grazing country; watch for cattle sharing the road. Eventually, the highway drops onto an undulating terrace, crosses the San Andreas Rift Zone, and reaches Fort Ross State Historic Park, which was the site of imperial Russia's farthest American outpost.

Fort Ross was initially settled by ninety-five Russians and forty Aleuts of the Russian-American Fur Trading Company in 1812. The group built a fourteen-foot-high timber stockade that featured forty cannons and corner lookouts. Warehouses, a jail, barracks, and the commandant's house were erected inside the compound, while a village surrounded it. The place was named "Rossiya" or Little Russia, and later corrupted to Fort Ross. The Russians set to work trapping sea otters and quickly brought the species to the verge of extinction. The colonists then turned to farming, but the damp climate and rodents decimated their efforts. In 1841, the Russians decided to cut their losses and sold the fort and all its property to John Sutter for $30,000. Sutter hauled everything, including 1,700 cattle, 940 horses and mules, and an arsenal of weapons to Sacramento. Most of the fort is now reconstructed and open as a living history exhibit. The park boasts an excellent visitor center with numerous interpretative exhibits. Hiking trails meander around the park over grasslands, through cypress groves, and above the rocky shore. The park also offers a twenty-eight-site campground tucked in a sheltered beach-side ravine.

The drive runs northwest along grassy terraces from Fort Ross. Sixteen miles north of Jenner it passes Stillwater Cove Regional Park, a pleasant overnight stop with twenty-three campsites. Salt Point State Park lies four miles farther up the coast. This scenic 4,000-acre park encompasses abrupt headlands that plunge into foaming surf, shallow valleys dense with cypress, pine, and redwood, sandy beaches rimmed with cliffs, and rocky tide pools nestled in quiet coves. The park not only offers seven miles of coastline, but includes the rolling hills east of the highway. Numerous trails thread the park. The 1.5-mile Stump Beach Trail leads along bluffs above the ocean and gives great views to January whale watchers. Visitors also enjoy excellent beachcombing, rockfishing, tide pool exploring, and abalone diving. The park's 178-site campground includes showers, restrooms, and tables.

Kruse Rhododendron State Reserve sits just up the highway from Salt

Point. This 317-acre nature preserve yields one of the Sonoma Coast's most beautiful natural wonders in April and May when its rhododendrons spread a canopy of pink blossoms throughout the second-growth forest. Nowhere else in California do rhododendrons grow in such profusion or as tall as the thirty-foot giants here. The reserve, reached via Kruse Ranch Road, can be explored by trail. A small picnic area sits at the parking lot.

Highway 1 continues north along the coast, running across a grassy shelf past Horseshoe and Rocky points to Stewarts Point. A small town here scatters along the bold promontory above the sea. The last eleven miles of the Sonoma Coast passes the Sea Ranch, a controversial luxury, vacation-home subdivision that was once part of a 17,500-acre Mexican land grant called Rancho de Herman. A battle between developers and conservationists culminated in the establishment of the California Coastal Commission and continued public access to ten miles of state-owned beach.

Past Sea Ranch, the highway crosses the Gualala River and enters Mendocino County and Coast. For the next ninety miles, the serpentine drive winds across a brooding landscape, traversing steep ridges, crossing numerous creeks and rivers, and swinging around coves. The ocean, always in sight, dictates geography and climate. Strong winds constantly scour the sea-facing bluffs, rippling fields of grass and sculpting exposed trees. It's a land that seems in eternal motion—cloud shadows trail across wooded hills; unceasing waves batter rocky headlands; and gray fog hides the earth's sharp edges, making forms uncertain and hazy.

Gualala, a derivation of the Pomo Indian word "wala'li" meaning meeting of the waters, lies at the mouth of the Gualala River. Until the 1960s, this small town was a bustling redwood lumber town. Nearby is Gualala Point Regional Park with trails, picnicking, and a campground. The river is popular with steelhead fishermen in winter. The drive continues up the coast through open meadows and Monterey cypress groves on broad marine terraces and reaches Point Arena after sixteen miles.

Point Arena, first sighted by Captain George Vancouver in 1792, was a rollicking seaport in the late 19th century. The nearby Point Arena Lighthouse, a six-story, automated beacon, warns sailors of underwater dangers. Until the first lighthouse was built in 1870, many ships found a watery grave here, including ten on a stormy November night in 1865. Visitors can tour the old lighthouse, marching up its 147 steps to a spectacular coastal view. Manchester State Beach hugs the coast for five sandy miles from the point. The park offers camping, beachcombing, surf fishing, and good bird watching. Elk, another old lumber town, sits fourteen miles up the road on Greenwood Creek. The town's last lumber mill closed in 1932, leaving a charming village of Victorian homes. Numerous sea stacks, their rocky pinnacles white with bird guano, stud nearby Greenwood Cove. Greenwood Creek Beach State Park is on the site of the old lumber mill and offers a mile-long stretch of beach.

Just north of Elk, the highway sweeps across the Navarro River and enters the heartland of the Mendocino Coast. The towns of Mendocino and Fort

Fort Ross State Historic Park, on California Highway 1 on the Sonoma Coast, sheltered early Russian colonists.

Bragg sit along this forty-mile-long coast, surrounded by some excellent state parks including Van Damme, Mendocino Headlands, Russian Gulch, and McKerricher parks. Van Damme and Mendocino Headlands are the first parks encountered.

Van Damme, three miles south of the town of Mendocino, spreads its 1,800 acres for five miles along the Little River. The park is covered with second-growth redwood forest and is laced with trails. Fern Canyon Trail winds for 2.5 miles through lush undergrowth. The Pygmy Forest section boasts dwarfed Bolander and Bishop pine, Mendocino pygmy cypress, and manzanita trees as old as 100 years that are only two feet tall and less than an inch thick. Acidic soils and poor drainage stunt the trees. The park has a popular seventy-one-site campground. Mendocino Headlands State Park sits just up the highway. This spectacular coastal slice is a monument to sea erosion with sea stacks and headlands carved by relentless waves. The park—offering hiking, whale watching, and excellent tide pools—forms a pristine greenbelt along Mendocino's west edge and preserves the town's unique shore from development.

Mendocino perches atop dramatic bluffs above its rugged coast. It's a quaint, rustic town with a New England ambience. Many of the town's Victorian homes were built by homesick pioneers who settled here during its 19th century lumber boom. The town was founded in 1852 by shipwrecked William Kasten and quickly became a logging center that shipped thousands of feet of redwood to San Francisco. After the last sawmill closed in 1937, Mendocino's fortunes slowly ebbed until the 1960s when it became an artist's colony. It's a trendy, stylish place today with boutiques, health-food restaurants, and galleries. A walk around the town's designated National Historic District reveals the charm of its gingerbread architecture and the wild beauty of its coastline. Be prepared on busy summer weekends for crowded streets and a lack of parking spots.

Russian Gulch State Park and Jug Handle State Reserve are just north of Mendocino. Russian Gulch features thick forests, a wide bay, and a thirty-site campground. Jug Handle preserves a staircase of five wave-cut terraces. Each level is 100 feet higher and 100,000 years older than the one below and is populated by different plant communities.

Fort Bragg, the coast's largest town between San Francisco and Eureka, is a working town, unlike its sister city to the south. Loggers, mill workers, and fishermen live here. The town was founded in 1855 as a military fort to keep Indians on the Mendocino Reservation. In 1867, the area was opened to settlers, and Fort Bragg became a lumber town. It still retains its working class roots with the local Georgia-Pacific mill. The town also boasts the only traffic lights along the scenic drive. The California and Western Railroad, affectionately called the "Skunk Train," is Fort Bragg's main tourist attraction. The track snakes forty miles inland through redwood forests to Willits. The trains run daily in summer and include both half- and full-day runs. The seventeen-acre Mendocino Botanical Gardens is another interesting stop.

MacKerricher State Park, the largest coastal state park on the drive, lies three miles north of Fort Bragg. The park is a superlative area, with sharp cliffs and headlands. It has one of northern California's longest beaches, windswept sand dunes, rocky islands, tide pools, fields of wildflowers, and a freshwater lagoon. A short trail leads out to Laguna Point, a good spot to sight gray whales December through April during their migration. Harbor seals are often seen here frolicking in the surf and sunning on rocks. The park features a secluded 140-site campground with restrooms, showers, and beach access.

The last twenty-six miles of Highway 1 along the coast travels a remote, lonely land. The road twists across marine terraces and drops down through shallow canyons. Roadside pullouts offer marvelous views and trails that lead to hidden beaches and coves. Westport is a small town with sparse services and was once the largest seaport between San Francisco and Eureka. In the 1880s, the town was the center of a massive freight operation that supplied inland cities. The completion of the railroad to Fort Bragg, however, spelled the beginning of the end for Westport. The highway straightens out north of Westport for a few miles. Westport-Union Landing State Beach lies along this road section. The park is a marvelous place to get away from crowds. A campground with 150 primitive sites scatters along the top of a lofty bluff and offers ocean views.

The drive continues up the coast and ten miles from Westport the highway turns inland and leaves the Mendocino Coast behind. The shoreline north of here, called the Lost Coast, is a ragged vastness of wild mountains, stormy beaches, and few people and roads. The last seventeen miles of California 1 follows a winding, old logging road. Obey the numerous caution signs and drive slowly. The road corkscrews up steep canyons past lush woodlands before emerging atop lofty ridges. Several pullouts yield excellent viewpoints. Eventually, the road begins spiraling down across ridge lines before spanning the South Fork of the Eel River and entering Leggett. U.S. 101 and the drive's end lies just outside Leggett. A northward turn leads to Eureka and the Redwood Country. A south turn heads to Ukiah, Santa Rosa, and San Francisco.

4 CALIFORNIA 12, 29 & 175
Sonoma-Napa Valley Drive

General description: A 132-mile-long drive that makes an open loop through the pastoral wine country of the Sonoma and Napa valleys.
Special attractions: Santa Rosa, Annadel State Park, Jack London State Historic Park, Valley of the Moon, Sonoma Valley, Sonoma, Sonoma State Historic Park, Napa, Napa Valley, wineries, Sugarloaf Ridge State Park, Bale Grist Mill State Historic Park, Bothe-Napa Valley State Park, Calistoga, Old Faithful Geyser, Mount St. Helena, Robert Louis Stevenson State Park, Clear Lake, Hopland, scenic views, hiking, photography, wine-tasting, camping.
Location: West-central California. The drive begins in Santa Rosa off U.S. 101 just north of San Francisco and ends at Hopland on U.S. 101.
Drive route numbers and names: California highways 12, 29, and 175, St. Helena Highway, Sonoma Highway.
Travel season: Year-round.
Camping: Several public campgrounds lie along the drive. On California 12 north of Sonoma are thirty-one-site Spring Lake Regional Park and fifty-site Sugarloaf Ridge State Park. Two campgrounds sit near Calistoga in the upper Napa Valley. Bothe-Napa Valley State Park offers fifty-eight sites and the Napa County Fairgrounds has forty-nine sites. More camping is west of the

Napa Valley at Lake Berryessa and Lake Hennessey. Many campgrounds lie off California 175 at Clear Lake. Loch Lomond Park has thirty-seven RV sites with hookups. Clear Lake State Park, north of Kelseyville, has 147 lake-side sites. Reservations for state park sites are necessary in summer. Call MISTIX at (800) 444-7275.

Services: All services including gas, food, groceries, and lodging are found at Santa Rosa, Sonoma, Napa, Yountville, St. Helena, Calistoga, Kelseyville, Lakeport, and Hopland.

Nearby attractions: Sonoma Coast State Beaches, Russian River, San Francisco area attractions, Golden Gate Bridge, Muir Woods National Monument, Point Reyes National Seashore, Golden Gate National Recreation Area, Fort Ross State Historic Park, San Pablo National Wildlife Refuge, Marine World Africa USA, Armstrong Redwoods State Reserve, Petaluma Adobe State Historic Park.

For more information: Napa Valley Visitors Bureau, 1556 First Street, Napa, CA 94559, (707) 226-7459. Sonoma County Convention and Visitors Bureau, 10 Fourth St., Suite 100, Santa Rosa, CA 95401, (707) 996-1033.

The drive: This 132-mile scenic drive makes an open loop between Santa Rosa and Hopland, both on U.S. 101. The drive, following three California highways, traverses California's wine country in the Sonoma and Napa valleys, crosses high, rolling mountains tangled with dense woods, and passes Clear Lake, which is the largest natural lake entirely within the state. Numerous historic sites line the highways, including the ranch and home of famed author Jack London, the Mexican colonial town of Sonoma, and the ghost town site of Silverado made famous by writer Robert Louis Stevenson.

The wine country offers pleasant weather year-round, with wet winters and dry summers. Expect cool temperatures between forty and sixty degrees and regular rain during winter. Seventeen inches of Sonoma's total annual rainfall of twenty-seven inches falls between December and February. Spring continues with rain but yields warmer days and wildflower-strewn hillsides. Temperatures become hot by June. Daily highs often creep into the nineties, and skies are generally clear and dry. Fog often shrouds the lower valleys on summer mornings. Autumn days, with the summer tourists gone and the vineyards ablaze with color, are warm and clear.

The drive begins by following California Highway 12 (Sonoma Highway) east from Santa Rosa and U.S. Highway 101. Santa Rosa has a population of 115,000 and is Sonoma County's largest city and economic hub. One of the city's best attractions is the Luther Burbank Home and Gardens. Luther Burbank, a renowned, self-taught horticulturist, worked here for fifty years improving and developing cultivated plants like Shasta daisies and Santa Rosa plums in the area's rich soils and mild climate. Burbank died in 1926 and is buried near his house, which is open daily to visitors. Other Santa Rosa points of interest include the Codding Museum of Natural History, the Sonoma County Museum, and the Ripley Memorial Museum. This museum houses world-wide memorabilia from local son Robert "Believe It or Not!" Ripley.

The highway quickly runs through Santa Rosa's eastern suburbs and swings southeast into the Sonoma Valley or the Valley of the Moon, a broad valley flanked by the Sonoma Mountains on the west and the Mayacamas Mountains on the east. This seventeen-mile-long valley, nicknamed the Valley of the Moon by local author Jack London in a popular novel, is home to more than thirty wineries. Sonoma is supposedly a local Indian word meaning "many moons."

Annadel State Park sits south of the highway immediately after entering the valley. This 5,000-acre park spreads over rolling hills broken by trickling streams and coated with oak woodlands and grassy meadows. Thirty-five miles of trails lace the hills, leading to lush canyons with redwoods, Douglas firs, and ferns. A popular hike leads three miles to Lake Ilsanjo, a good lake to fish for black bass. The lake's name is derived from its former owners—Ilsa and Joe. Spring Lake Regional Park, just northwest of Annadel, offers a thirty-one-site campground next to the seventy-two-acre lake.

Hood Mountain Regional Park and Sugarloaf Ridge State Park drape over the Mayacamas Mountains across the valley from Annadel. Both parks boast a variety of plant communities spread across steep mountain sides and slicing canyons. Sugarloaf Ridge, a rugged 2,500-acre park, reaches a high point of 2,729 feet atop Bald Mountain. Over twenty-five miles of trail snake across the park, passing big leaf maples, madrones, coast redwoods, several oak species, and, in springtime, some 187 flower species that include owl's clover, iris, lupine, Indian paintbrush, and periwinkle. The views from both Bald and Hood mountains are marvelous. Fifty campsites, with tables, food lockers, and water, scatter through an evergreen forest at Sugarloaf. Hikers should carry water and watch for poison oak and rattlesnakes.

The drive follows the verdant Valley of the Moon for eighteen miles from Santa Rosa to Sonoma, twisting down the valley past sun-drenched vineyards and several small towns such as Kenwood, Glen Ellen, El Verano, and Boyes Hot Springs. Numerous back roads explore the countryside, many making excellent and safe bike tours. Eight wineries including Kenwood Vineyards, lie in residential Kenwood. Kenwood hosts the World Championship Pillow Fight every Fourth of July. Just down the road sits the old resort community of Glen Ellen and Jack London State Historic Park. The 800-acre park, lying west of the scenic drive, creeps up the northeast flank of Sonoma Mountain.

Jack London was born in San Francisco in 1876 and became one of the best known and most successful writers of his time with books like *White Fang* and *The Call of the Wild*. In 1905, London and his second wife Charmian bought acreage in Sonoma Valley and established the Beauty Ranch. By 1911, at age thirty-five, he had acquired more than 1,100 acres and work began on his four-story Wolf House mansion. The house, however, mysteriously burned down in 1913 only days before the Londons were to move in, leaving fragmented stone walls. London died in 1916 and was buried under a lava boulder on a grassy hill beside two pioneer children. Charmian London built the House of Happy Walls nearby, which today houses a collection of London's papers, rejection slips, library, travel souvenirs, and memorabilia.

CALIFORNIA 12, 29 & 175: SONOMA-NAPA VALLEY

To CA
Hwy. 20

Clear
Lake

29

Lakeport

To Ukiah

Lakeport
Peak

Clear
Lake
State Park

175

Big Valley

Hopland

Kelseyville

Mt.
Konocti
1,310 ft.

Clearlake

29

Lower Lake

101

Mt.
Hannah
1,212 ft.

Loch
Lomond

Cobb

Boggs Mtn.

29

Cloverdale

Cobb
Mtn.

175

Collayomi
Valley

Middletown

Pine Mtn.
1,011 ft.

ALEXANDER VALLEY

MAYACAMA MOUNTAINS

Mt. St. Helena
1,425 ft.

Robert Louis Stevenson
State Park

128

Sugarloaf Mtn.
910 ft.

Healdsburg

29

NAPA

Calistoga

Bothe-Napa Valley
State Park

Bale Grist Mill
State Hist. Park

St. Helena

Lake
Hennessey
Recreation
Area

Sugarloaf Ridge
State Park

Oakmont

VALLEY

Haystack Mtn.

Santa
Rosa

Annadel
State Park

Kenwood

12

Jack London
State Hist. Park

Valley of the Moon

Mt. Veeder

Yountville

California

Sonoma Mtn.
2,299 ft.

Sonoma

Napa

29

To I-80
and
Vallejo

101

Sonoma Valley

0   5   10   15
Miles

121

To San
Francisco

To U.S. 101

Several easy trails stroll around the state park, exploring the same paths London rode.

The old resort towns of El Verano and Boyes Hot Springs are just north of Sonoma. Boyes Hot Springs, the geographical center of the valley, is famed for its thermal mineral springs. An Englishman named Captain Henry E. Boyes developed the springs after learning of their medicinal powers.

Sonoma, one of California's oldest and most historic towns, lies on the undulating hills between the Mayacamas Mountains and the watery delta of Sonoma Creek above San Pablo Bay. Originally established as California's northernmost mission in 1823 to counter the Russian presence at nearby Fort Ross, the town was laid out by Comandante Alferez Mariano Vallejo around a spacious central plaza, the largest in California, and named Pueblo de Sonoma. Low-slung adobe "haciendas" or houses and "palacios" or palaces were erected, and Vallejo built a prosperous fiefdom. On June 14, 1846, Sonoma fell into the hands of a group of armed American settlers and trappers angered by the Mexican law that prohibited them from owning property. The group was led by explorer Captain John C. Fremont. They took over Sonoma without a shot, declared California an independent republic, and raised the Bear Flag over the town plaza. The flag, the basis for today's California flag, featured a red stripe, a star in memory of the Lone Star Republic in Texas, and a crudely drawn bear. Shortly afterward, Sonoma and California came under the American flag as part of the spoils of the Mexican-American War. Vallejo remained in Sonoma as a leading citizen and land baron, became a delegate to California's first constitutional convention in 1849, and was elected a state senator and mayor of Sonoma.

Sonoma features many frontier buildings, including the Mission San Francisco de Solano, the Vallejo home, and the Sonoma Barracks that are preserved in Sonoma State Historic Park. Sonoma, besides being the cradle of modern California, is also the birthplace of the state's viticulture. The mission padres planted grape vines in the early 1800s and made rustic wines. In 1856, Count Agoston Haraszthy, a Hungarian emigrant, planted the first major American vineyard with European grapes and founded Buena Vista Winery. The winery is east of Sonoma on a eucalyptus-lined lane. It offers tasting and tours of the original stone wine cellar as well as aging caves built by Chinese workers in 1862. In town itself is Sebastiani Vineyard, a large winery with a comprehensive tour and complimentary samples. Besides wine, travelers can also sample Sonoma's famous cheeses at the Vella Cheese Company with its superb Monterey cheeses and the Sonoma Cheese Factory, home of the famed Sonoma Jack cheeses. Sonoma offers all visitor services. The visitors bureau on the Plaza doles out free information on the region.

The drive turns south in Sonoma and continues for a few miles to Schellville where the highway bends abruptly eastward. The drive runs past ranches, grazing cattle and horses, vineyards, and undulating hills coated with tawny grass at the southern end of the Mayacamas Mountains. After eleven miles, Highway 12 intersects California 29 just south of Napa. The city of Napa sits astride the Napa River at the southern end of the thirty-mile-long

Historic downtown Sonoma, one of California's oldest towns, sits along the Napa Valley drive.

Napa Valley, California's most famous wine region.

The Napa Valley is considered with the Sonoma Valley as one of the world's great wine regions. It offers porous, well-drained soils and a dry Mediterranean climate conducive to growing excellent grapes. While early American settlers grew grapes from cuttings from Sonoma's mission vineyards, Charles Krug is considered the valley's first true vintner after introducing Riesling grapes in 1861. The valley's acclaimed vintages today are dry wines. Some of the valley's grapes include Pinot Noir, Riesling, Chardonnay, Cabernet Sauvignon, Chenin Blanc, and others. More than 200 wineries with some 32,000 acres of vineyards carpet the valley floor. Napa wine connoisseurs still agree with writer Robert Louis Stevenson's 1880 assessment of California wines as "bottled poetry."

The Napa Valley, because of its superb climate, fine lodging and dining, pastoral beauty, and excellent wines, is deservedly popular with visitors. Weekends, particularly in autumn when the grapes are crushed, are hectic with bumper to bumper traffic. Better to travel on weekdays and avoid the rush. Most valley wineries offer tours, and some require reservations and charge tasting fees. Beginning tasters are well-advised to take the informative tours at the larger wineries like Robert Mondavi before exploring the small vineyards. Current winery lists with addresses and phone numbers are found at local chambers of commerce. It's best to call ahead to smaller wineries for hours and tours. A good sampling of the valley's wines and wineries often includes stopping at a large, medium, and small winery, preferably in different parts of the valley as each has its own distinctive wines. Select a designated, non-drinking driver in advance when touring the wine country, and remember to drink sensibly.

The drive turns north of California 29 and quickly enters the city of Napa, the southern anchor and business center for the prosperous valley. The word "napa," like so many California place names, is an Indian word meaning grizzly bear or derived from "napo," meaning house. The name was given to Vallejo's large land grant here and later applied to the county. Napa now is a large sprawling city that began in 1848 as a river port on the San Pablo Bay and later became a busy tannery town.

The drive runs north on route 29 for twenty-five miles to Calistoga, passing through the heart of the Napa wine country and the picturesque towns of Yountville and St. Helena. Yountville, nine miles north of Napa via a four-lane highway, is a quaint, up-scale village with numerous historic stone buildings. In 1836, North Carolina trapper George Yount built the valley's first house and planted the first vineyard here on a Mexican land grant. The town is also home to the Veterans Home of California and numerous chic shops and restaurants. Nearby is Domaine Chandon, makers of fine sparkling wines, and S. Anderson Vineyard. St. Helena, like neighboring Yountville, is a town of expensive shops and restaurants. The Robert Louis Stevenson Museum is housed in a wing of the Silverado Museum. The collection is a must-see for the Stevenson aficionado and includes over 8,000 items from his life and literature. The exhibits detail Stevenson's first childhood letters, first editions of his treasured books, manuscripts and letters, drawings, and photographs. Nearby is the Napa Valley Wine Library with more than 3,000 books on wine and wine making.

Most of the Napa Valley's better-known vintages are produced on the eight-mile section between Yountville and St. Helena. Robert Mondavi Winery, one of the largest, sits west of the highway at Oakville. Other wineries on this highway stretch include Beaulieu, Girard, Rutherford Hill, Sutter Home, Spring Mountain, and Heitz Wine Cellar. At St. Helena lie Christian Brothers, Beringer, and Krug wineries. Beringer Vineyards, open since 1876, offers its famed aging caves dug by Chinese workers, the ornate Rhine House mansion, and an excellent thirty-minute tour followed by a tasting. Charles Krug Winery is the valley's oldest and boasts four distinctive tours. It's Viticulture Field Seminar is offered every Friday and open to only twenty participants. It explores all facets of Napa Valley wine making. The popular Cabernet Sauvignon Seminar discovers this fine grape and its hearty wines. North of St. Helena are Frog's Leap, Deer Park Winery, and Burgess Cellars.

Two of the valley's premier champagne makers—Hanns Kornell Champagne Cellars and Schramsberg—sit north of St. Helena. Schramsberg, the first hillside winery in Napa Valley, ages its exquisite sparkling wines in 125-year-old caves hollowed out of volcanic ash deposits. Robert Louis Stevenson spent an afternoon in 1880 with founder Jacob Schram tasting wines in the cellar. He later wrote, "To Mr. Schram this was a solemn office...and he followed every sip and read my face with proud anxiety. I tasted all. I tasted every variety and shade of Schramberger...." Today, the vineyard offers sales but no tasting.

Two state parks also lie in the northern Napa Valley. The Bale Grist Mill State Historic Park, a few miles north of St. Helena, preserves a flour mill built by English doctor Edward T. Bale in 1846. Bothe-Napa Valley State Park straddles the mountain ridges just south of Calistoga. The 1,700-acre park spreads along Ritchie Creek and offers numerous hiking trails, a picnic area, a fifty-site campground with showers, and a swimming pool.

Calistoga crowns the northern end of the Napa Valley, nestled in the narrow valley between lofty peaks. Mormon entrepreneur Samuel Brannan platted the town in 1859 as a luxurious spa to attract well-heeled San Franciscans. Numerous hot springs were the main attraction. The local Indians called the area "Colaynomo" or Oven Place, but Brannan, after opening his grand hotel, called it Calistoga. Legend says that when he announced his new Saratoga of California, he muddled his speech saying it was the Calistoga of Sarifornia. The town remains a popular tourist haven. Visitors still bathe in the hot springs, take hot mud baths, and explore the upper valley's wineries, including the elite Cuvaison, Stonegate Winery, and Chateau Montelena. More wineries lie northwest of Calistoga on California Highway 128 in the Alexander Valley. The Sharpsteen Museum and Sam Brannan Cottage make a good stop in Calistoga and includes a detailed diorama of the town in 1865.

Volcanism coupled with the San Andreas Rift system explains the underground hot springs at Calistoga as well as the geology of the Napa and Sonoma valleys and the surrounding mountain ranges. The northwest-to-southeast-trending valleys were formed by faults associated with the famed San Andreas Fault to the west. The valley floors filled with gravel and silt washed from the highlands, forming rich, porous soils that are ideal for grape-growing. The soils here also impart unique taste characteristics to valley wines. Deposits of volcanic ash and rust-colored volcanic rocks blanket the area mountains. Most of the volcanoes that erupted lie north of Napa Valley around Clear Lake. Hot rock does, however, lie just underground at Calistoga, creating the bubbling hot springs and the unique sixty-foot-high Old Faithful Geyser. A petrified forest, encased and preserved by volcanic ash, lies just west of Calistoga. The largest log stretches 126 feet long and 8 feet in diameter.

Highway 29 turns north in Calistoga, swings through vineyards at the

California Highway 175 twists across the Mayacama Mountains north of the Napa Valley.

mountain base, and begins swiftly spiraling northward above Jericho Canyon. The drive climbs into the mountains, its narrow lanes spiraling up through dense oak thickets and past glades of wind-rippled grass. After five miles, it reaches a saddle east of 4,344-foot Mount St. Helena and Robert Louis Stevenson State Park.

The 3,200-acre park, mostly wilderness, drapes over the chaparral, oak, and pine-covered slopes of Mount St. Helena. The peak is one of the highest in the Coast Ranges and towers over the surrounding countryside. An unsubstantiated local myth says the peak was named for a Russian princess. In truth, it and the Napa Valley town were named in 1855 for the St. Helena Division of the Sons of Temperance. The park is, of course, named for the famed Scottish author Robert Louis Stevenson who honeymooned with his new wife Fanny Osbourne at the abandoned town site of Silverado on Mount St. Helena's flanks in May of 1880. He later wrote the classic *Silverado Squatters*, a slim volume that detailed his experiences in the Napa country. Stevenson wrote of the park's dominant peak, "The mountain...feeds in the springtime many splashing brooks. From its summit you must have an excellent lesson in geography....Three counties, Napa, Lake, and Sonoma, march across its cliffy shoulders....Its sides are fringed with forest, and the soil, where it is bare, glows warm with cinnabar."

A rough parking area is located atop Mount St. Helena's eastern shoulder at a high saddle. Here sit the ruins of the old Toll House on the old Calistoga-Lakeport stage road that Highway 29 now follows. A trail begins here and winds west a mile to a granite, book-shaped marker that commemorates old Silverado and the Stevensons' honeymoon site. The trail scrambles west to a fire road and leads four miles to the mountain's summit, some 4,000 feet above the Napa Valley. The view from atop is astounding on a clear day. The blue Pacific Ocean glimmers to the west; Mount Diablo lifts its grassy flanks to the southeast; and to the north Mount Shasta and Lassen Peak poke above the horizon, their snowcapped summits glimmering like distant alabaster towers.

From the ridge line, the drive drops steeply northward and follows St. Helena Creek to Middletown, a small town lying mid-way between Calistoga and Lower Lake. The drive turns northwest here on California Highway 175 and heads up the broad Collayomi Valley. The quiet highway runs through grassland and forest on the valley floor, passing small ranches with grazing cattle. After about five miles, the road begins climbing through a forest of gray pine, oak, and manzanita. Two miles later, the road crests at 2,600-foot Whispering Pines, a secluded, cool residential community is set amongst towering sugar pines. The highway twists northwestward, passing a succession of small communities, Boggs Mountain State Forest, and crossing brushy, tree-choked canyons. As the road drops, it follows the broad valley of Cole Creek, with shade from oak trees dappling the asphalt. After eighteen miles, Highway 175 rejoins Highway 29 and runs west around Mount Konocti to Kelseyville.

Mount Konocti, a conical 4,200-foot peak, dominates the Clear Lake area. The peak and surrounding area is part of the Clear Lake volcanic field, a dormant region of recent volcanoes and lava flows. Konocti is built of volcanic cinders and lava. It stopped erupting some 250,000 years ago, although some activity on its northeast base occurred only 10,000 years ago. Numerous earthquakes and a large underground pocket of molten magma that create fumaroles and hot springs indicate the area is still geologically active. Clear Lake, the largest natural lake totally within California with 43,000 acres, formed when landslides blocked its western drainage to the Russian River, and lava flows blocked its eastern drainage. The Clear Lake area is an excellent rock hounding area, offering "Lake County diamonds" or excellent quartz crystals. A good spot to find the crystals is on Perini Road southwest of Lower Lake. Other collectible rocks found include calcite, chert, jasper, and obsidian.

The area around Kelseyville is renowned for its excellent pears. Benjamin Kelsey founded the town in 1847 when he bought land from General Vallejo. Local Pomo Indians, however, killed Kelsey in 1849 for harsh treatment of Indian laborers. The Indians ceded their lands here in 1851 for "Ten head of beef cattle, three sacks of bread and sundry clothing." Today, orderly pear and walnut orchards march across the rolling hills around the small quiet town of Kelseyville. Clear Lake State Park lies on the lake shore just north of town. The park offers two miles of shoreline, water-skiing, swimming, fishing for crappie, catfish, perch, bass, and bluegill, and 147 campsites in four campgrounds.

The drive traverses Big Valley west of Kelseyville, passing orchards and vineyards and reaches the southern outskirts of Lakeport after eight miles. Turn south on Highway 175 here. California 29 continues north into Lakeport. The scenery along the next eighteen miles is simply stunning. The drive corkscrews up precipitous slopes and deep canyons to the forested crest of the Mayacamas Mountains before dropping steeply down to Hopland and the Russian River. Dense forest and thick chaparral lines the serpentine roadway; marvelous views of Clear Lake and the surrounding mountains unfold from each pullouts. Little traffic is encountered on this lonely road section. The drive ends on U.S. 101 at Hopland. The town's main industry used to be hops for brewing beer until the 1950s. Now vineyards and wineries flourish in the surrounding Sanel Valley. Fetzer Vineyards, the largest winery here, offers a large, in-town tasting room. The excellent Hopland Brewery, a micro-brewing operation, opened in 1983 and operates a brew-pub. Numerous crafts and antique stores make Hopland a popular shopping stop. Travelers can return to the San Francisco Bay area by turning south on U.S. 101. Squaw Rock, just south of town, is a popular summer swimming hole on the Russian River.

| 5 | CALIFORNIA 1 |
| | *Carmel to Morro Bay* |

General description: A 122-mile-long highway that twists down the scenic central California coastline from Carmel to Morro Bay.
Special attractions: Carmel, Mission San Carlos, Point Lobos State Reserve, Garrapata State Park, Big Sur Coast, Andrew Molera State Park, Pfeiffer Big Sur State Park, Julia Pfeiffer Burns State Park, Los Padres National Forest, Hearst-San Simeon State Historical Monument, William R. Hearst Memorial State Beach, San Simeon State Beach, Cayucos State Beach, Morro Strand State Beach, scenic views, camping, hiking, whale-watching, photography.
Location: Western California between San Francisco and Los Angeles. The drive runs from Monterey to Morro Bay, twelve miles from San Luis Obispo and U.S. 101.
Drive route number and name: California Highway 1, Cabrillo Highway.
Travel season: Year-round. Watch for fog along the drive in summer. Heavy winter rains make the pavement slick and may create landslides that close the highway.
Camping: Several public campgrounds lie along the drive in state parks and Los Padres National Forest. Andrew Molera State Park offers several

The Bixby Bridge spans a precipitous gorge between rugged headlands along the Big Sur Coast.

primitive, walk-in, tent sites; Pfeiffer Big Sur State Park has 217 sites; San Simeon State Beach has two campgrounds with seventy and 134 sites; and Morro Bay State Park offers two campgrounds with 115-sites and 104 sites. Reservations, particularly in summer, are strongly recommended as the campgrounds are very busy. Call MISTIX at (800) 444-PARK for reservations. Kirk Creek and Plaskett Creek campgrounds in the national forest are at the drive's north end just off the highway. Several private campgrounds also lie along the drive.

Services: All services are available in Monterey, Carmel, Morro Bay, and San Luis Obispo. Limited services are found along the drive.

Nearby attractions: Monterey, Cannery Row, Monterey Bay Aquarium, Monterey State Historic Park, Pinnacles National Monument, Fremont Peak State Park, San Juan Bautista State Historic Park, Morro Bay Museum of Natural History, Pismo State Beach, San Luis Obispo County Historical Museum, Mission San Luis Obispo de Tolosa.

For more information: Big Sur Chamber of Commerce, P.O. Box 87, Big Sur, CA 93920, (408) 667-2100. Monterey Peninsula Visitors and Convention Bureau, 380 Alvarado St., P.O. Box 1770, Monterey, CA 93942-1770, (408) 649-1770. Morro Bay Chamber of Commerce, 895 Napa St., Suite A-1, Morro Bay, CA 93442, (805) 772-4467.

The drive: This 122-mile-long scenic drive follows California Highway 1 and twists along the spectacular Big Sur Coast between Carmel and Morro Bay along central California's Pacific shoreline. The road is simply one of the world's most breathtaking drives, a must-do adventure for any California traveler. Here, the steep ridges of the remote Santa Lucia Range plunge down to a rocky, wave-battered coast, making an abrupt transition from wild peak to wild ocean. The roadway follows this transition zone, snaking along precipitous headlands, crossing grassy meadows above ragged coves, and traversing thirty-three bridges that span deep canyons and gorges. It's a superb landscape that serves as a fitting boundary between North America and the Pacific Ocean.

The climate along the Big Sur Coast is mild year-round. Around Monterey Bay on the drive's north end, the weather varies little between winter and summer. Only ten degrees difference separates the mean temperatures for August and January making the climate here the most uniform of anywhere in the United States. Summer brings thick fog banks that wrap the coast in gray shrouds. The fog usually burns off by mid-day, but temperatures are often cool. Bring a sweater for those days. Inland temperatures on the mountains and valleys above the coast can be hot with daily highs reaching into the nineties. Thunder storms are infrequent, although light showers may accompany the fog. The upper part of the drive between Big Sur and Carmel is cooler and damper than the southern section. Autumn brings warm, clear days until winter storms sweep off the Pacific in December. Heavy rains lead to frequent landslides along the road. Forty-two land slides blocked the highway during the wet winter of 1982-83. One took over a year to clear away. The greenery in spring adorns the coastal meadows and forests, and the days are clear and breezy with occasional showers.

Monterey is considered the birthplace of California. Juan Rodriguez Cabrillo, a Portuguese sailor exploring for Spain, discovered Monterey Bay in 1542. California Highway 1 is called the Cabrillo Highway in honor of California's first European explorer. In 1602, Sebastian Vizcaino celebrated mass under Monterey's own "Plymouth Rock," an old spreading oak tree. Almost two centuries later, explorer Gaspar de Potola and Father Junipero Serra established a presidio and mission on the bay's fertile south shore; and the town, called Monterey, grew into a lively port and the provincial capital of Alta California. Monterey later became a major fishing port and fish cannery, immortalized in John Steinbeck's classic 1945 novel *Cannery Row* as "a poem, a stink, a grating noise, a quality of light, a tune, a habit, a nostalgia, a dream." Today, the "Sardine capital of the world" attracts tourists to stroll its charming streets. Monterey retains its historic flavor with more 18th and 19th century building than any other California town. The self-guided "Path of History" winds 2.7 miles through the downtown past white-washed adobe buildings with red tile roofs. Other popular attractions include Steinbeck's Cannery Row, Fisherman's Wharf, Monterey State Historic Park, and the spectacular Monterey Bay Aquarium. The aquarium explores sixty-mile-long Monterey Bay's diverse habitats with its 10,000-foot-deep

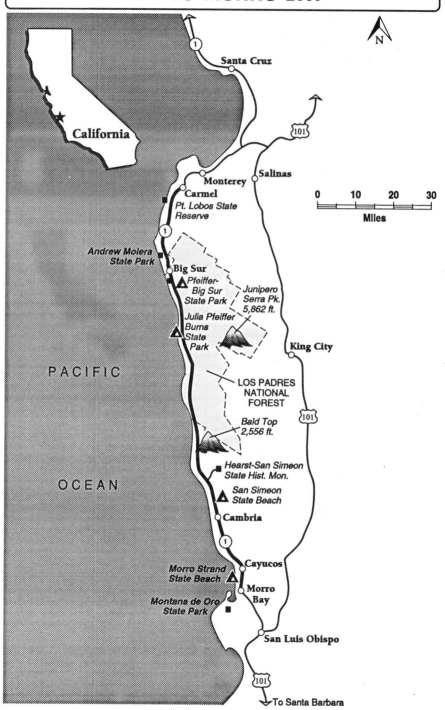

N

Santa Cruz

California

Monterey   Salinas
Carmel
Pt. Lobos State
Reserve

0   10   20   30
Miles

Andrew Molera
State Park

Big Sur
Pfeiffer-
Big Sur
State Park

Junipero
Serra Pk.
5,862 ft.

Julia Pfeiffer
Burns
State
Park

King City

PACIFIC

LOS PADRES
NATIONAL
FOREST

Bald Top
2,556 ft.

OCEAN

Hearst-San Simeon
State Hist. Mon.

San Simeon
State Beach

Cambria

Cayucos

Morro Strand
State Beach
Morro
Bay

Montana de Oro
State Park

San Luis Obispo

To Santa Barbara

canyons, kelp beds, and tidal flats.

The drive begins in the arts town of Carmel just south of Monterey on California Highway 1. Carmel is a picturesque town nestled along Carmel Bay. Carmel is one of California's least commercial towns, yet it is also one of the most popular. Visitors flock to play golf on its many championship courses, including prestigious Pebble Beach Golf Links, to shop its exclusive stores and galleries, and to admire the scenery at Point Lobos State Reserve. Carmel also boasts a bohemian past of famed writers, artists, and photographers who rejoiced in the area's supreme natural beauty. The artist's colony included writers Jack London, Mary Austin, Lincoln Steffens, Upton Sinclair, and Robinson Jeffers, and photographers Ansel Adams and Edward Weston. Jeffers, the poet laureate of Big Sur Country, lived in Tor House on the Carmel Bay coast. This distinctive American poet embodied the region's strong spirit of place and invoked its wildness and freedom in his powerful poetry— "...each November great waves awake and are drawn/ Like smoking mountains bright from the west/ And come and cover the cliff with white violent cleanness."

The drive drops down from Carmel, crosses the Carmel River, and passes Carmel River State Beach, a generally uncrowded stretch of sand bordered by windswept cypress and eucalyptus trees. Good birding is found in the river's marsh delta. A mile past the state beach lies Point Lobos State Reserve, perhaps California's most beautiful coastal park land. This 1,276-acre nature preserve of rocky headlands, wave-carved coves, narrow shell-strewn beaches, and sea stacks, juts into south Carmel Bay. Its six-mile coast is a wonderful place of relentless surf and wind. Tide pools teeming with life—sea urchins, hermit crabs, starfish, anemones—are exposed on the rough shore at low tide. Numerous birds including sea gulls, comorants, brown pelicans, and herons soar overhead. Colonies of barking sea lions populate the quiet coves, leading to the point's early Spanish name "Punta de los Lobos Marinos" or Point of the Sea Wolves. Sea otters are often seen frolicking in the surf or off-shore kelp beds. The California Sea Otter Refuge begins south of Point Lobos and runs down to Big Sur. The reserve is also well known for its diverse flora, with more than 300 plant species inhabiting its terrain. It's a good place to see the elegant Monterey cypress, a rare tree that grows only on Point Lobos and nearby Cypress Point. These gnarled, twisted trees, buffeted by fierce coastal winds, line the park's rocky cliffs and headlands. To preserve the park's beauty, only 450 visitors are allowed into the park at any one time. Plan to come early or wait in line along the highway on weekends. Park visitors will agree with Robert Louis Stevenson, who supposedly modeled Spyglass Hill in *Treasure Island* after Point Lobos, that the site is "the most beautiful meeting of land and sea on earth."

The drive runs through Carmel Highlands and enters Big Sur Country past Point Lobos. This is a spectacular stretch of coast where the Santa Lucia Range plunges into the blue Pacific Ocean. The Santa Lucias, also called the Big Sur Hills, spread southward from the Carmel River to the Cuyama River. Much of the range is administered by Los Padres National Forest, part of which is the remote 250,000-acre Ventana Wilderness Area. The range high point is 5,862-foot Junipero Serra Peak.

The drive's next thirty miles clings to the seaward face of the Santa Lucias above the crash of the Pacific surf. The road is narrow with numerous pullouts. Use them to enjoy the scenery or allow traffic to safely pass. The first stop is 2,800-acre Garrapata State Park along the coast just north of Soberanes Point. This day-use park land, named by the Spanish for the lowly wood tick, boasts gleaming white beaches flanked by granite buttresses, arches, and grottos. Some good trails lace the bluffs above the water and the coves offer fishing for greenling and surf perch. A good trail climbs east from the highway 1.5 miles up Soberanes Creek to a verdant grove of redwoods nestled in the chaparral-covered hills.

The highway twists south from Garrapata past Kaiser and Rocky points to the Bixby Creek Bridge, a dramatic concrete span that arches over Bixby Creek's deep gorge. The famed bridge measures 718 feet long and 260 feet high and consumed some 6,600 cubic yards of concrete poured into forms supported by 300,000 board feet of Douglas fir. The bridge, also called Rainbow Bridge, was completed in 1932. The highway itself was finished in 1937, hacked out of the remote coast by convict labor who battled violent weather and tough engineering problems for nine years. The road cost more than $10 million or $71,000 per mile. The coast here at the turn of the century was one of California's least accessible regions. In the 1890s, Dr. John Roberts, a Monterey physician, often made house calls along the coast by riding on horseback on a spiraling wagon track. He gradually mapped and plotted a road course that ran from Monterey to San Luis Obispo. Roberts and state senator James Rigdon estimated the cost of the road to be $50,000 and got legislation passed in 1919 to construct the road. In the late 1950s, state engineers and land developers sought to modernize and straighten the road, turning it into an interstate-like highway. Big Sur's landowners realized the folly of the plan and fought to preserve the coast. The highway, withdrawn from the state freeway system, was dedicated in 1966 by Lady Bird Johnson as California's first official scenic drive.

The drive hugs the coast and then climbs away from a bridge to a lofty viewpoint above Hurricane Point. Good views of the ocean and the north coast are found here. Look to the south to see shipwrecks near Point Sur at low tide. The road drops southward, crosses the Little Sur River, and edges around Little River Hill to Point Sur. This rocky point was once nicknamed "the graveyard of the Pacific" for its numerous offshore shipwrecks including the *S.S. Los Angeles* in 1873. The automated Point Sur Lighthouse that now graces the site is operated by the Coast Guard. This 34-acre spit of land is also a state park. Regular ranger-led tours visit the lighthouse. The point also makes a great spot for winter whale watching. Massive fifty-ton California gray whales, California's state mammal, make an annual 12,000-mile round-trip migration south to Baja California from Alaska in autumn to breeding and birthing grounds in Mexican waters before heading north with the spring. Bring a pair of binoculars to look for these gentle giants surfacing off-shore.

California Highway 1 follows the rugged Big Sur Coast, one of California's most spectacular shorelines.

The highway bends southeast after Point Sur and traverses a wide bench between the mountains and the sea. After a few miles, it passes 2,088-acre Andrew Molera State Park along the lower section of the Big Sur River. The usually uncrowded park offers several trails, a two-mile-long beach, and a primitive fifty-site-walk-in campground a quarter mile from the highway parking lot. This area, bounded on the north by the Little Sur River and the south by the Big Sur River, was part of an 8,949-acre Mexican land grant called Rancho El Sur granted in 1839. The coast here was called by the early Spanish "El Pais Grande del Sur" or the Great Land of the South. Americans shortened it to Big Sur.

It's past Point Sur that Big Sur aficionados consider the "true" Big Sur to begin. A town called Big Sur stretches the six-mile-length of the Big Sur River Valley with scattered houses and a few stores along Highway 1. This backwater, picturesque valley has long been an artist's colony, attracting those who felt that even Carmel was too civilized. Novelist Henry Miller lived here from 1947 to 1964. He wrote of Big Sur: "That same prehistoric look. The look of always. Nature smiling at herself in the mirror of eternity."

Past Molera State Park, the highway swings inland and follows the Big Sur River valley southeast through abrupt wooded mountains. Pfeiffer-Big Sur State Park, one of California's most popular state parks, is soon encountered. This small 821-acre park abuts the Ventana Wilderness Area and is flanked by Pfeiffer Ridge and Cabezo Prieto. A thick woodland of oak, sycamore, big-leaf maples, willows, cottonwoods, and redwoods crowd the river valley, while trees that prefer drier climes, oak, chaparral, and the endemic Santa Lucia fir scatter across the higher ridges. The spectacular coastal redwoods grow in isolated groves here. Their thick, fire-resistant trunks lift skyward, casting a canopy of sun-dappled shade over the moist, fern-covered forest floor. An excellent trail wanders through the redwoods to Pfeiffer Falls. Other trails climb into the nearby wilderness area. The park offers 217 wooded campsites. But reservations are advised through MISTIX.

A mile past the state park Forest Road 19S05 drops down narrow Sycamore Canyon to scenic Pfeiffer Beach. This ragged coast is lined with rocky, wave-battered crags, and narrow sand beaches. It was the first place settled on the Big Sur coast when the Pfeiffers, for whom the beach and state park are named, homesteaded here in 1869. Another excellent side-trip begins at Andrew Molera State Park and follows the old Coast Road for eleven miles to Bixby Bridge. This dirt road offers spectacular views of Big Sur Country as it corkscrews up and over lofty ridges and peaks, but it may be impassable when wet.

Past the Sycamore Canyon turn the road rolls down to Nepenthe and its wide vista almost 1,000 feet above the azure Pacific Ocean. Filmmaker Orson Wells once owned a cabin here. Just south of Nepenthe sits the Henry Miller Memorial Library, an unassuming house among tall redwoods. This small library is open by appointment only; it preserves books, manuscripts, and paintings by one of Big Sur's most famous bohemian residents. Miller willed his personal collection to long-time friend Emil White, who in turn donated it to the Big Sur Land Trust for further preservation.

The Cabrillo Highway hugs the coast for the next sixty miles, occasionally venturing down near the pounding surf but usually edging along precipitous, chaparral-shrouded mountain sides high above the rocky strand. Except for the narrow band of asphalt-covered road, this remote, rugged land still remains as Spanish explorer Juan Cabrillo saw it in 1542, fifty scant years after Columbus' discovery of the New World. He noted in his journal, "All the coast passed this day is very bold; there is a great swell and the land is very high. There are mountains which seem to reach the heavens, and the sea beats on them."

Julia Pfeiffer Burns State Park, about seven miles south of Nepenthe, is another great park on the coast. Excellent hiking trails thread across the steep hillsides, dropping down to two miles of rocky coastline, and walking up trickling creeks lined with redwoods near the southern end of their range. One hike passes Saddle Rock to the cliffs above Waterfall Cove where a waterfall drops into the surf far below. The park has some walk-in and group camping, picnic facilities, as well as winter whale-watching programs.

The drive continues south, swings around Lopez Point, and enters the northern section of Los Padres National Forest. A couple miles later, the road passes thirty-three site Kirk Creek Campground and tiny Mill Creek Picnic Area. A prison labor camp for 150 well-behaved San Quentin inmates sat at Kirk Creek. The inmate's sentences were reduced three days for every two worked, and escape attempts into the dry, unpopulated surrounding country were rare. The Nacimiento-Ferguson Road, the only road over the Santa Lucia Range, twists east over the range crest to U.S. 101. A side-road climbs to the summit of 5,755-foot Cone Peak and overlooks the vast Ventana Wilderness to the north. Inquire at a national forest office for road conditions.

The small community of Pacific Valley sits on a wide marine terrace below the mountain escarpment. A national forest ranger station here dispenses information, maps, and wilderness permits. A short hike east from the station climbs to seventy-five-foot-high Salmon Creek Falls. This area offers some good coastal access on public lands. Sand Dollar Picnic Area and forty-four site Plaskett Creek Campground sit along this road section. Jade Cove south of Plaskett Point boasts excellent jade hunting along the cobbled beaches. The beaches and cove are unseen from the highway; look for signs and pullouts. A path drops down a stairway on a cliff to the cove. Two jade types are found here—rare Nephrite jade and common green Monterey jade. Over a period of months in 1971, three divers excavated an eight-foot-long, 9,000-pound boulder of nephrite jade valued at $180,000. At Willow Creek is a picnic area above the rocky beach. Higher is Willow Creek Vista on the highway with scenic views of the coast receding to the southeast horizon.

Past Willow Creek, the highway uncoils across precipitous ridges high above the ocean. Numerous pullouts allow scenic views. Drive carefully and slowly through this section; maximum speeds are less than thirty miles an hour. The road passes several rugged headlands—Ragged Point, Breaker Point, Point Sierra Nevada, and Point Piedras Blancas—that jut into the

A hiker crosses a surf-washed beach along the Big Sur Coast.

heaving water. Piedras Blancas, named for its white, guano-covered rocks, has a 145-foot-high lighthouse. The area is used for marine wildlife studies, including the thick kelp forest that covers the bay south of the lighthouse. The kelp is anchored to the ocean floor and grows to heights of 100 feet and serves as home to numerous sea creatures. A walk along the beach reveals tangles of kelp with remains of life clinging to the damp seaweed, including baby octopi, skeleton shrimp, sea spiders, sponges, and kelp crabs. The area also offers good spots to sit above the ocean and watch sea otters frolic in the kelp beds.

The landscape changes dramatically after Piedras Blancas as the road crosses grassy marine terraces above the low, rocky coastline. The chaparral-covered mountains rise beyond the bench. William Randolph Hearst Memorial State Beach lies near San Simeon. It offers good sunbathing, picnicking, and fishing. High above San Simeon atop the rounded hills sits California's second busiest tourist attraction—the Hearst San Simeon State Historic Monument. This extravagant castle was built by publishing magnate William Randolph Hearst beginning in 1919. The Hearst Castle, with 100 rooms including thirty-one bathrooms, two libraries, and a billiards parlor, is adorned with art treasures from around the world. The first-floor vestibule is decorated with 2,000-year-old mosaic tiles from Pompeii. The mansion cost more than ten million dollars, or as much as the total cost of Highway 1. The estate, donated to California by the Hearst Corporation in memory of its maker, can be toured daily. It takes almost two days to see the entire place.

A few miles past the turn to the Hearst estate lies San Simeon State Beach. This great beach, accessed by several roadside parking areas, spreads along the shore beneath low, broken cliffs topped by windswept grass. The state park land also offers two excellent campgrounds on the east side of the highway. San Simeon Creek Campground has 134 sites and Washburn Campground offers seventy sites on the rolling grassland.

Cambria, three miles south of San Simeon Beach, is nestled in a broad valley carved by Santa Rosa Creek. Groves of Monterey pine mix with open grasslands on the bold, rolling hills surrounding the town. The pine is endemic to California and grows in a very restricted range around Monterey, Ano Nuevo Point, two islands off Baja California, and around Cambria. It prefers sandy soils from marine sediments and moisture-laden summer fogs. Monterey pine, along with close relatives knob cone and Bishop pines, once grew across much of coastal California in a mild climate. All three pines grow today in relic stands. The Monterey pine, however, is widely used worldwide for reforestation and ornamental purposes.

The drive runs southeast from Cambria up broad Perry Creek valley and down Ellysly Creek and reaches the north end of scallop-shaped Estero Bay. The road heads east and then south through Cayucos, past Cayucos and Morro Strand state beaches to the town of Morro Bay on the tiny inlet of Morro Bay. The town is dominated by 576-foot-high Morro Rock, named by early Spanish explorers for its bold headland. The rock is also called the "Gibraltar of the Pacific." It is the interior remains of an ancient volcano that once lifted its cone here. South of the rock are large middens or piles of broken seashells left by the early Chumash Indians. Some artifacts found here are as old as 6,000 years. Morro Bay and Morro Rock are both wildlife preserves, inhabited by numerous birds, including falcons, great blue herons, egrets, and 250 other bird species living or wintering here. The bay, sitting along the Great Pacific Flyway, is an important rest stop for migrating birds. The bay and its fertile estuary is considered one of the nation's top bird watching spots. The town offers an excellent Museum of Natural History that explores the surrounding hills and ocean habitats. While the scenic drive ends at Morro Bay, Highway 1 bends inland at Morro Bay and runs as a four-lane highway another twelve miles to U.S. 101 and the historic town of San Luis Obispo.

General description: A 110-mile-long drive that begins on the western edge of the San Joaquin Valley, follows long grassy valleys formed by the San Andreas Rift Zone and traverses the edge of the Gabilan Range to Hollister.

Special attractions: San Andreas Rift Zone, Pinnacles National Monument, San Benito River, Gabilan Range, hiking, scenic views, camping, rock climbing, bicycling.

Location: West-central California. The drive begins on Interstate 5 in the San Joaquin Valley, heads west on California 198, then north on California 25 to Hollister just south of San Jose.

Drive route number: California highways 198 and 25.

Travel season: Year-round.

Camping: Only one campground lies along the drive—Pinnacles Campground, Inc. This private campground, with 125 shaded sites, is in Bear Valley on dead-end California 146 just off the drive before Pinnacles National Monument is reached.

Services: All services are available in Coalinga and Hollister. Don't plan on finding any services along the drive.

Nearby attractions: Fremont Peak State Park, San Juan Bautista State Historic Park, Monterey State Historic Park, Monterey Bay Aquarium, Monterey State Beach, Point Lobos State Reserve, Natural Bridges State Beach, Santa Cruz, Monterey, Mission Nuestra Senora de la Soledad, Santa Lucia Range, Los Padres National Forest.

For more information: Pinnacles National Monument, Paicines, 95043, (408) 389-4485.

The drive: This 110-mile scenic drive follows California highways 198 and 25 and traverses a series of long fault-line valleys formed by the San Andreas Rift Zone. The route passes along the east side of the Gabilan Range, which is one of the inner Coast Ranges between Coalinga in the San Joaquin Valley and Hollister east of Monterey Bay. The countryside the drive runs through is unpopulated and almost pristine, broken only by a few ranches or fences. The pastoral land offers a rare beauty and subtle charm, not overpowering like nearby Yosemite or the Big Sur Coast. Each season brings its own rhythm and distinct flavor. After spring rains, the rumpled land is verdant with green grass and sprinkled with colorful wildflowers. Summer heat desiccates the savannas and turns the straw-dry grass a tawny brown. This is a drive to savor, to slow down and admire the view, to stop and watch the wind ripple the grass, to watch a hawk soar overhead, and to appreciate the here and now.

The weather along the drive is typically Mediterranean with hot, dry summers and cool, rainy winters and springs. Winter and spring bring rain and cool temperatures sweeping in from the Pacific. Expect highs between fifty and seventy degrees. Summers are generally hot, with daily highs climbing to 90 or 100 degrees. The dry heat punishes the land, pulling moisture from the grasses, trees, and streams. Occasional clouds or showers blot the storm of sunlight.

The drive begins at the isolated intersection of Interstate 5 and California Highway 198 on the west side of the agriculturally developed San Joaquin Valley. Gas, food, and lodging are all available at this road junction. The first three miles run west to the junction of routes 198 and 33 and then south nine miles to Coalinga. The road rolls over undulating grass-covered hills called Anticline Ridge before dropping past irrigated fields to the Pleasant Valley and Coalinga. This area is dotted with oil wells, part of the Coalinga Oil Field. Coalinga, at 162 feet high, is a small community nestled against grassy hills on the west side of Pleasant Valley. The town is home to oil and farm workers and offers all services to travelers.

Leaving Coalinga, the highway climbs into the hills of the Diablo Range and follows the winding trickle of Wartham Creek westward. The Diablo Range, a series of low mountains seamed with abrupt rain-carved canyons, runs northwest above the San Joaquin Valley to 3,849-foot Mount Diablo just east of San Francisco Bay. The road twists and turns along the creek, passing ranch homes, grazing cattle and horses, and steep sand-colored hills. Stately cottonwood trees scatter along the creek bed, and junipers dot the hillsides. As the road gains elevation, oaks blanket the hills with blotches of dark green. Farther up the drive, the road and canyon straighten; spindly gray pines appear on the hills. "Digger" or gray pines, a common conifer on California's hot lowland slopes, have thin, ten-inch-long, gray needles that droop raggedly from its branches. The needles deflect much of the drying sunlight and offer small evaporative surfaces. The gray pine generally thrives in association with blue oak, another drought-tolerant tree. Oaks are typical California trees. Of the state's thirteen species, eleven oaks are endemic to the California Floristic Province.

Twenty-one miles from Coalinga the drive climbs away from Wartham Creek, crosses a divide, and drops into 2,300-foot-high Priest Valley. This picturesque valley, flanked by Twin Peaks and Round Mountain on the northeast and Mustang Ridge on the southwest, is as pretty a place as anywhere in California. Spreading oaks stud the grassy hillsides. Gray pines, cottonwoods, willows, and dense meadows line Lewis Creek as it winds across the valley. The valley was named in the early 1850s when William Galman and Captain Walker found a priest and 100 Indians encamped here while capturing wild horses. The valley is also the site of the last stand of the infamous bandit Joaquin Murrieta in 1853. After being brutally wronged by American miners, Murrieta vowed revenge and systematically murdered all the offenders. He and his gang then took up banditry. The state put a $5,000 reward on his death or capture and the hunt was on. Captain Harry Love and twenty rangers took the challenge and tracked Murrieta to an arroyo here in July of 1853. He was ambushed at night and killed. His head was cut off and

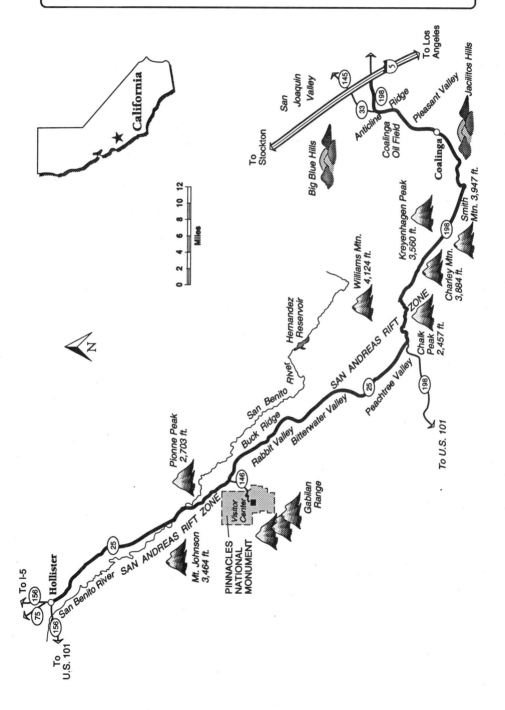

Scattered oaks and tawny grasslands cover rough hills above the San Andreas Fault in Rabbit Valley on California Highway 25.

taken to San Jose as proof of his demise. The head, preserved in alcohol, was later exhibited all over California.

After a few more miles, the highway climbs out of the valley floor up steep hillsides to the top of Mustang Ridge, a long ridge along the San Andreas Fault that separates Priest Valley and Lewis Creek from Peachtree Valley to the west. Spectacular vistas up Lewis Creek are seen from the drive as it climbs. The road switchbacks steeply with seven percent grades down the western slope of Mustang Ridge, reaching the broad floor of Peachtree Valley four miles from the ridge crest. The highway intersects California Highway 25 in the valley. Turn north on route 25. Highway 198 continues west to U.S. 101 just south of King City.

Highway 25 runs northwest up the Peachtree Valley along the seep of San Lorenzo Creek. Dry savanna country, green in spring and tan in summer, covers the valley floor and the mountain sides. Occasional oaks lurk among the grasslands. Fields of wheat, watered by sprinklers, grow alongside the drive. For twenty miles, the highway traverses Peachtree Valley, turns up Lewis Creek into Bitterwater Valley, and then up Rabbit Valley. The bucolic landscape here, with hump-backed ridges sweeping away from the sunny valley floor in great tawny grasslands and dense live oak thickets, belies the angry nature of the underlying earth.

The land at first seems to hold no great, mysterious secrets. But underground hides California's most famous and most studied earth feature—the San Andreas Fault. California is splintered with faults, most running southeast to northwest through long, linear valleys like Peachtree, Bitterwater, and Rabbit valleys. The San Andreas Fault or Rift Zone is the dividing line between the North American crustal plate and the Pacific plate and runs more than 600 miles from the Sea of Cortez in northern Mexico to the Mendecino Coast north of San Francisco. The Pacific plate is slipping northwest on an average of two inches a year. Often the plates lock together until they spring apart, moving with a sharp jolting earthquake. A 1857 quake on the Carrizo Plain south of here recorded an amazing thirty-three-foot slippage. Hollister, at the drive's terminus, rocks almost everyday with small, sometimes imperceptible earthquakes. A 1985 quake in Cienaga Valley, just south of Hollister off route 25, broke and spilled a 20,000-gallon wine keg in the Almaden winery. The winery's main building is built atop the fault itself, which is slowly wrenching the building apart.

Past Rabbit Valley, the drive climbs over a slight divide and runs up another high, narrow valley flanked by Buck Ridge on the east and the rugged Gabilan Range on the west. The road passes wheat fields and Dry Lake, a parched lake bed. Keep an eye out for pronghorn antelope grazing along the grassy roadside. The highway bends west past the San Benito turnoff, crosses a ridge, drops into Bear Valley, and reaches the intersection with California Highway 146. An excellent side trip turns west on 146 and travels five miles to the visitor center at Pinnacles National Monument.

Pinnacles National Monument is truly one of California's least known and least appreciated national park lands. The 16,222-acre monument, administered by the National Park Service, preserves a ragged jumble of eroded spires, buttes, buttresses, ramparts, aretes, and cathedrals in the otherwise pastoral Gabilan Range. Huge boulders and fallen debris form a roof over sharp, narrow canyons where streams carve underground caverns. The rock here is volcanic rhyolite and breccia deposited around a huge, 8,000-foot-high volcano some twenty-two million years ago and 195 miles to the south near Lancaster. The volcano, built atop the San Andreas Rift Zone, then began creeping northwest along the fault to its present position. The other portion of the volcano called the Neenach Formation still lies alongside the fault far to the south. Erosion did the rest of the work, sculpting, molding, and scouring the rock into its eerie, fractured shapes. The park remains a lesson in geology that tells tales of the uplifting and tearing down of great mountains, the long procession of life, and the earth's constant change.

Chaparral covers eighty-two percent of the monument and is the dominant ecosystem. It flourishes on steep slopes with coarse soil and scanty water. The common scrubby plants of chaparral include chamise, buckthorn, holly-leaved cherry, and manzanita. The riparian plant communities along meager streams are the park's most species-rich areas, with tall shade trees, including sycamores, cottonwoods, willows, and oaks, and a lush undergrowth of moss, ferns, and flowers. Lichens, the rock colonizer, inhabit the monument's rocks, spreading slowly across their surface, taking thirty years to cover a square inch and slowly breaking down the solid rock to soil. Most of Pinnacles is a wilderness area that harbors diverse wildlife. Birds include the ubiquitous turkey vulture and raven, screech owls, prairie falcons that nest in rocky aeries, scrub jays, nuthatches, quail, acorn woodpeckers, hawks, and owls. Mammal species are raccoon, blacktail deer, mountain lion, bobcat, skunk, gray fox, pocket mice, and deer mice. Hikers need to keep a wary eye out for rattlesnakes, a common resident of the hills and scree slopes.

Pinnacles offers visitors a range of outdoor opportunities. A private 125-site campground sits just east of the monument boundary on route 146 with tables shaded by towering oaks. Twenty-six miles of maintained trails lace the monument. The Bear Gulch Visitor Center exhibits the monument's geology, including a seismograph recording daily action on the nearby San Andreas Fault, natural history, and history. A few good hikes leave near the visitor center. The Moses Spring/Bear Gulch Caves Trail climbs up to several of the park's caves. The excellent 5.3-mile High Peaks Trail ascends steeply to the High Peaks, the rocky heart of Pinnacles. The Chalone Peak Trail reaches the monument's high point—3,304-foot North Chaldone Peak. The monument also offers excellent rock climbing on steep, pocketed rock and up slender spires. Springtime is the prime time to visit Pinnacles, with a blaze of wildflowers spreading carpets of color across the ridges and meadows.

The drive runs north from the Pinnacles turnoff up Bear Valley. After five miles, the highway leaves the broad fault valley, rolls across a few shallow canyons, and drops alongside the meandering San Benito River as it flows toward Monterey Bay. The river valley broadens as the road runs north. The forested Gabilan Range, beloved by author John Steinbeck, loom to the west. The range's northernmost mountain is 3,169-foot Fremont Peak, part of Fremont Peak State Park. Here, in 1846, Captain John C. Fremont raised the American flag on California soil in defiance of the Mexican government. The park has a campground and a trail to the mountain summit. Marvelous views unfold of Monterey Bay, Salinas Valley, and San Benito River Valley. Fields of grapes, part of the Almaden wine district, line the drive. The road turns away from the river at Paicines, skirts the east side of Swanson Bluff, and follows Tres Pinos Creek. A few miles further, it passes through Tres Pinos and low rolling hills covered with grass. The drive then drops into broad Hollister Valley. Three miles later it enters Hollister, which is the center of a rich agricultural region. A few miles west of Hollister on California 156 sits Mission San Juan Bautista, a state historic park that preserves the fifteenth Spanish mission in California; it was established in 1797. The surrounding town is a popular visitor attraction and still retains the ambience and flavor of a nineteenth century California town. A little further west lies Monterey and Santa Cruz on the shores of Monterey Bay.

General description: California Highway 96 twists alongside the Klamath and Trinity rivers for 147 miles through deep canyons and over densely wooded ridges in northern California.

Special attractions: Klamath River, Trinity River, Pacific Crest Trail, Klamath National Forest, Six Rivers National Forest, rafting, swimming, steelhead and salmon fishing, camping, hiking, backpacking.

Location: Northwestern California just south of the Oregon border. The drive runs from Interstate 5 six miles north of Yreka to Willow Creek and California route 299 forty miles east of Arcata on the Pacific coast.

Drive route number: California Highway 96.

Travel season: The highway is open year-round. Watch for wet pavement, heavy rain, and occasional snow in winter.

Camping: Nine campgrounds sit along the drive on national forest lands. The campgrounds from east to west are Tree of Heaven (twenty-one sites), Sarah Totten (seventeen sites), O'Neil Creek (eighteen sites), Fort Goff (five sites), Dillion Creek (twenty-one sites), Pearch Creek (eleven sites), Bluff Creek (eleven sites), Aikens Creek (twenty-nine sites), and Tish Tang (forty sites). Several other campgrounds lie just off the drive, including Boise Creek, Fish Lake, and Beaver Creek. Private RV parks are found along the drive.

Services: All services are in Yreka and Willow Creek. Limited services are found along the drive—including gas, food, and lodging—at Happy Camp, Orleans, Weitchpec, and Hoopa.

Nearby attractions: Marble Mountain Wilderness Area, Red Buttes Wilderness Area, Rogue River National Forest, Yreka, Mount Shasta, Salmon-Trinity Alps Wilderness Area, Russian Wilderness Area, Redwood National Park, Prairie Creek Redwoods State Park, Smith River Scenic Byway, Pacific coast beaches, Eureka.

For more information: Klamath National Forest, 1312 Fairlane Rd., Yreka, CA 96097, (916) 842-6131. Six Rivers National Forest, 507 F Street, Eureka, CA 95501, (707)442-1721.

The drive: California 96 twists for 147 miles through the deep gorges of the Klamath and Trinity rivers in the remote Klamath Ranges of northwestern California. The Klamath River, running from southern Oregon's Upper Klamath Lake through the Cascade and Klamath mountains to the Pacific Ocean, marks the southern and eastern boundary of the rumpled Siskiyou Mountains. The Scott Bar, Marble, and Salmon mountains stretch south of the river. In California, the 265-mile-long Klamath River is second only to the Sacramento River in the amount of water it empties into the Pacific. This is a rugged land seamed with precipitous canyons and lorded over by densely forested peaks. The drive offers travelers a chance to roam far from

California's well-used highways into a sparsely populated region with less than five people per square mile. The area teems with wildlife such as the legendary and elusive man-ape Sasquatch. Numerous pullouts line the road for scenic views and river access. Allow at least six hours to drive the narrow, winding route.

The climate along the Klamath River drive is generally moderate year-round. Summer temperatures vary from the upper nineties at the drive's desert origins on Interstate 5 to seventies and eighties in the thick forests 100 miles down river. Rain showers occasionally fall in summer at the lower elevations. The rainy season begins in October when the leaves change and continues through the winter. Expect cool, cloudy days with intermittent to heavy rainstorms. Snow sometimes falls along the highway but usually blankets the ridges and peaks above the river. The worst storm in recorded history occurred during the winter of 1964-65 when heavy rains and early snows saturated the Klamath Ranges. In mid-December 1964, moist tropical air that dashes against the coastal mountains further soaked the ground and melted the snowpack. The water, unable to soak into the sodden ground, ran into the already swollen Klamath and Eel rivers. The rain continued unabated for days, and towns along the Klamath were evacuated as the river rose to record levels. Roadside signs today mark the river level that reached depths of 100 feet and washed out much of the highway.

The drive begins six miles north of Yreka at the intersection of Interstate 5 and California 96. Turn west on route 96. Yreka, the largest town in the area, nestles against rolling grassy hills along Yreka Creek. The town boasts a proud pioneer past that started, like many California settlements, with the discovery of gold. Miners en route to the Scott Bar gold fields from Oregon camped here in 1851. The next morning Abraham Thompson found flecks of gold clinging to the grass roots his pack mules were eating. The discovery brought more than 2,000 miners in just a few weeks and Thompson's Dry Diggins was born. The town underwent five name changes in the next year before settling on Yreka, a Shasta Indian word meaning "north mountain." The town's numerous gold-rush era buildings, preserved on the National Register of Historic Places, can be toured with a free walking guide from the chamber of commerce. A display of gold nuggets at the Siskiyou County Courthouse and the Klamath National Forest Interpretative Museum are also well worth seeing.

A roadside rest area sits along the Klamath River immediately after exiting from the interstate. The road swings down along the bottom of the river canyon, a position it will occupy for the next 128 miles to Weitchpec. Junipers and chaparral clot the dry grassy slopes above the highway, while oaks line the river bank. At two miles, the Shasta River and California 263 from Yreka join the drive. The elevation along the drive is the highest here at 2,039 feet. The road wends westward, passing rocky crags and entering Klamath National Forest. The 1.7-million-acre forest offers five wilderness areas, four National Wild and Scenic rivers, and lots of untrampled, remote space. Tree of Heaven Campground sits below the road on a bowknot river bend; it has

Dense forests line the Klamath River and California Highway 96.

twenty-one campsites. A mowed lawn, shaded by fruit and nut trees, spreads among the campsites.

The drive continues west past Cayuse and Gottville river access points, and at eighteen miles goes through Klamath River, a small village on the river flood plain at 1,661 feet elevation; the town has limited services. A few miles beyond here the canyon broadens and high forested ridges outline the Siskiyou Mountains to the north. This is California's northernmost mountain range, stretching across the Oregon border. The timbered slopes have been heavily logged. South of the road tower 4,173-foot Bearcat Mountain and 5,493-foot Bald Mountain. Oak Knoll Ranger Station and McKinney River Access lie along the eleven-mile highway segment between Klamath River and Horse Creek. Just before Horse Creek, the road crosses the river on a girder bridge to the south bank. Tall pines mat the north-facing slopes while the warmer, grassy, south-facing slopes are sparsely sprinkled with oak and shrubs. As the road runs west, the canyon narrows and steep ridges rear up overhead.

The sixteen miles from Horse Creek to Seiad Valley is simply beautiful. The deep river swells through long placid pools before tumbling over water-worn boulders. Dense forest shades the banks and plentiful wildlife can be spotted from the road—including graceful, long-legged great blue herons and white egrets stalking the river shallows, beavers that attracted early trappers into these rugged canyons, and plentiful waterfowl such as pintail ducks, Canada geese, five species of grebes, and cormorants. Freshwater "riparian" habitats along rivers, streams, and lakes are California's most species-rich plant and animal communities. Riparian areas support eighty-three percent of the state's amphibian species, forty percent of its reptiles, and forty-two percent of its mammals. Common amphibians found here are the western toad, bullfrog, and Pacific giant salamander. Numerous reptiles also live in the forest, including sagebrush lizard, western skink, rubber boa, California mountain king snake, three types of garter snakes, and the western rattlesnake, which is commonly found in brushy, rocky areas along streams and rivers.

Five miles southwest of Horse Creek the Klamath River intersects with the Scott River. This small river runs south from the Scott Bar Mountains and the Trinity Alps. Scott Bar, three miles south of the drive on County Road 7F01, is a dilapidated townsite where miners including John Scott panned for gold along the river's gravel bars in 1850. By 1863, the placer deposits were mined out, although weekend prospectors still search here for the elusive metal. The Klamath River itself has also yielded gold from its river gravel. A prospecting party followed the river's length, panning gold from every promising bar along the way. Even today, dredges operate on placer claims on the river. A couple good campgrounds sit along the Scott River farther south from Scott Bar.

Sarah Totten Campground, with seventeen sites, is a mile down from the Scott River by the small town of Hamburg. Huge tailings piles left by placer miners lie along the Klamath here. O'Neill Campground lies another five miles down river and five miles beyond is Seiad Valley, a small village on the river's north bank. A New York farmer settled in this wide valley in 1854 and made a small fortune by growing potatoes and selling them to prospectors for fifteen cents a pound. The Pacific Crest Trail drops north down Girder Creek and crosses the river just west of here; it then climbs steeply north over 6,011-foot Upper Devil's Peak before twisting along the Siskiyou crest into Oregon. Small Fort Goff Campground, with five sites, sits alongside the drive four miles west of Seiad Valley.

The drive and river begin a southward march just past Fort Goff. The forest thickens along the river, with towering Douglas fir and pines blanketing the surrounding mountain peaks. The river begins alternately cutting down into abrupt bedrock gorges and meandering across wide, grassy meadows lined with willows. The Klamath Ranges, composed primarily of ancient seafloor sediments like mudstone and sandstone that were recrystallized by heat and pressure into metamorphic rocks, are an extension of the Sierra Nevada. The two ranges separated some 140 million years ago. The best place to see the Klamath Ranges' old seafloor rocks is in the shallow gorges exposed by the Klamath River. Ten miles south of Fort Goff the highway climbs away from the river, which winds below in entrenched meanders past Williams and Morgan points. After a couple miles, the road drops down a steep, forest-lined corridor to a broad valley and Happy Camp.

Happy Camp, at 1,085 feet, calls itself the "Steelhead Capital of the World" for its excellent fishing opportunities. The town was once an isolated mining area. Now it is a base for many outfitters for fishing and rafting expeditions. Gold and jade is still mined here, and it also is a popular jumping-off spot for backcountry visitors to the Siskiyou and Marble Mountain wilderness areas.

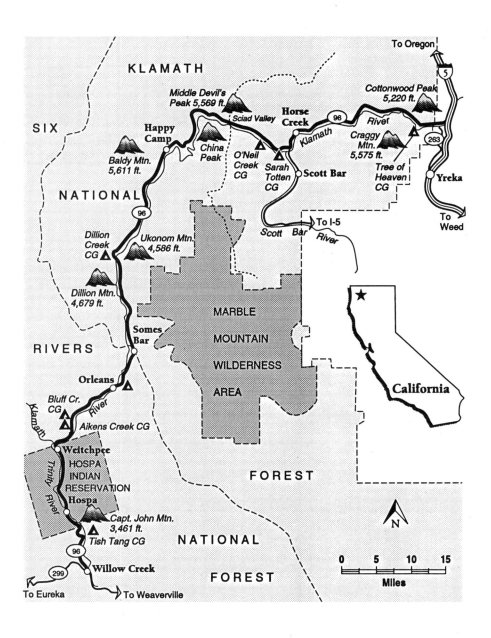

Fishermen flock to the Klamath River every fall for the steelhead and salmon run. More are caught in the Klamath River than any other California stream. A joint project between the native Karuk Indians and the California Department of Fish and Game is returning the chinook salmon to the Klamath and its tributaries. The fish are reared in ponds, imprinted with water from various tributaries, and then released in the hope that they will return to spawn in their imprinted waters. Pristine lakes in the surrounding mountains yield great rainbow, brown, and brook trout fishing.

The Klamath River also is known as one of California's best rafting rivers. The river's relatively slow flow, lack of huge rapids, and warm water attracts flotillas of rafts, kayaks, and canoes. The easy access afforded by Highway 96 allows numerous one or two day float trips of different lengths and difficulties. Happy Camp is a popular put-in for Class III runs that typically take three days. The river section from Interstate 5 to Happy Camp is mostly flat water with occasional Class II riffles. River guides and rental boats are available in Happy Camp.

From Happy Camp to Weitchpec, a distance of sixty-six miles, the river plunges south through a deep gorge lined with steep, forested ridges that climb to lofty 4,000-foot peaks. The canyon is mostly a narrow V-shaped chasm that occasionally opens into a wide valley. The drive follows the river, sometimes clinging shelf-like to the steep slopes above. Numerous river pullouts line the road, allowing easy access to the river below. Some good campgrounds lie along the road—Dillion Creek in Klamath National Forest, and Pearch Creek, Aikens Creek, and Bluff Creek campgrounds in Six Rivers National Forest. Dillion Creek has twenty-one sites scattered along a forested bench above Dillion Creek and is an excellent stop-over. A trail drops down from the campground to Dillion Creek and its fabulous, cliff-lined swimming holes, with deep, clear water. Other points of interest along the drive include Somes Bar and the trailhead for the nearby 242,000-acre Marble Mountain Wilderness Area. Somes Bar is a small town located on the confluence of the Klamath and Salmon rivers. The nearby Marble Mountain Wilderness Area has seventy-nine mountain lakes, several long limestone caves, verdant meadows, and glacier-polished peaks that climb to elevations of 7,000 feet. The town of Orleans lies another eleven miles down stream at an elevation of 400 feet. It offers all visitor services, including gas, food, lodging, and RV parks.

The rugged mountain country from Seiad Valley to Orleans is the ancestral homeland of the Karuk Indians. The tribe, only recently recognized by the federal government as a distinct cultural group, still occupies the area and uses their sacred ceremonial grounds at "Kota-mein" near Somes Bar and "Inam" at Clear Creek. The Karuk traditionally lived in villages and harvested the land's rich game and plants. Acorns, salmon, eels, deer, and ducks provided much of their diet. The Karuk are renowned for their exquisite basketry woven for food gathering and storage, carrying infants, and finely woven caps for ceremonies.

This remote land is also the home of Sasquatch or Bigfoot, the legendary

Morning sunlight glints off the Klamath River along California Highway 96.

man-ape that roams northern California. Numerous sightings here describe a creature seven to ten feet tall, weighing as much as 500 pounds, with thick fur, long arms, an erect posture, and huge footprints. A 1967 home movie captured the elusive animal on film, although biologists still argue about the film's veracity. Two young women from Happy Camp reportedly found a dead Sasquatch on a forest road in 1967, but they didn't report their grisly discovery until 1971 and were unable to relocate the exact site and remains that would have proven whether or not Bigfoot really exists.

Weitchpec sits on a bluff above the rocky confluence of the Klamath and Trinity rivers. The drive leaves the Klamath River here, which bends sharply northwest and flows to the Pacific. The road crosses the river on a high bridge, passes through the small hamlet of Weitchpec, and begins a torturous, twisting run southward above the precipitous gorge of the Trinity River. The road, carved into rock, hugs the steep mountain side for almost four miles before descending into the broad Hoopa Valley and the Hoopa Indian Reservation. The 100-square-mile reservation was established in 1865 after twelve bloody years of war between the Hoopa Indians and encroaching white settlers. The drive runs across broad meadows on the Trinity's floodplain and then past houses and businesses in the town of Hoopa, the reservation's administrative center.

The highway climbs out of the Hoopa Valley at its south end over densely forested ridges. Ancient Indian Village Vista Point is a good viewpoint that overlooks the valley to the north and the deep canyon of the Trinity River to the east. Tish Tang Campground nestles in the forest here. The road drops back down along the river's gravel banks, swings through pastures studded with grazing cattle and horses, crosses Willow Creek, and climbs up to the town of Willow Creek and the drive's end at its intersection with California Highway 299. A turn west leads across the Coastal Range to Arcata and the scenic Redwood Coast. A turn east heads up the winding Trinity River to historic Weaverville and on to Redding at the north end of the Central Valley.

8 LAVA BEDS NATIONAL MONUMENT SCENIC DRIVE

General description: A forty-mile-long drive that makes an open loop through Lava Beds National Monument, passing cinder cones, vast lava flows, lava tube caves, the site of the Modoc Indian War, and the wetlands of Tule Lake National Wildlife Refuge.

Special attractions: Lava Beds National Monument, Lava Beds Wilderness Area, Cave Loop Road, lava tube caves, Schonchin Butte, Schonchin Lava Flow, Devil's Homestead Lava Flow, Modoc War historic sites, Captain Jack's Stronghold, Tule Lake National Wildlife Refuge, Modoc National Forest, petroglyphs, wildlife, waterfowl, hiking, backpacking, caving, camping.

Location: Far northeastern California. The drive's northern terminus on California 139 is four miles south of Tule lake and eight miles south of the Oregon border. The southern end is twenty-seven miles north of Canby and California 299.

Drive route numbers and names: Modoc Forest Road 97 (Tionesta Road), Modoc Forest Road 10 (Lava Beds National Monument Road), Modoc County Road 120, Modoc County Road 111.

Travel season: Year-round. The drive is sometimes icy or snowy in winter.

Camping: Indian Well Campground east of the monument's visitor center has forty sites with water, restrooms, picnic table, fire ring, and grill. Water and flush toilets are only available in the summer season. Winter camping is free. Several campgrounds lie in adjoining Modoc National Forest, including Medicine Lake, Headquarters, and Hemlock south of the monument.

Services: All services are available in Tulelake and Canby, California and Merrill, Oregon.

Nearby attractions: Clear Lake National Wildlife Refuge, Lower Klamath National Wildlife Refuge, Mount Shasta, Klamath National Forest, South Warner Wilderness Area, Cedar Pass-Fandango Pass scenic drive, Buckhorn Back Country Byway, Goose Lake, Glass Mountain Geologic Area.

For more information: Lava Beds National Monument, Box 867, Tulelake, CA 96134, (916) 667-2282. Tulelake Chamber of Commerce, 619 Main, Tulelake, CA 96134, (916) 667-5178.

The drive: The Lava Beds National Monument scenic drive traverses forty miles of wild country on the edge of the Modoc Plateau of northeastern California. It's a rare landscape of spreading lava flows studded with black cinder cones, a once-violent land filled with the silent sound and fury of recent volcanism. The Modoc Plateau, covering all of northeastern California, is the southern part of the greater Columbia Plateau. This immense 200,000-square-mile area encompasses eastern Oregon and parts of Washington, Nevada, Utah, Idaho, Wyoming, as well as California. The Columbia Plateau built up over the last thirty million years as a long succession of lava flows, pouring out of surface vents and fissures. It flooded the land with thousands of feet of basalt and rhyolite and left only high peaks and volcanoes poking island-like above the sea of lava. The flows varied from 10 to 200 feet in thickness. Geologists estimate that more than 100,000 cubic miles of lava formed the plateau. While ancient stair-stepped lava plateaus surround Lava Beds National Monument, the flows and cones seen here are much more recent. The Callahan lava flow in the monument's southwestern corner is only 1,100 years old, while others formed in the last 100,000 years.

The climate at Lava Beds is generally dry with temperatures ranging from a record low of minus 18 degrees to a high of 102 degrees. The monument receives just over fifteen inches of precipitation annually and more than forty-one inches of snow each winter. Elevations up to 5,600 feet ensure chilly weather anytime of the year, and snow has been reported in every month except August. May through October is the best time to visit. Spring highs are in the fifties and sixties, with cool nights and occasional showers. Summer can be hot, with temperatures approaching 100 degrees. July, the warmest month, averages a high of eighty-two degrees daily. But be prepared for chilly nights. Heavy thunderstorms can douse the monument, even though it is usually dry. Winter highs hover around forty degrees, with nights in the low twenties. Tule fog often envelopes the monument, riming junipers and sagebrush with a crystal coat of ice.

The scenic drive begins twenty-seven miles north of Canby on California Highway 139. Turn west from the highway onto Modoc Forest Road 97. The turn is marked Lava Beds National Monument. The drive follows Forest Road 97 for two and a half miles before turning onto Forest Road 10. The entire drive is a paved, two-lane roadway with numerous scenic and interpretive pullouts. For the next few miles, the road crosses a gently undulating landscape blanketed with sagebrush, grasses, junipers, and scattered ponderosa pines. After a few more miles, the road skirts the southern edge of a huge lava flow punctuated with rounded cinder cones. Watch for marked side roads that run north to East Sand Butte and 4,661-foot Big Sand Butte.

Southwest of the drive looms the Medicine Lake volcano, a huge blister-like volcano spotted with numerous recent cinder cones. Recurrent eruptions over many millennia erected a rounded shield volcano here with gently sloping sides. The magma chamber under the summit later emptied through side vents, causing the peak to collapse inward and form a six-mile-long, 500-foot-deep caldera. Medicine Lake, a popular fishing and boating lake, nestles its sparkling blue waters in the caldera's depths. Earthquakes under the mountain indicate to geologists that the volcano is not dead yet. Glass Mountain Geologic Area is another interesting point on the mountain. Sharp, glassy obsidian found here forms a 950-year-old lava flow on the volcano's east flank. The highlands are reached by Forest Road 49 along the drive. Three campgrounds surround Medicine Lake.

At nine miles from the beginning, the drive swings around Little Sand Butte and three miles later enters Lava Beds National Monument. The 46,821-acre monument, with more than 28,000 acres of established wilderness, preserves some of America's best volcanic features such as lava flows, lava tube caves, and cinder cones, as well as historic and archeological sites from the Modoc Tribe and plant and animal communities similar to those in the nearby Great Basin Desert. The national monument was established by presidential proclamation in 1933 and is literally blanketed by volcanic rock. The monument boasts the greatest concentration of lava tube caves in the United States, with more than 200 located so far. The longest, Catacombs Cave, stretches 6,900 feet underground. Other caves reach depths of 150 feet with several surveyed levels. Besides its geologic attractions, the monument offers a wealth of wildlife—including migrating birds on the Pacific Flyway that shelter over at nearby Tule Lake Unit of Klamath Basin National Wildlife Refuge.

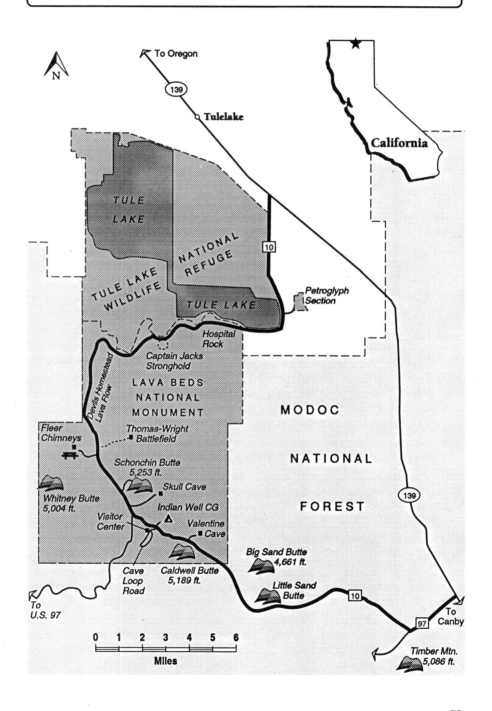

To Oregon

139

Tulelake

California

10

TULE LAKE

NATIONAL REFUGE

TULE LAKE WILDLIFE

TULE LAKE

Petroglyph Section

Hospital Rock

Captain Jacks Stronghold

Devils Homestead Lava Flow

LAVA BEDS NATIONAL MONUMENT

MODOC

Fleer Chimneys

Thomas-Wright Battlefield

NATIONAL

Schonchin Butte 5,253 ft.

Skull Cave

Whitney Butte 5,004 ft.

Indian Well CG

FOREST

139

Visitor Center

Valentine Cave

Cave Loop Road

Caldwell Butte 5,189 ft.

Big Sand Butte 4,661 ft.

Little Sand Butte

10

To U.S. 97

97

To Canby

Timber Mtn. 5,086 ft.

| 0 | 1 | 2 | 3 | 4 | 5 | 6 |

Miles

After entering the national monument, the drive runs northwest past 5,189-foot Caldwell Butte, Valentine Cave, and over an old lava flow sprinkled with western juniper and sagebrush on the way to the monument's visitor center. The center offers free information about the monument, as well as displays of natural history, geology, and history. Indian Well Campground, with forty sites, lies a half mile east of the visitor center. The sites, spread among junipers and cinders, have tables and grills. Water and flush toilets are available from May through September. In winter, all water is turned off, but camping is free. Nightly campfire programs occur in summer.

A good introduction to the monument's caves is Mushpot Cave near the visitor center. The cave is the only lighted one at Lava Beds and offers interpretive displays on the formation of lava tubes. Two basic cave types are found in the United States—limestone solution caves and lava tube caves. Lava tubes are caves that were once filled with flowing, molten lava. As lava advances downhill, the surface quickly cools and hardens into a thick crust. The rigid basalt surface acts as a good insulator, keeping underground lava fluid. The lava drains like a river down a tube or cavity toward the front edge of the flow. After the main volcanic vents stop spewing magma from the earth's mantle, the tube empties and leaves an open cavity beneath the surface. Some master tubes can run for miles, often branching to form distributary tubes.

The two-mile-long Cave Loop Road west of the visitor center is an excellent place to discover the variety and beauty of the Lava Beds' caves. This area has the monument's largest concentration of caves and many are easily accessible from numerous parking areas. Some caves have ladders or stairways that drop from the surface to the cave floor. Maps for many of the caves are available at the visitor center. Be sure to carry at least three sources of battery-powered light, as well as extra batteries. Carry a light for each explorer and never go alone. It's wise to wear a hardhat. There are many sharp and jagged lava chunks in the cave ceilings. Dress warmly, the caves are cool and moist, even in summer. If you plan on going to undeveloped caves in the more remote parts of the monument, be sure to check in at the visitor center. It is unlawful to eat, smoke, or carry glass containers in the caves. The center also lends flashlights and bump hats to spelunkers. The caves on the loop road include: Catacombs Cave, the connected Hercules Leg and Juniper caves, Golden Dome Cave, and Hopkins Chocolate Cave.

Past the visitor center, the drive swings around another cinder cone called Crescent Butte and then runs northwest through a sparse woodland of western juniper and mountain mahogany. Lava Beds sits on the boundary between two great ecosystems—the Great Basin Desert to the east and the Cascade Mountains to the west—and encompasses plants and animals characteristic of both. The monument at first glance appears somewhat barren. Life, however, has secured a firm foothold on the seemingly inhospitable lava beds. Lichen, the rock colonizer, covers the lava surface and slowly breaks the basalt down to soil. Sagebrush and grasses coat much

The Lava Beds scenic drive crosses the recent Devil's Homestead Lava Flow in Lava Beds National Monument.

of the monument's lower elevations, while woodlands of juniper and pine blanket the higher southern reaches. Six pine species, including ponderosa, knob cone, Jeffrey, and sugar, are found here as well as white fir and incense cedar. Spring and early summer brings a colorful display of wildflowers.

The monument's three main ecosystems—pine forests, sagebrush grasslands, and brush lands harbor an astonishing variety of life with more than 283 wildlife species. Mammal species total forty-eight. Mule deer are the most common large mammal, with hundreds migrating onto the monument during winter from the snowy Medicine Lake highlands. Other mammals at the monument include: pronghorn, bobcat, porcupine, striped skunk, kangaroo rat, yellow-bellied marmot, pika, and twelve bat species.

Lava Beds National Monument and the surrounding Klamath Basin is renowned for its large numbers of raptors, with twenty-five species recorded here. The area's plateaus and ridges, rimmed with basalt cliffs, make perfect aeries for hawks, owls, and eagles. More bald eagles winter along Tule Lake than anywhere else south of Alaska. Common raptors seen include turkey vultures, sharp-shinned hawks, red-tailed hawks, prairie falcons, barn owls, and great horned owls. The birds are often seen wheeling over the lava beds, looking for mice, rats, squirrels, and snakes. Eight different snake species live at Lava Beds. Some interesting snakes are the Rocky Mountain rubber boa, a type of boa constrictor, the rare ringneck snake, the semi-poisonous desert night snake, and the western rattlesnake. Rattlesnakes, while common here, are rarely seen. But visitors should use caution when hiking and when crawling into caves. Rattlesnakes are sometimes found on ledges near cave entrances.

The drive rolls northwest past cinder cones and old lava flows. Spectacular views unfold of high plateaus and the Warner Mountains to the east and Tule Lake to the north. A side road drops east to Skull Cave. This large cave, named for bighorn sheep skulls found inside, has a seventy-five-foot-high chamber and a floor covered with ice year-round. Nearby is a 0.8-mile trail that leads to Big Painted Cave and Symbol Bridge. Outstanding pictographs painted by Indians, including the Modoc culture, adorn both sites. Unfortunately, vandalism has defaced many of the rock art panels. Remember, look but don't touch. Finger oils transmitted to the delicate paintings hasten their ruin.

A mile and a half up the drive another road heads west to Merrill Cave. This is an excellent cave with perennial ice in its lower level. During winter beautiful icicles and ice crystals form on the cave walls and ceiling. The 3.4-mile Whitney Butte Trail begins at the cave parking area and travels west around 5,004-foot Whitney Butte. Schonchin Butte, a 5,253-foot cinder cone, looms north of the drive past the Merrill Cave turnoff. Another side road turns off the drive and leads to a hiking trail that climbs steeply to a fire lookout atop the peak. It offers marvelous 360 degree views of the surrounding lava fields and Tule Lake Basin. The side road is unsuitable for trailers.

Past the butte the drive runs onto a rolling sea of black lava, the crests frozen and twisted against the sky. A pull off leads to the short trail to Balcony and Boulevard caves. Another side road runs west to Fleener Chimneys. The chimneys are spatter cones that formed when lava spattered around a vent along a fissure. Magma, forced up through the vent, bubbled explosively and tossed molten rock onto the cone's steep sides. Rivers of lava also flowed out of vents here and meandered north for three and a half miles forming the Devil's Homestead Lava Flow. The Fleener Chimneys, one of the Lava Beds' first attractions, were more than 100 feet deep. Visitors, however, dropped rocks into the deepest hole and eventually filled it. The chimneys are slowly being restored to their former depth.

The drive drops northward, passes Black Crater and the trail to Thomas-Wright Battlefield, and dips down onto the Devil's Homestead Lava Flow. This flow looks almost new with only lichen and a scattering of juniper and rabbitbrush on the black lava. A pullout in the middle of the flow makes a good stop to look at a fairly recent flow. Both types of hardened lava—"aa" and "pahoehoe"—are seen here. Both words are Hawaiian. When the lava left the vents at Fleener Chimneys, the fluid pahoehoe lava ran north in the wide valley. By the time the lava reached today's drive, it had cooled, lost dissolved gases, and turned into viscous aa lava. Pahoehoe forms a ropy-textured surface when it cools, whereas aa is chunky, jagged, and heaped into loose ridges.

After crossing the half-mile-wide lava flow, the drive edges onto the east flank of Gillem Bluff, a long ridge striped with bands of basalt that stair-step upward. The road runs along a grassy bench above Devil's Homestead Lava Flow. A viewpoint on a cliff edge gives a great view of the torturous lava

A spelunker explores a rough side passage in Hopkins Chocolate Cave in Lava Beds National Monument.

landscape to the east. Three miles from the lava flow the road bends east along the wildlife refuge border and follows old lava flows above Tule Lake. Several stops along here explain key historic sites of the Modoc Indian War.

The Modoc Indians lived in the Klamath and Tule Lake basins along the California-Oregon border for hundreds if not thousands of years. Archeological evidence suggests the area was inhabited as long ago as 11,500 years. The Modocs had a hunting and gathering society, following the deer and other game into the neighboring mountains in summer and coming back to more permanent camps around Tule, Lower Klamath, and Clear lakes. Here were plentiful waterfowl, fish, roots, seeds, and tule reeds. But by the 1860s, American settlers came to the valley and asked the U.S. government to move the Modocs to a reservation. They were placed on the Klamath Reservation with the Klamath and Snake Indians, their ancestral enemies. The arrangement was unsatisfactory and some of the Modocs led by their young leader Kientpoos, nicknamed Captain Jack, left the reservation and went back to their homeland. On November 28, 1872, army troops were sent out to bring the Modocs, "by force if necessary," back to the reservation. Hostilities broke out and the war began.

The Modocs, after murdering some valley settlers in retribution, retreated into the lava beds and made their stand in a rugged area of lava trenches, shallow caves, and rough terrain now called Captain Jack's Stronghold. More than 300 troops made their way through thick fog on January 16, 1873, to capture the fifty Modoc men, women, and children. But the Modocs, using the natural fort to their advantage, routed the troops in the fog, killing nine, wounding twenty-eight, and capturing plenty of guns and ammunition. The government then decided to try to resolve the issue peacefully, and a Peace Commission was organized by President Ulysses Grant. Several meetings took place and the issue was unresolved. The Modocs wanted to live on their homeland and the U.S. government wanted them moved to the reservation. A militant Modoc faction, convinced that the army would leave if their leaders were killed, prodded Captain Jack into agreeing to help murder the commission. At an April meeting several Modocs opened fire on the four unarmed commissioners, killing General Thomas Canby and Reverend Thomas. The army then began a siege of the stronghold, but upon capturing it a few days later on April 17, they found it deserted. The Modocs, under cover of night, had retreated across an unguarded lava plateau. On May 10 the Modocs attacked an army camp at Dry Lake, but were soundly defeated. The Indians quarreled, split into several splinter groups, and headed out of the area. A group led by Hooker Jim was captured, and Hooker Jim agreed to track down Captain Jack. Captain Jack surrendered on June 1, and California's only major Indian war was over. Captain Jack and three other Modoc leaders hanged in October 1873, and the surviving Indians were shipped to a reservation in Oklahoma. The Modoc tribe and culture virtually disappeared as many Indians died of disease. About 200 Modocs live in Oklahoma today as descendants of the original 155 captured Indians. Some 300 people of Modoc ancestry also live in southern Oregon and northern California, descendants of those Modocs who never left the reservation during the war.

The first of the drive's historic sites is located where the road bends east. This is Gillem's Camp, the 1873 site of army headquarters during the six-month Modoc War. A few small ruins with interpretive signs is all that remains. A mile farther lies Canby Cross where General Canby was assassinated by Captain Jack. The drive runs across grass-covered lava flows to Captain Jack's Stronghold. Here, an interesting loop walk explores the natural lava battlements, stopping at various points of interest including shelter caves and firing positions. A small picnic area sheltered by junipers is located at the parking area. Two miles east lies Hospital Rock, site of a small army encampment during the Modoc War.

Two roadside wildlife turnouts overlook Tule Lake along the monument's northern border, offering views of ducks and geese bobbing on the lake surface. Tule Lake is known for its spectacular displays of birds, particularly waterfowl. The semi-annual migrations of birds along the Pacific Flyway include lengthy stops at the Tule Lake Unit of the Klamath Basin National Wildlife Refuge, just north of the monument. The wetlands here support literally millions of birds. In autumn more than a million ducks and a half-million geese rest and recuperate on their long journeys from the Arctic to winter's warmer climes. Springtime brings nesting waterfowl that dot the lake's placid water. The drive section along the Lava Beds' northern boundary skirts the edge of Tule Lake. The Wildlife Refuge Tour Route is a dirt road that parallels the drive and gives great views of twenty duck species along with geese, pelicans, herons, cormorants, and others. A pair of binoculars is handy to help with species identifications. Good views of snowcapped Mount Shasta, a huge stratovolcano that looms in the west, are found along the drive here.

The drive dips down, leaves the Lava Beds, and runs across a dike next to Tule Lake. The lake, occasionally thick with waterfowl, is fringed by reeds and marsh, while irrigated fields spread to the south. Almost two miles later, the drive intersects Modoc County Road 111. Turn north or left here. A short distance along the road, a turn leads to the Petroglyph Section of Lava Beds National Monument. A sand-colored volcanic cliff face here is etched with Indian petroglyphs or rock art. The drive continues north, skirting the east edge of the lake and passing wheat fields, grain elevators, egrets wading in a roadside canal, and red-winged blackbirds perched atop wavering tule reeds. The road ends on California Highway 139 four miles south of the town of Tulelake. A left turn heads to Tulelake and Oregon, and a right goes south on California Highway 139 to Canby.

9 CEDAR PASS-FANDANGO PASS SCENIC DRIVE

General description: This eighty-one-mile drive loops over the Warner Mountains via Cedar and Fandango passes in northeastern California, passing ranch lands, rugged mountain scenery, a dried alkali lake bed, and Goose Lake.

Special attractions: Warner Mountains, Goose Lake, Cedar Pass, Fandango Pass, Cedarville, Modoc National Forest, hiking, camping, panoramic views.

Location: Far northeastern California. The drive begins six miles north of Alturas at the junction of U.S. 395 and California 299.

Drive route names and numbers: California Highway 299, Surprise Valley Road, Modoc County Road 1, Fandango Pass Road, Forest Road 9, U.S. 395.

Travel season: Year-round. The paved highway sections on U.S. 395 and California 299 are open year-round. Watch for heavy snow and icy roads. The Fandango Pass Road closes in early winter and reopens in late spring.

Camping: Two national forest campgrounds, Cedar Pass and Stough, sit along California 299 near the Cedar Pass summit. Otherwise low-impact, primitive camping is permitted in Modoc National Forest off the drive and on adjoining BLM lands. Goose Lake State Park just across the border in Oregon has a peaceful lake-side campground with showers.

Services: All services are found in Alturas and Lakeview, Oregon. Limited services are in Cedarville and Fort Bidwell.

Nearby attractions: Modoc National Forest, Barrel Springs Back Country

Byway, Lava Beds National Monument, Klamath Basin National Wildlife Refuges, South Warner Wilderness Area, Buckhorn Back Country Byway, Goose Lake State Park (Oregon).

For more information: Modoc National Forest, 441 N. Main Street, Alturas, CA 96101, (916) 233-5811. Modoc County Chamber of Commerce, 522 S. Main, Alturas, CA 96101, (916)233-4434.

The drive: Northeastern California is a remote, hidden land, a place of broad volcanic plateaus, barren lava, cinder hills, fault-block mountains, wide valleys, and trickling creeks. The unpopulated region of California's outback forms a boundary between the state's fertile interior valleys and lush coastal ranges and the arid Great Basin Desert in Nevada. The area encompasses two of the state's geomorphic provinces—the Modoc Plateau, part of the greater Columbia Plateau, and the Basin and Range province. This eighty-one-mile scenic drive explores the austere region's diversity, climbing over two passes in the Warner Mountains, traversing Surprise Valley, and passing Goose Lake. The drive offers stunning views—lofty mountains fringed with snow cornices, watery mirages that dance over desiccated lake beds, the dull-gray sheen of sagebrush blanketing rounded ridges and hillocks, and distant peaks that gleam with snow like alabaster towers.

Traffic along the drive's seventy-one paved miles and ten gravel miles is light and mostly local. The ten-mile section over Fandango Pass is graded gravel and generally one-and-a-half lanes wide. This section is easily driven in a passenger car except after heavy rain when parts might be muddy and slick. Winter snow closes Fandango Pass. But the rest of the drive remains open.

Summer and autumn are the best times to drive the roads, with daily highs falling between seventy and 100 degrees. The record high for the area is a sweltering 112 degrees. It is cooler in the Warner Mountains than the surrounding valleys. Rainfall is sporadic, with occasional thunderstorms crackling over the mountain crest. The area has severe winter weather with freezing temperatures and heavy snow atop the peaks. Temperatures can fall as low as minus thirty-five degrees, but daytime highs are usually in the thirties. Up to eight inches of snow may fall on the valley floors, while up to eight feet may blanket the higher elevations. Cold weather begins in November and often lasts until May. Spring tends to be short, with warm, breezy days.

The scenic drive begins six miles north of Alturas where U.S. 395 intersects California Highway 299. Turn east on route 299. Alturas, the county seat of immense Modoc County, nestles among rolling hills along the Pit River on the gentle western flank of the Warner Mountains. Alturas means "valley on the mountaintop" in Spanish. It was settled in the early 1870s as ranchers and homesteaders took up residence in the grassy valley. The town, far from California's population centers, boasts an old West ambience; it is surrounded by sheep and cattle ranches; its side streets are quiet and tree lined; and it claims Modoc County's only two traffic lights.

CEDAR PASS-FANDANGO PASS SCENIC DRIVE

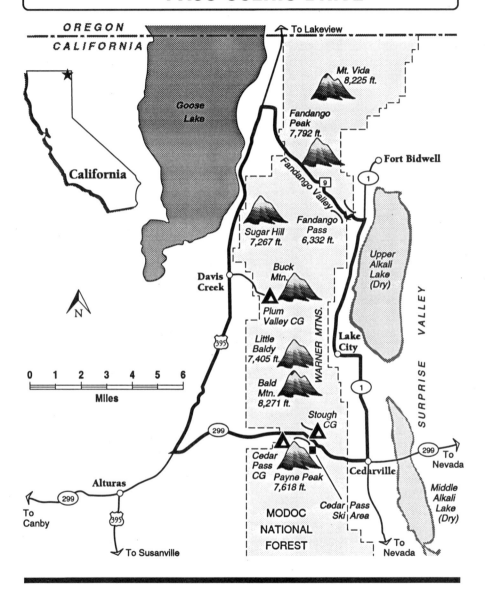

The Modoc County Historical Museum offers a collection of more than 400 pioneer guns and Indian artifacts, including projectile points, spears, and baskets. Just south of town off U.S. 395 lies the 6,280-acre Modoc National Wildlife Refuge. An auto tour route loops through the refuge's wetlands, allowing visitors to glimpse waterfowl on their bi-annual migrations.

The drive steadily climbs east from the North Fork of the Pit River over undulating basalt ridges. A forest of western juniper coats the rolling hillocks. After a couple miles, the highway emerges onto a sagebrush-covered bench and reaches an elevation of 5,000 feet. The road drops into a shallow valley and follows Thomas Creek eastward. The trickling creek, densely lined with towering cottonwoods and willow thickets, is broken by wide grassy meadows and scattered ranches. Ponderosa pines crowd the hill sides south of the creek.

To the south and east, looms the Warner Range, an impressive eighty-mile-long sierra studded with rounded peaks seamed with deep canyons. These isolated mountains are a raised fault-block range of old volcanic rock. The Surprise Valley fault scarp forms a steep, precipitous face on the range's east side, while the western slope gently tilts upward to the range crest. Several Warner summits top 9,000 feet, including Eagle Peak, the 9,892-foot high point. Much of the range's rugged character is protected in the 69,000-acre South Warner Wilderness Area with its wind-ruffled lakes, wildflower-strewn meadows, and abundant recreational opportunities. One of the best walks is the twenty-six-mile Summit Trail along the range crest south of the scenic drive. Inquire at the Modoc National Forest office in Alturas for wilderness permits and hiking information.

The scenic drive follows the only highway over the Warner Range as it climbs alongside Thomas Creek. As it ascends, the climate cools. Pines and firs mat the moist north-facing slopes, while sagebrush and juniper are scattered across the slopes north of the asphalt. Cedar Pass Campground, its seventeen camp sites shaded by tall conifers, sits just below the pass summit at 5,900 feet. Past the campground the canyon narrows. It is hemmed in by steep scree slopes and bold cliffs. Outcrops of breccia, a volcanic rock of ash and cinders, protrude out of the mountainside north of the highway. Almost three miles from the campground, the drive crests the top of 6,305-foot Cedar Pass. Bald and Cedar mountains lift their rocky bulks to the north above Summit Canyon. The first road over the pass was built by pioneer John Bonner in 1869, and the modern road generally follows the same route.

The road drops steeply down Cedar Creek Canyon on the eastside of the pass. Just below the summit, a short side-road climbs to Stough Reservoir and an eight-site national forest campground. Another turn leads south to Cedar Pass Ski Area, a small ski slope with a beginner hill, T-bar lift to advanced runs, and groomed cross-country trails. The highway twists down the canyon and empties onto the western side of the broad Surprise Valley and Cedarville at 4,630 foot elevation.

Visiting Cedarville is like taking a big step back in time. It's a rural, friendly town that, except for a few modern amenities, looks like it just woke up to the twentieth century. The town is the oldest in these parts; it got its start in 1865 when a Mr. Townsend built a cabin here. Indians killed him that same year, and his widow sold the place to John Bonner and William Cressler. They used it as a trading post and store, supplying passing emigrants on the Lassen-Applegate Trail and settlers in Surprise Valley. The old Cressler-Bonner

The Warner Mountains loom above a ranch barn in Surprise Valley along the Cedar Pass-Fandango Pass scenic drive in northeastern California.

Trading Post, a weather-worn, log cabin with a shake roof, stands in a town park. Cedarville still serves as a supply center for neighboring ranches in the Surprise Valley and across the border in Nevada.

The drive turns in Cedarville on Modoc County Road 1 (Surprise Valley Road). It then runs north along the sloping western edge of the huge valley. The Surprise Valley, so named because of the surprise registered by a party of 1861 emigrants on seeing the fertile, green valley floor after crossing the torturous Nevada desert, is a wide basin dotted with verdant hay fields, grazing cattle, and three dried lake beds—Upper, Middle, and Lower Alkali lakes. The valley was formed as a down-faulted basin between two uplifted mountain ranges. It was an immense lake not long ago that stretched down the valley's seventy mile length. During the last ice age it filled with runoff, but over the last 10,000 years the lake shrunk as the climate warmed and dried, leaving only these three huge sand pans. Water occasionally covers the lakes with a thin sheet that reflects the sky, clouds, and nearby peaks.

Just over nine miles from Cedarville, the drive enters Lake City, another old settlement. Not much is left of the town now save a few clapboard homes surrounded by spreading cottonwood trees and orchards, but this site was once a busy town. Its first cabin was erected in 1864, and a sawmill began operations the next year. By 1868, Lake City offered a post office, saloon, hotel, log schoolhouse, and store.

The road runs north from Lake City on old shoreline terraces above Upper Alkali Lake. Green pastures dotted with cattle cover the gentle slopes between the lake and roadway. The Warner Mountains lift their lofty escarpment to the west with sagebrush and juniper on the lower slopes giving way to pine and fir forests up high. Snow cornices line the upper ridge lines against the cobalt sky.

Ten miles from Lake City the Surprise Valley Road intersects with Forest Road 9 (Fandango Pass Road). Turn west on it. It's worth a side-trip to continue north a few miles to Fort Bidwell at the head of the Surprise Valley. Fort Bidwell is the farthest northeast of any town in California. It was an important military site that provided protection from Indians for emigrant travelers and early settlers, beginning in 1866. The fort was abandoned in 1892 and used as an Indian school. The only remaining building is the fort hospital. The Fort Bidwell General Store exhibits some local military artifacts and serves as the community grapevine. The BLM's Barrel Springs Back Country Byway begins just east of Fort Bidwell and climbs east onto high mesas along the California and Nevada border. Several hot springs dot the area around Surprise Valley, including the Menlo Baths just south of Fort Bidwell. Ask at the Fort Bidwell General Store or the national forest office in Cedarville for directions.

The dirt Fandango Pass Road begins climbing immediately. Switch backs steeply ascend slopes blanketed with gray sagebrush. A mixed pine and fir forest clings to the mountainside. After a couple miles, the road enters Modoc National Forest. As the road climbs, climate and plant communities change, making the highlands a cool refuge from the hot valleys below. Groves of quaking aspen that turn gold in the autumn nestle in moist side-canyons; forests of ponderosa, Jeffrey, white, and lodgepole pine, white fir, and mountain mahogany spread a patchwork carpet over the rolling mountains. Marvelous views of Surprise Valley and rugged Nevada ranges to the east spread out below the twisting road. Four miles and almost 2,000 vertical feet from the road's start at the valley floor, it crosses the summit of 6,332-foot Fandango Pass.

Fandango Pass is a significant site in California history. It was here, atop this lonely saddle, that two pioneer trails converged. The Applegate-Lassen Trail, established in 1846, traversed Nevada's barren northwestern corner from the Humboldt River on the California Trail to this rugged highland. The Applegate Trail ran northwest from here across the lava beds near Tule to the fertile Willamette Valley in the Oregon Territory; the Lassen Cutoff, established by guide Peter Lassen in 1848, turned south and meandered down to the northern gold mines in California. An historic marker atop the pass commemorates these two great emigrant trails.

The narrow road descends northwest through a pine and fir forest above the Fandango Valley, a flattish valley covered with sage and flanked by high ridges. Glimpses of Goose Lake appear through the trees. The drive quickly reaches the valley floor and runs along the ecotone where woodland and sagebrush meet. This valley edge is the tragic site of the Fandango Pass Massacre. In the early 1850s, an emigrant party of men, women, and children camped in this pretty valley, finding joy in its woodlands and flowing water after the arid tedium of northwestern Nevada. In their evening revelry, the group danced the Spanish fandango unaware that hostile Indians had surrounded their camp. The warriors attacked the merry makers without warning and killed all but two in a short, bloody struggle. News of the massacre quickly reached the military and a detachment of cavalry was sent to seek retribution. The Indians were surrounded and slain, and the valley and nearby pass were named for that last, ill-fated fandango.

After a few miles, the open valley narrows and the drive runs through pine woodlands broken with grassy meadows. At Buck Creek Fire Station, a national forest outpost, the road becomes paved. Heading northwest it crosses juniper-covered benches before turning abruptly west and dropping onto sloping pasture land above Goose Lake. Fourteen miles after leaving Surprise Valley the road ends on U.S. 395, eastern California's main north-south highway. The scenic drive turns south on route 395 toward Alturas. A right turn heads north past Goose Lake State Park on the Oregon side of the state line and runs to Lakeview nineteen miles north of the road junction.

The remaining twenty-eight miles on the drive follow U.S. 395 south back to its intersection with California 299. The road traverses a wide sagebrush bench, part of an ancient wave terrace above Goose Lake. The lake, like the Alkali lakes in Surprise Valley, sits in a fault-block valley. It too filled in prehistoric times with runoff from melting glaciers, forming a wide shallow lake. The drying climate as well as irrigation demands have shrunk Goose Lake to a fraction of its former size. The whole southern lake floor is now a dusty playa below the roadway, although sagebrush and pastures have slowly reclaimed some of the lake bed. The lake has also shrunk away from its former outlets, including the North Fork of the Pit River; this makes the lake's water increasingly alkaline.

Heading south the road drops down through ranches and farmland on the old lake bed. The Warner Range forms a rugged eastern horizon. A turnoff at Davis Creek wends up Forest Road 11 to Plum Valley Campground, and then on over the range to Lake City. Davis Creek, a roadside stop, is named for an early prospector killed here in 1868. The area is famed for its obsidian mines including the Rainbow Mine.

South of Davis Creek, the drive leaves the old lake bed, climbs over some low juniper-coated rises, and drops into the narrow, winding canyon of the Pit River. The river, usually a mere trickle in summer, meanders through willow-lined banks beneath the basalt cliffs of the canyon rim. West of the canyon stretches Devil's Garden. The high tableland of lava flows is covered with California's largest stand of western juniper, more than 300,000 acres. As the highway runs south, the valley slowly broadens and cattle graze on its fertile floor. Fanciful exposures of rhyolitic volcanic ash sculpted into pinnacles, tepees, and hoodoos line the road in places. The drive ends shortly afterwards at the highway's junction with state route 299. Continue on to Alturas six miles ahead.

10 CALIFORNIA 89
Lassen Volcanic National Park Drive

General description: A thirty-five-mile paved highway that twists around 10,457-foot Lassen Peak, passing numerous geothermal features and evidence of recent volcanism in Lassen Volcanic National Park.

Special attractions: Lassen Peak, Sulphur Works, Bumpass Hell, Lake Helen, Lassen Winter Sports Area, Kings Creek, Summit Lake, Nobles Emigrant Trail, Manzanita Lake, Lassen Volcanic Wilderness Area, Pacific Crest Trail, visitor center, hiking, camping, backpacking, fishing, picnicking, rock climbing, cross-country skiing, downhill skiing.

Location: Northeastern California. The drive's northern terminus is just over fifty miles east of Redding and Interstate 5 via California Highway 44. The southern end of the road is approached by California 89 from Truckee and California 36 from Red Bluff.

Drive route name and number: California Highway 89, Lassen Park Highway.

Travel season: Due to extremely heavy snowfall, as much as fifty feet a winter, the highway closes by the end of October and doesn't reopen until it is fully plowed in late May or early June. The road is open, however, to the

Lassen Winter Sports Area on the volcano's southern slopes. Expect winds, chilly temperatures, and snow. Carry chains and extra warm clothes. Occasional thunderstorms and even snow can make the pavement slick in summer.

Camping: Four National Park Service campgrounds are located along the drive. Southwest Campground, with twenty-one walk-in sites, is at the south entrance to the park. North and South Summit Lake campgrounds, with a total of ninety-four sites lie in the forest alongside Summit Lake. Crags Campground's forty-five sites open only when the other camping areas are filled. Manzanita Lake Campground, with 179 sites, is the most popular and prettiest campground in the park. A concession service operates here, selling food, drink, showers, and gas. Three other campgrounds scatter across the remote eastern part of the park and several Forest Service campgrounds lie north along route 89 and Hat Creek, including Big Pine, Hat Creek, Cave, Rocky, Bridge, and Honn campgrounds.

Services: Services are limited in Lassen Park at Southwest Entrance and Manzanita Lake. Gas is available only at Manzanita Lake in the park. The only lodging in the park is at Warner Valley near the park's southeast corner away from the drive. Otherwise limited services are available along the highways north and south of the park. Full services are offered in Redding, Red Bluff, and Susanville.

Nearby attractions: Lassen National Forest, Plumas National Forest, Feather River, Lake Almanor, Thousand Lakes Wilderness Area, Caribou Wilderness Area, Subway Cave and other lava tube caves in Hat Creek Valley, Eagle Lake, Susanville, Latour State Forest, McArthur-Burney Falls Memorial State Park, Ahjumawi Lava Springs State Park, Yuba Pass scenic drive.

For more information: Lassen Volcanic National Park, P.O. Box 100, Mineral, CA 96063-0100. (916) 595-4444.

The drive: Lassen Peak dominates northern California's skyline like no other peak except its sister volcano Mount Shasta, seventy miles to the northwest. Lassen's bulk lends to its conspicuousness. Lifting abruptly from surrounding forested ridges to its snowcapped 10,457-foot summit, Lassen Peak anchors the southern end of the Cascade Range. This mercurial mountain chain marches north from Lassen Peak into southern British Columbia, its crest endowed with majestic, symmetrical peaks, including Mount Rainier, Mount Hood, Mount Shasta, and Lassen Peak. These lofty mountains, all currently dormant volcanos, display the classic volcanic shape, with long graceful slopes that arc upward to the summit. The Cascades form the eastern boundary of some 300 active volcanoes that ring the Pacific Ocean. This is the only live volcanic area in the continental United States in the twentieth century, evidenced by the explosive 1980 eruption of Mount St. Helens and Lassen Peak's activity between 1914 and 1921.

The Lassen Park drive wends thirty-five miles through 106,000-acre Lassen Volcanic National Park on California Highway 89, traversing a spectacular mountain landscape. The mountain, raw with volcanic violence, dominates the drive, always towering above the twisted roadway. A host of bizarre and interesting volcanic features scatter along the highway, including mud pots, fumaroles, boiling lakes, and hot springs—a reminder that geology is not just exposures of rock but a living, dynamic force. Gentler touches of life soften the rugged landscape. Meadows, lush with summer wildflowers, and dense coniferous forests of pine and fir carpet roadside ridges. Tumbling creeks fed by melting snow rush over rounded boulders and pool in deep ponds. The park harbors eight distinct plant communities that are home to some 250 vertebrate species and is California's least known and visited national park. It also offers a host of outdoor recreation from hiking on Lassen Peak to fly-fishing in a pristine lake.

Lassen Park's climate can be summed up in one word—snow. As much as 700 inches of snow falls in the park, making an average thirty-foot-deep snowpack. Severe winters characterize the area, with frigid temperatures, fierce winds, and unpredictable moisture-laden storms that blow off the Pacific Ocean. The scenic drive is closed by winter snow, generally from late October through May, although the southwest entrance remains open to the Lassen Winter Sports Area. After the road opens in early summer, it slices through deep drifts on the upper elevations. The park's summer weather is sunny and cool, with chilly nights. Daily highs generally rise to the sixties and seventies. Occasional thunderstorms or snow showers can make roads slick. Be prepared for adverse conditions, especially if hiking on the higher mountains. Autumn is pleasant here. Expect warm, clear days, cold nights, and few crowds.

The scenic drive, following California Highway 89, begins at the park's southwest entrance. Route 89 is a long highway that runs from Mount Shasta south through Truckee and South Lake Tahoe. It can be reached from Susanville and Red Bluff via California 36. The drive runs north from its intersection with Highway 36 along the edge of a high ridge. The road cuts through a lush red fir forest as it climbs above 5,000 feet. The drive reaches the Lassen Volcanic National Park boundary after four miles.

The park was first protected as a national monument by President Theodore Roosevelt in 1907 as part of the greater 1.5-million-acre Lassen Peak Forest Reserve. A bill was introduced in Congress in 1912 to make the area a national park, but little happened until Lassen erupted on May 30, 1914. The national publicity accorded this geological phenomena led to the creation of Lassen Volcanic National Park in 1916. More than 80,000 acres of the park were designated wilderness in 1972.

A mile after entering the park, the road passes the entrance station. Beyond sits the Southwest Information Station, with park information and displays, and the Lassen Chalet offering basic visitor services. Nearby sits Southwest Campground with twenty-one walk-in sites at an elevation of 6,700 feet. The campground is open in winter. The Lassen Winter Sports Area spreads across the ridges to the west. This small, friendly ski area, open from mid-November to April, is seldom crowded and offers lessons and a variety

Lassen Peak towers over Lake Helen and the Lassen Peak Highway. Lassen Volcanic National Park.

of runs for skiers. The southwest entrance also serves as a winter gateway for cross-country skiers and snowshoers. Some of the best Nordic tours follow the snow-covered highway to Lake Helen and Kings Creek Meadows. A spectacular tour ends at Bumpass Hell, with stunning views of the steaming thermal area surrounded by snow. Registration is required for all day and overnight winter trips. Register at the ranger station.

The two-lane highway edges north above the deep canyon of West Sulphur Creek and after a mile reaches Sulphur Works, the park's most accessible thermal area. A short trail leaves the roadside parking area and wanders past hot springs, bubbling mud pots, and fumaroles. As at all thermal areas in the park, stay on the trail. The water is extremely hot, in excess of 195 degrees Fahrenheit, and thin crusts and unstable footing around the springs can lead to disaster. The distinctive rotten eggs aroma of hydrogen sulphide permeates the air. The Sulphur Works is part of the central vent system of Mount Tehama, a massive volcano that stood here long before Lassen Peak.

The ring of peaks that surrounds the Sulphur Works—9,235- foot Brokeoff Mountain, 9,087-foot Mount Diller, 8,886-foot Pilot Pinnacle, and 8,204-foot Mount Conrad—are all remnants of Mount Tehama, a stratovolcano that reached above 11,000 feet with an eleven-mile-wide base. The peak built up some 600,000 years ago by long volcanic episodes. Tehama eventually wore away through thermal activity that allowed its soft slopes to be easily eroded by rain, runoff, and glaciation. A wide rim resembling a caldera was left behind.

Lassen Peak, considered the world's largest plug dome volcano, arose over 20,000 years ago, long after Tehama's collapse, when a giant mass of lava pushed up through a vent on Tehama's north side. The peak formed not by eruptions like other volcanos, but like a giant lava mushroom shoved up the vent. The thick, syrupy lava, instead of flowing downhill, solidified as it grew until the dome towered over the worn-down volcanos surrounding it and plugged the underground vent.

Past the Sulphur Works, the drive swings across the steep slopes of 7,968-foot Diamond Peak. The ragged peak, strewn with steep cliffs and crags, is the solidified remains of one of Mount Tehama's main vents, which carried magma from deep underground reservoirs to the surface. It was named for glittering quartz and calcite crystals that stud its rocks. On the east side of Diamond Peak and Pilot Pinnacle the highway climbs above precipitous Little Hot Springs Valley. The road continues past this glacier-carved valley, and after a few miles passes Emerald Lake and Emerald Point. The emerald-green lake, lying in a basin etched out by glaciers, is at an elevation of 8,000 feet. The forest here in the Hudsonian or subalpine life zone creeps upward to Lassen's 9,000-foot timberline. Life at this altitude is hardened by harsh conditions that prevail much of the year. Snow drifts as deep as forty feet, and ferocious winds scour the open ridges. Dwarf forests of whitebark pine scatter across the drier slopes, while mountain hemlock thrive in sturdy clumps on moist, shaded slopes. Pioneer naturalist John Muir called the hemlock "singularly graceful in habit," and said "the finest groves I have yet

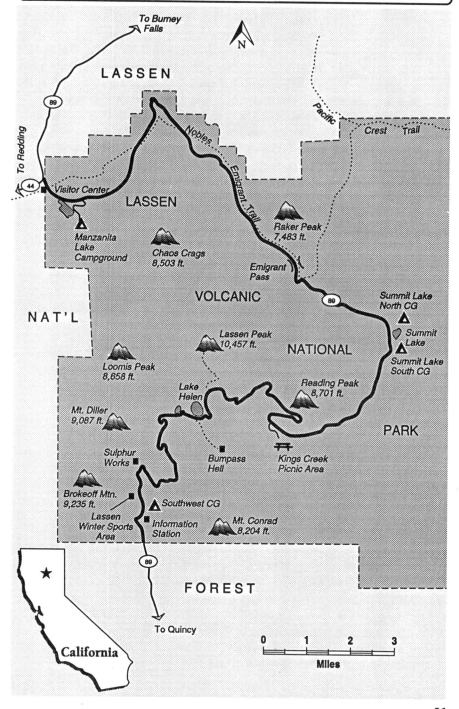

To Burney Falls

N

LASSEN

89

To Redding

44

Visitor Center

LASSEN

Manzanita Lake Campground

Chaos Crags 8,503 ft.

Nobles

Emigrant Trail

Raker Peak 7,483 ft.

Emigrant Pass

89

Pacific

Crest Trail

Summit Lake North CG

Summit Lake

Summit Lake South CG

VOLCANIC

NAT'L

Lassen Peak 10,457 ft.

NATIONAL

Loomis Peak 8,658 ft.

Lake Helen

Reading Peak 8,701 ft.

Mt. Diller 9,087 ft.

PARK

Sulphur Works

Bumpass Hell

Kings Creek Picnic Area

Brokeoff Mtn. 9,235 ft.

Southwest CG

Lassen Winter Sports Area

Information Station

Mt. Conrad 8,204 ft.

89

FOREST

To Quincy

★

California

0   1   2   3

Miles

found are on the southern slopes of Lassen's Butte." The nearby viewpoint offers superb views of the park's southern canyons and its volcanic peaks.

The trailhead to Bumpass Hell begins just past Emerald Lake at a large parking area about eleven miles north of the park entrance. The trail is a three-mile round-trip that threads across the top of a glaciated cirque, passing striations etched into glacial-polished rock by glaciers. Glacial erratics or large glacier-deposited boulders balance on bedrock along the trail. After winding through groves of whitebark pine and mountain hemlock, the trail emerges on the western rim of a steaming ten-acre basin—Bumpass Hell. This spectacular thermal area, Lassen Park's largest, is named for Kendall Vanhook Bumpass who discovered it and subsequently lost a leg by accidently stepping into one of the boiling springs while showing the area to visiting reporters. The trail drops steeply down to a series of boardwalks that explore the area. Stay on the trail and avoid having a Bumpass accident. The crust is fragile around the springs and will break under body weight.

Bumpass Hell is a seething caldron of bubbling mud pots, boiling hot springs, sulphur vents, and mineral-stained water. The area, which lies outside of Tehama's caldera, is heated by cooling magma deep underground. Surface water from melting snow and rain percolates down until it turns into steam from the heat of the magma chamber and returns to the surface. The water at this altitude boils at 198 degrees, rather than the 212 degrees at sea level. Much of the water, however, is hotter because of underground superheating under pressure. The circulating hot water deposits dissolved minerals around the springs. More valuable ores such as gold are often deposited by hot water at great depths underground.

From the Bumpass Hell parking lot, the drive skirts the edge of Lake Helen, a spectacular glacial lake that lies at 8,164 feet. Lassen Peak looms north over the lake, which remains frozen up to eight months of the year. The water temperature remains a chilly thirty-nine degrees even in late summer. The lake was named for Helen Tanner Brodt, who, in 1864, was the first woman to ascend Lassen Peak. The peak's first recorded ascent was in 1851 by Grover Godfrey. A picnic area sits on the lake's eastern shore.

The Lassen Peak Trail lies another mile up the road. The 2.5-mile-long trail switchbacks 2,000 feet up steep rocky slopes to the peak's lofty 10,457-foot summit. All northern California unfolds below. To the east lie dark, forested ridges and in the far distance stretch shadowy ranges in Nevada. Northward spreads the dark Modoc Plateau broken by the snowcapped Warner Range. Mount Shasta gleams to the northwest, its shoulders capped with brilliant snow. Westward lies the Sacramento Valley with the Klamath Ranges standing above the haze. The long ridge of the Sierra Nevada marches southeastward. Late summer or early fall is the best time to climb the mountain, otherwise heavy snow covers the trail. Early-season climbers should carry an ice-axe. The round-trip ascent takes about four hours. Be prepared for strong winds and inclement weather. Carry a raincoat, suntan lotion, sunglasses, water, and a hat.

The drive reaches its 8,512-foot high point just beyond the Lassen Peak

Brokeoff Mountain, the remnants of a huge volcano, lifts craggy ridges above the Lassen Peak Highway. Lassen Volcanic National Park.

parking area and drops over the mountain's southeastern flank. Magnificent views down the Warner Valley toward broad Lake Almanor and of the rough volcanic peaks in the park's eastern half stretch out below the winding highway. Prospect Peak, a prominent peak to the northeast, is an 8,338- foot shield volcano in the park's northeast corner. At its base is the perfectly symmetrical Cinder Cone, a 700-foot-high cone built by violent eruptions that tossed ash and cinders from its central vent. A sea of lava surrounds the cone. Argonauts on the Nobles Emigrant Trail in 1850 and 1851 reported the cone's eruptions, although scientists now say it erupted some 100 years earlier. The road descends and passes from woodlands inhabited by whitebark pine and mountain hemlock into dense stands of stately red fir broken by meadows strewn with wildflowers in summer.

The Kings Creek Meadows, about four miles below the road summit, are the largest of these mountain meadows. The highway skirts the Upper Meadow. Kings Creek meanders placidly in wide curves across the damp grassland, while steep ridges cloaked in red fir surround the bucolic valley. The meadow was once a lake, but water borne debris and silt carried by Kings Creek slowly filled it. The summer floral display includes alpine gentian, fawn lily, false hellebore, and lupine. Nearby is Kings Creek Picnic Area with cool sites scattered through the forest. A trail heads south here to Cold Boiling Lake, a bubbling clear lake, and around Bumpass Mountain to Bumpass Hell; a turn-off trail twists five miles to the southwest park entrance. Another trail begins below the Upper Meadow and drops 1.5 miles to Kings Creek Falls, a rushing cascade in a narrow volcanic gorge. Lassen Volcanic National Park offers more than 150 miles of trails, including seventeen miles of the famed Pacific Crest Trail.

The drive bends northeast from the meadows and runs along the southern flank of Reading Peak, an 8,701-foot plug volcano formed in the same way as Lassen Peak. The peak is named for Major Pierson Reading, first settler in Shasta County and leader of the third recorded ascent of Lassen Peak. The road gradually loses elevation as it runs northward, and four miles from Kings Meadows it reaches picturesque 6,695-foot Summit Lake. The small lake, surrounded by a dense forest of red fir, lodgepole pine, and whitebark pine, sits atop the summit or divide between the north-flowing Pit River drainage and the south-flowing Feather River drainage. Two popular campgrounds, North Summit Lake with forty-six sites and South Summit Lake with forty-eight sites, sit on the lake shore. A nearby ranger station provides trail information and backcountry permits for the adjoining Lassen Volcanic Wilderness Area to the east.

The road turns northwest at Summit Lake and crosses two-mile-long Dersch Meadows along the East Fork of Hat Creek. After 2.5 miles, the drive dips down over Hat Creek's west fork, a lively creek draining Lassen Peak's eastern slope. A parking area allows access to shallow Hat Lake, a shrinking lake that formed when a mud flow unleashed on Lassen Peak blocked the creek's path on May 19, 1915. Volcanic sediment carried by Hat Creek has quickly filled the lake, leaving this small remnant which will soon become a meadow like Kings Meadows.

From Hat Lake to the park's northwest entrance, the drive crosses destructive evidence of Lassen Peak's last violent eruptions. The peak, until Mount St. Helens' activity, was the only active volcano in the continental United States in the twentieth century. Even today, despite Lassen's deceptively calm demeanor, geologists consider it an active volcano that could erupt sooner rather than later. Early settlers considered the peak an extinct volcano, so it was somewhat surprising when on May 30, 1914, the mountain belched forth a gaseous column and ejected lava and debris onto its upper slopes. A new vent opened in the summit crater and Lassen erupted 150 times over the next year. In May 1915, lava overflowed the crater rim and seeped down its slopes. The molten rock melted the peak's heavy snowpack sending an avalanche followed by devastating mud flows down into Hat and Lost creeks. The next day the peak exploded a mushroom cloud of ash and steam over 25,000 feet into the air, a frightening sight visible as far away as Sacramento. An avalanche of steam and gas rocketed down Lassen's northeastern slopes, decimating forests like mere match sticks. This swath of destruction, the Devastated Area, borders the drive just north of Hat Lake. The fallen trees along the flow's edge all lie facing downhill from the volcano, and the great pines standing along the mud flow's edge still retain scars where their bark was shredded off that violent day. Today, young stands of lodgepole pine and quaking aspen slowly fill in the Devastated Area. After this eruption, Lassen's fury abated and by 1917 most volcanic activity had ceased.

The drive follows the old Nobles Emigrant Trail from Hat Creek to the park's northwest corner. The Nobles Trail was laid out as an alternative to the longer Lassen Trail, which ran from Fandango Pass to the northern end of the Sacramento Valley in the early 1850s. The Nobles Trail traversed the rough country from Black Rock in Nevada to Fort Reading, now Redding, California. This short-cut route proved popular and its ruts are still visible today. Parts of the trail were used as recently as 1931 when the present highway was completed. William Nobles laid out the trail and sold the route to Shasta City businessmen for $2,000 in 1852. The Lassen Trail and Lassen Peak were named for Peter Lassen, a Danish pioneer who guided parties along his trail beginning in 1848. Lassen was reputed to be a terrible guide. One party supposedly forced him at gunpoint to climb the peak that now bears his name to ascertain their correct location.

Northwest of the Devastated Area, the road passes west of 7,483-foot Raker Peak, a 1,200-foot-high shield volcano named for California representative John Raker who pushed passage of the 1916 bill that created Lassen Volcanic National Park. Hot Rock, alongside the drive, is a large lava boulder carried down by the 1915 mud flow. Mature forests of white fir, incense cedar (not a true cedar), sugar pine, and ponderosa pine, untouched by the volcanic devastation, cover the hillsides above the drive. One of the nation's largest white firs, measuring 168 feet high, grows on the roadside.

Past Hot Rock, the drive leaves Lost Creek and swings around the northern end of Chaos Crags. These rumpled mountains are a group of four smaller, more recent lava plug domes than neighboring Lassen Peak. Geologists say they are about 1,000 years old, with their last activity reported in 1850. When the crags arose, steam blasts undermined their northern flank and scattered a massive landslide of boulders northward. The drive crosses this area of broken talus, called the Chaos Jumbles. A pygmy forest grows on porous soil patches among the boulders.

The highway descends east from Chaos Jumbles and quickly reaches Reflection Lake and Manzanita Lake. Reflection Lake, at 5,880 feet, offers a perfect reflection of Lassen Peak and Chaos Crags on peaceful summer evenings. Wide Manzanita Lake is named for the manzanita bushes that clot its shores. The lake gives a spectacular view of Lassen's bold, bulky outline that looms to the south, rising 4,625 feet above the peaceful lake. In summer, fishermen line its shores, swimmers cool off in its clear water, and waterfowl rest on its waters during fall migrations. Manzanita Lake Campground, with 179 sites, sits in thick forest above the lake's eastern shore. This pleasant campground offers private sites and a nearby concessionaire sells groceries, gas, and showers. From Manzanita Lake, the drive turns northwest, passes the park entrance station, and reaches the park boundary at route 89's junction with California Highway 44. A left turn on Highway 44 drops through pine forests to Redding at the head of the Sacramento Valley. Highway 89 continues north, dropping down along Hat Creek and passing numerous forest campgrounds and a huge lava flow pockmarked with lava tube caves, including Subway Cave. The highway continues north to Burney.

Quaking aspen on the Yuba Pass drive.

General description: A seventy-five-mile highway that begins in Nevada City, crosses the South and Middle forks of the Yuba River, and follows the North Fork of the Yuba River to the 6,701-foot summit of Yuba Pass.

Special attractions: Nevada City, South Fork Yuba River, Middle Fork Yuba River, Tahoe National Forest, North Fork Yuba River, Downieville, Sierra City, Yuba Pass, camping, hiking, fishing, four-wheeling, swimming, gold panning.

Location: East-central California. The drive begins in Nevada City at the intersection of state routes 49 and 20 north of Interstate 80 and ends at California 89 twenty-nine miles north of Truckee.

Drive route number: California Highway 89.

Travel season: Year-round. The drive receives heavy snow in winter and may be temporarily closed. Adequate snow tires and chains are advised.

Camping: Tahoe National Forest campgrounds along the drive include Oregon Creek, Shenanigan, Lower Carlton, Upper Carlton, Fiddle Creek, Indian Valley, Rocky Rest, Ramshorn, Cannon Point, Union Flat, Loganville, Haypress, Wild Plum, Lodgepole, Sierra, Chapman Creek, Lincoln Creek, and Yuba Pass. The lower elevation ones along the river tend to fill up early in summer. The higher ones near the pass summit are cool and shaded. Numerous other forest campgrounds lie on side roads off the main highway.

Services: All services are found in Nevada City, Downieville, and Sierra City including gas, food, and lodging. Limited services are at North San Juan and Camptonville.

Nearby attractions: South Yuba Trail, Malakoff Diggings State Historic Park, Donner Pass, Donner Lake, Donner Memorial State Park, Truckee, Lake Tahoe, Desolation Wilderness Area, Plumas Eureka State Park, Empire Mine State Historic Park.

For more information: Tahoe National Forest, Highway 49 and Coyote Street, Nevada City, CA 95959, (916) 265-4531. Sierra County Commission on Tourism, P.O. Box 473, Downieville, Ca 95936.

The drive: The Yuba Pass scenic drive follows California Highway 49 for seventy-five miles from Nevada City to the North Fork of the Yuba River. It parallels the river through several historic mining towns before climbing over 6,701-foot Yuba Pass on the crest of the Sierra Nevada. The road dips through deep river gorges, traverses high wooded ridges, passes the remains of California's gold rush days, and offers numerous recreational opportunities from camping and fishing to snowmobiling and cross country skiing. The winding, paved highway has numerous turnouts for sight-seeing and takes at least three hours to drive.

The weather along the drive is typical Sierran, with hot summers in the low canyons and cool temperatures in the higher elevations. Expect summer highs in the nineties in the lowlands and seventies atop the pass. Occasional thunderstorms build over the mountains, dropping a curtain of rain across the peaks. Autumns are pleasant, with warm clear days and chilly nights. Winter brings severe storms that dump deep snow across the high country. Be prepared when driving in winter by bringing extra warm clothes, a sleeping bag, food, and tire chains. The highway may be closed after harsh storms. Spring brings warmer temperatures and rivers full of runoff. The lower elevations begin turning green by April.

The drive begins in 2,520-foot-high Nevada City at the intersection of California highways 20 and 49. Turn north on route 49. Nevada City lies five miles northeast of Grass Valley and twenty-eight miles north of Interstate 80. Nevada City, one of California's most picturesque gold rush town, sprawls along the wooded hills above Deer Creek. The town arose when miners began probing rich placer deposits along Deer Creek in 1849. It ran through a succession of names—Caldwell's Upper Store, Deer Creek Dry Diggin's, and Coyoteville—before settling on Nevada after the severe winter of 1850; Nevada is Spanish for "snow- covered." When the neighboring state stole its name a few years later, City was added. The town quickly grew and soon almost every square foot around Nevada City and nearby Grass Valley was being worked. Much of the gold excavated in the Nevada City and Grass Valley mining district came from underground mines that followed gold-quartz veins along the contact of granite and metamorphosed sedimentary rocks. By 1856 the town had burned down three times. Eventually, more than $400 million in gold was extracted from the earth, with the last mine closing in the early 1950s. Nevada City today is one of the gold country's prettiest towns, with white-steepled churches, narrow winding streets lined with shops, and lovely autumn colors when the surrounding sugar maples and oaks blaze with color. It's a good place to explore on foot. The chamber of commerce offers a brochure for walkers to discover the town's historic attractions—including Firehouse Number 1, the Nevada Theatre, and the National Hotel, which has operated continuously since 1856 and claims to being the oldest operating hotel west of the Rockies.

The highway runs north from Nevada City and drops down through a mixed forest of oak and gray pine into the steep canyon of the South Yuba River, one of the river's three forks that drain the northern Sierra Nevadas. The river, named by the Spanish "Rio de las Uvas" or River of Grapes for the tangled vines along its banks, supposedly yielded more gold in its thick gravel deposits than any other American river system. Almost seven miles north of Nevada City, the drive sweeps across the river and its narrow granite gorge on a concrete bridge. The Independence Trail, along Rush Creek a mile before the river crossing, is a wheelchair-accessible trail that follows the abandoned Excelsior Ditch flume for seven miles into the South Yuba River canyon and allows physically challenged visitors to enjoy the Sierra foothills.

After crossing the river, the highway quickly climbs away from the river

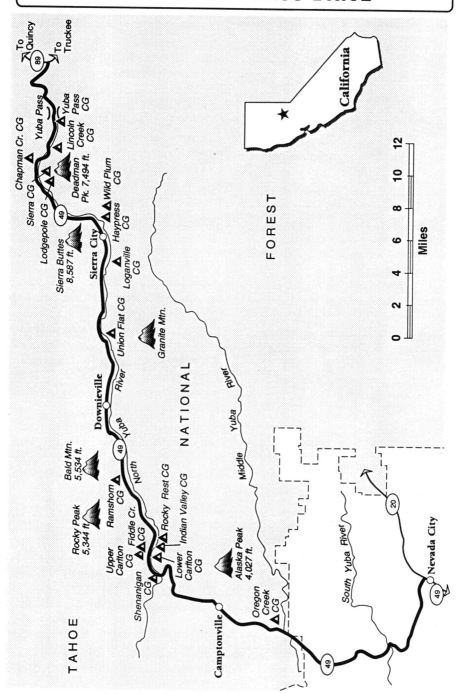

11

CALIFORNIA 49: THE YUBA PASS DRIVE

over chaparral and oak-covered ridges and swings around rounded Bunker Hill. Four miles from the river, the drive passes a side road that heads east to Malakoff Diggins State Historic Park, a monument to the destruction that mining can cause. The diggings were thick gravel deposits filled with low-grade gold ore on San Juan Ridge, a long ridge that was once an ancient river bed. To get at the ore required a large hydraulic mining operation that washed the gravel into long sluice boxes and yielded only ten cents a cubic yard. From 1866 until 1884, the Malakoff Diggins were the site of the world's largest hydraulic mine and employed hundreds of men who literally re-sculpted the ridge in search of gold. The mine was an ecological disaster even by the lax mining standards of that era. The land was laid waste with eroded ravines, mountains of gravel, and a countryside denuded of forest. Silt swept down the Yuba River choking waterways in the Central Valley, damming irrigation canals, burying crops and fields, and muddying San Francisco Bay almost 200 miles away. Public outrage led by farmers and landowners led to passage of the Federal Anti-Debris Act in 1883, which almost overnight closed down the Malakoff mine. Travelers today can walk on trails that wander across the Bryce Canyon-like bluffs above the mine and explore the remains of this destructive mine. Water has filled the bottom of the 7,000-foot-long pit creating a huge lake. The 3,400-acre park is also used for picnicking, fishing, and camping.

The drive continues across the rolling San Juan Ridge under a canopy of pine, fir, and oak. On its north side lies the town of North San Juan, another gold rush village. It was named by Mexican War veteran Christian Kientz, who thought a hill he found gold on in 1853 resembled a hill with a prison in Mexico called "San Juan de Ulloa." The town boasted a population of 10,000 when it headquartered the nearby Malakoff Diggins. Now the town has a population of about 125.

The highway drops down from North San Juan, enters the immense Tahoe National Forest, and crosses the Middle Fork of the Yuba River. On the river's north side is a turn to the Oregon Creek Day Use Area, a pleasant picnic site and swimming hole along the river bank. The river is flanked by dense Sierran forest of oak, pine, and incense cedar (not a true cedar). The river winds west through a shallow, rocky canyon and the seventeen-site Oregon Creek Campground is nearby.

The road climbs alongside Oregon Creek from the river and reaches an intersection with the Marysville Road after three miles. A Tahoe National Forest ranger station sits at the junction. A turn down the side road leads to New Bullards Bar Reservoir and several forest campgrounds. The narrow, twisting highway steadily rises through a tree-lined corridor to Camptonville, another sleepy mining town that's home to a small number of residents. A national forest office here provides camping, hiking, and fishing information. After a few miles, the road crosses into Sierra County, crests a hilltop, and begins spiraling around Indian Hill to the North Fork of the Yuba River. The highway is extremely narrow and winding through here, with a maximum speed of twenty miles per hour. The drive crosses the Yuba River on a wide

Swimmers in the Yuba River along California Highway 49. Yuba Pass Drive.

concrete bridge span. A couple pullouts here allow access to the river below and excellent late-summer swimming.

The North Fork headwaters arise to the east atop Yuba Pass on the Sierra divide and run swiftly westward to a confluence with its other forks before draining into the Central Valley at Marysville. The scenic drive along state route 49 parallels the river through its wooded canyon for thirty-seven miles to the pass summit. Numerous national forest campgrounds, a couple historic towns, and spectacular scenery line the highway. Yuba's North Fork, the most active placer stream in California, is famed for its rich gold deposits. Mining dredges scatter along the river from Shenanigan Flat to Downieville, floating in deep pools below tumbling rapids. Most of the river is worked by legal mining claims. Amateur prospectors can search the river for their own pot of gold, but be sure to do it legally. Although hanging claim-jumpers from the nearest oak is out of the question these days, claim-jumping is not fondly looked upon. Check at the ranger station in Camptonville for maps detailing where recreational gold-panning is allowed.

After crossing to the river's north bank, a succession of fine campgrounds line the highway—Shenanigan, Upper Carlton, Lower Carlton, Fiddle Creek, Indian Flat, Rocky Rest, and Ramshorn. All make good summer base camps to swim, fish, hike, pan for gold, or relax under shady trees. The river and road, heading east, follow the bottom of a deep V-shaped gorge. The river sliced the canyon into the firm bedrock over the last few million years as the

Sierras rose. Thick forests of oak and pine blanket the canyon walls. Its floor of ancient sedimentary and volcanic rocks were altered by intense heat and pressure, while volcanic crags from ancient eruptions punctuate the craggy ridge lines silhouetted against the turquoise sky.

Downieville, the next historic point of interest along the route, sits astride the confluence of the Downie and Yuba rivers. The town was founded in 1849 and first called The Forks. It was later renamed for Major William Downie, who supposedly said he would toss a pan of gold dust into the street if the town was named for him. By 1852, Downieville's population had swollen to more than 3,000. Miners flocked in to dig the rich gravels, some yielding as much as $300 a pan. The Tincup Diggings were named because its owners worked each day until a tincup was filled with the precious metal. Other stories include miner Jim Crow finding gold flecks in a cooking pot after boiling a fourteen-pound salmon and Frank Anderson, the first miner to pan here, taking $12,900 out of a sixty-square-foot claim in eleven days. In the 1850s, the North Yuba River was diverted from its channel so the river bed gravel could be laboriously processed. After a few years, the placer gold ran out, and miners began hard-rock mining on a few gold-quartz veins. But another mother lode was never found. The town also saw its share of disastrous fires and floods. The great 1938 flood wiped out most of the original buildings, except for scattered houses clinging to hillsides above the river. It's a quiet, restful place these days. California's only original gallows, now a state historic monument, stands outside the Sierra County Courthouse. Other worthwhile sights include the Sierra County Museum and Downieville Heritage Park.

The drive continues above the river for thirteen miles to Sierra City. The road traverses on south-facing slopes through a forest of pine, incense cedar, and oak, and then passes Union Flat and Loganville campgrounds. Sierra City, another old mining town, sits below the 8,600-foot Sierra Buttes, which lift their ragged, snowcapped crowns to the north. In 1850 it got its start, like neighboring Downieville, from placer gold deposits in the Yuba River. Over the next twenty years, miners honeycombed the Sierra Buttes with tunnels and dug out a fortune in gold ore. The Monumental Mine yielded a 100-pound nugget worth $25,000 in 1860. But tough times lay ahead as avalanches from the buttes wiped out the town in 1852, 1888, and 1889. Sierra City now offers several informative attractions. Best is the Sierra County Historical Park at the Kentucky Mine. The mine, preserved as an historical site, boasts its original machinery and offers tours of the mine and stamp mill. Haypress and Wild Plum forest campgrounds lie just east of Sierra City along Haypress Creek.

The drive swings north from Sierra City, paralleling the river and steadily climbs into a broad valley. Sierra City is the western limit of glaciation in this part of the Sierra Nevada. The highway follows a wide U-shaped valley to Yuba Pass, in contrast to the abrupt V-shaped gorge to the west carved by the river. As the road climbs, it passes through lateral moraines, huge piles of boulders and gravels pushed to the side as ancient glaciers crept down valley.

The road climbs above 5,000 feet and passes small waterfalls, including Loves Falls, and cascades along the tumbling river. About five miles from Sierra City at Bassetts, a gravel side road called the Gold Lakes Highway heads north to some forest campgrounds and several excellent lakes formed from glaciation. Sand Lake, Sardine lakes, Goose Lake, and Gold Lake offer fishing, boating, and swimming. Sand Pond, near Sardine Campground just off the drive, is considered one of the Sierra's best swimming holes. The area is part of Sierra Buttes Recreation Area, which also is popular in winter for cross-country skiing and snowmobiling.

Past Bassetts the highway meanders east along the river, rapidly climbing toward the pass summit. Some quiet campgrounds scatter along the drive, offering great overnight stays among the lodgepole pine and red fir forest. The best campground, however, is the last—Yuba Pass Campground. This twenty-site campground sits atop the broad 6,701-foot summit of Yuba Pass by a wide grassy meadow flanked with quaking aspen and towering red fir. The summit is a popular cross-country ski area in winter. The word Yuba was first applied to the river by Captain Sutter in 1840 after a Maidu Indian village that sat at the river's mouth.

The highway descends the east slope of the pass through a thick fir forest that changes to pine and cedar in the warmer climes of lower elevations. The abrupt escarpment here is a fault scarp that forms the eastern face of the Sierra Nevada. Three miles from the summit, the road leaves Tahoe National Forest. A lofty viewpoint lies a mile further, providing a stunning vista of the Sierra Valley to the east. The valley, like Lake Tahoe, is a down-dropped graben flanked by faults. The Middle Fork of the Feather River empties the broad valley that was once the bottom of a great mountain lake. Sierra Valley was discovered by black explorer and mountain man James Beckwourth in 1851 while searching for a feasible wagon route over the northern Sierras. The following year he established a trading post and hotel in the valley. The lush valley provided livestock, hay, and timber to the gold boom at Sierra City and Downieville over the range and later to the silver rush at Nevada's Virginia City. The valley's wetlands today are a popular stopover for migrating waterfowl. Large deer herds also winter over here away from the deep mountain snow. Sierra Valley sits astride two great North American ecosystems—the High Sierra woodlands of pine and fir and the Great Basin Desert with its characteristic sagebrush and juniper communities. Highway 49 ends a few miles later at its junction with California 89 on the valley's western edge at a lumber mill. Truckee and Interstate 80 lie thirty miles south on route 89. Quincy and Lassen Volcanic National Park sit in rough, wooded country a couple hours to the north.

12

CALIFORNIA 89
South Lake Tahoe to Truckee

General description: A forty-two-mile, two-lane paved highway that traverses the scenic west shore of Lake Tahoe and follows the Truckee River Canyon.

Special attractions: Lake Tahoe, Fallen Leaf Lake, Emerald Bay, D.L. Bliss State Park, Sugar Pine State Park, Squaw Valley, Tahoe National Forest, hiking, camping, rock climbing, boating, skiing, cross-country skiing, backpacking.

Location: East-central California near the Nevada border. Truckee, the drive's northern terminus, sits almost twenty miles west of Nevada on Interstate 80.

Drive route number and name: California Highway 89, Emerald Bay Road.

Travel season: The highway is open year-round. Heavy snow and ice can make the road dangerous in winter. Use proper snow tires and chains, and carry extra clothing.

Camping: There are many campgrounds along the scenic drive. Fallen Leaf Campground, near South Lake Tahoe, offers 205 sites among towering pines. Bay View, Kaspian, Meeks Bay, and William Kent all have first-come, first-served sites. Camp Richardson has 230 sites, some with hook-ups. The city of South Lake Tahoe operates a municipal campground in town. Sugar Pine Point and D. L. Bliss state parks both have excellent campgrounds. Granite Flat, Goose Meadow, and Silver Creek national forest campgrounds lie along the Truckee River north of the lake.

Services: All services are at South Lake Tahoe, Tahoe City, and Truckee.

Nearby attractions: Desolation Wilderness Area, Carson Pass, Donner Summit, Lake Tahoe State Park (NV), Donner Memorial State Park, Yuba Pass, Carson City, Fort Churchill to Wellington Back Country Byway (NV).

For more information: Lake Tahoe Basin Management Unit, U.S. Forest Service, 870 Emerald Bay Road, Suite 1, South Lake Tahoe, CA 96150, (916) 573-2600. Lake Tahoe Visitors Authority, 1156 Ski Run Blvd., South Lake Tahoe, CA 96150, (916) 544-5050, (800) AT-TAHOE.

The drive: This forty-two-mile-long drive follows California Highway 89 from South Lake Tahoe to Truckee and traverses some of the state's best scenery. The road runs along the lake's west shore and then north through the Truckee River Canyon to Interstate 80. Lake Tahoe itself is unsurpassed— a glistening jewel cupped in a wide basin surrounded by snowcapped mountains. Lake Tahoe is twenty-two miles long and twelve miles wide, with a shoreline of seventy-two miles; it is 1,645 feet deep, which makes it the tenth deepest lake in the world and third deepest in North America after Canada's Great Slave Lake and Oregon's Crater Lake. The lake's deepest point lies ninety-two feet lower than Carson City. Sixty-three streams and

Emerald Bay, surrounded by forests and granite crags, lies along Lake Tahoe's western shore and the California Highway 89 drive.

rivers flow into the lake, but only one, the Truckee River, drains it. Because of its depth, the lake never freezes and is famed for its extreme clarity. The lake contains so much water that it could cover California with a fourteen inch layer.

The Tahoe Basin offers an excellent year-round climate with an average of 307 days of sunshine annually. Summers are mild and warm, with highs usually in the seventies and eighties and occasional afternoon thunderstorms. Spring is cool and breezy. Falls are gorgeous, with warm Indian summer days, golden aspen leaves, and chilly nights. Winter brings an average of 213 inches of snow a year along the lake shore. The area is famed for its Sierra ski resorts, including Squaw Valley, site of the 1960 Winter Olympics. In winter expect cold days and colder nights. The drive is regularly plowed and sanded after snowstorms. But be prepared for adverse conditions by carrying tire chains and warm clothing.

The scenic drive begins at the intersection of California Highway 89 and U.S. 50 in South Lake Tahoe, just a few miles over the state line. Turn north on 89. South Lake Tahoe is the largest town on the lake shore with a population of 21,000 and attracts more than 2.5 million visitors annually. Many come in winter to sample neighboring ski areas like Heavenly Ski Resort. The area is one of California's most popular vacation spots. In summer, tourists marvel at the lake, enjoy the cool climate, play golf, mountain bike and hike the myriad trails, and relax on the town's three beaches. Besides gaming in South Lake Tahoe's Nevada-side casinos, popular activities include riding the one-mile-long Heavenly Aerial Tram for a spectacular panoramic vista of the lake and the Sierra Nevada and cruising across the lake on a stern-wheel paddle boat. The Lake Tahoe Historical Museum, along U.S. 50 in town, acquaints visitors with the area's colorful past.

The highway quickly leaves South Lake Tahoe's suburban developments and enters the U.S. Forest Service's Lake Tahoe Basin Management Unit, which administers all forest lands in the Tahoe Basin. Upon entering the forest, the Pope-Baldwin Recreation Area is immediately encountered. This area is now managed by the Forest Service and was once the summer home of many of California's affluent elite. Elias J. Baldwin built the opulent Tallac Hotel and Tallac House casino here in the pine woods in 1879. The lavish hotel boasted a ballroom, string orchestra, tennis courts, and boat rides. After Baldwin's death in 1909, the hotel's fortunes declined; and his widow had it razed. Wealthy San Franciscans Emanuel Heller, George Pope, and Lloyd Tevis bought the land and erected grand summer cottages. Their heirs donated the property to the Federal Government because of maintenance costs and high taxes. The area is now the center of the Forest Service's Lake Tahoe interpretative programs.

Tallac Historic Site is three miles from the highway junction with U.S. 50. The historic site preserves 150 acres with the scattered remains of the Tallac Resort along with the three summer estates. The Tallac Museum serves as the site's interpretative center with ranger-led tours that explore the lake's rich turn-of-the-century past. Many special events and programs occur here

12

CALIFORNIA 89:
SOUTH LAKE TAHOE TO TRUCKEE

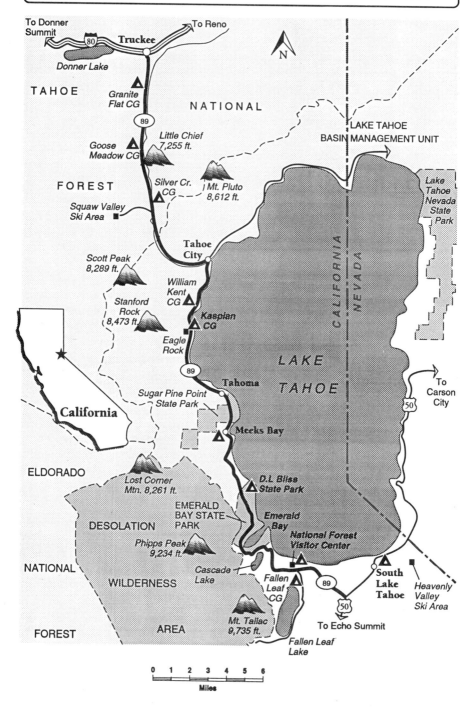

To Donner Summit

To Reno

Truckee

80

Donner Lake

TAHOE

Granite Flat CG

89

NATIONAL

Goose Meadow CG

Little Chief 7,255 ft.

LAKE TAHOE BASIN MANAGEMENT UNIT

FOREST

Silver Cr. CG

Mt. Pluto 8,612 ft.

Lake Tahoe Nevada State Park

Squaw Valley Ski Area

Scott Peak 8,289 ft.

Tahoe City

William Kent CG

CALIFORNIA NEVADA

Stanford Rock 8,473 ft.

Kaspian CG

Eagle Rock

89

Tahoma

LAKE TAHOE

To Carson City

50

California

Sugar Pine Point State Park

Meeks Bay

ELDORADO

Lost Corner Mtn. 8,261 ft.

D.L. Bliss State Park

EMERALD BAY STATE PARK

Emerald Bay

National Forest Visitor Center

DESOLATION

Phipps Peak 9,234 ft.

NATIONAL

Cascade Lake

Fallen Leaf CG

89

South Lake Tahoe

WILDERNESS

50

Heavenly Valley Ski Area

FOREST

AREA

Mt. Tallac 9,735 ft.

To Echo Summit

Fallen Leaf Lake

N

0 1 2 3 4 5 6
Miles

throughout the summer, including the Valhalla Summer Festival of Arts and Music. A schedule is available from the nearby Forest Service Visitor Center.

The visitor center, lying just off the drive three miles north of South Lake Tahoe, offers a wide range of activities, displays, trails, and information. The center's six interpretative trails give a broad overview of the natural history and history of the Lake Tahoe area. The half-mile Rainbow Trail passes through pine forest and meadow. Along the way is the interesting Stream Profile Chamber. The underground, plate-glassed chamber peers into the stream ecology of Taylor Creek, exploring the life-cycle of trout and the importance of marshes and meadows that filter and preserve Tahoe's clear water. Autumn visitors can also witness the spawning run of crimson-colored kokanee salmon digging and defending their egg nests. The Lake of the Sky Trail provides an easy stroll to Tahoe's south shore, offering interpretative displays on the impressions of the area's first explorers. The Trail of the Washoe discovers the culture of the ancient Washoe Indians who journeyed from the Carson Valley to this area, a favorite summering spot rich in game and fish. The other trails—Tallac Historic Site Trail, Forest Tree Trail, and Smokey's Trail—all reward the inquisitive hiker. Other visitor activities include ranger-led programs, regular campfire programs at the center's amphitheater, bicycling, and fishing. Pope and Baldwin beaches and the Kiva Picnic Area complete the area's opportunities.

Campers flock to the popular 230-site Camp Richardson and the 205-site Fallen Leaf Campground. Camp Richardson is operated by a concessionaire on a non-reservation basis; Fallen Leaf Campground is a pleasant, well-spaced campground surrounded by towering sugar and Jeffrey pines. Fallen Leaf Lake was formed by a glacial moraine and sits just south of the campground. Rugged 9,735-foot Mount Tallac looms west of the lake. At the end of the Fallen Leaf Road is a popular trailhead for visitors venturing into 63,475-acre Desolation Wilderness Area, the single most-visited wilderness in the United States. Permits are required to hike and camp in this spectacular section of the Sierras to minimize human impact on the area's fragile ecosystems. The permits are free and available from the Forest Service.

The drive runs northwest, passing Cascade Lake, another pretty glacial moraine lake nestled in a hollow above Lake Tahoe. The road switchbacks away from the lake onto a high ridge and enters scenic Emerald Bay State Park, which, coupled with adjoining D. L. Bliss State Park, protects six miles of Lake Tahoe's magnificent shoreline.

Emerald Bay is the real heart of today's Lake Tahoe. It's a beautiful sparkling bay gouged out by ancient glaciers that spilled eastward from the Sierra crest. This watery jewel is surrounded by thick forest and is one of California's most photographed and seen natural wonders. Inspiration Point sits high above the bay's southwest edge. It gives a spectacular view and offers interpretative displays on the area's unique history. Far below lies Fannette Island, the lake's only island. At the head the bay hides Vikingsholm Castle, a Scandinavian-style mansion built in 1928 by heiress Lora Knight and fashioned after an 11th century Norse fortress. Vikingsholm is part of the state park now. A mile-long trail drops down from Emerald Bay Overlook on the bay's west end to the mansion. Tours are scheduled throughout the summer. The Emerald Bay Overlook is a good place to park and explore the surrounding mountains. Glacier-polished granite east of the road offers great viewpoints to sit and meditate on the lake's subtle grandeur. A short hike heads west from the parking area to Eagle Falls on the edge of the Desolation Wilderness Area. The area also offers excellent rock climbing on the many buttresses and small crags above the parking area.

Lake Tahoe has long attracted visitors. First the Washoe Indians summered along the lake shore, finding the cool climate and abundant game to their liking. Tahoe itself is a Washoe word meaning "lake of the sky." The first Anglo-Americans to see the lake were John C. Fremont and his expedition cartographer Charles Preuss from atop Red Lake Peak just north of Carson Pass on February 14, 1844. Fremont noted in his journal that "We had a beautiful view of a mountain lake at our feet, about fifteen miles in length, and so entirely surrounded by mountains that we could not discover an outlet." The discovery of the Comstock silver lode in Nevada brought waves of emigrants and miners through the Tahoe Basin, beginning in 1859. Then young Samuel Clemens, not yet Mark Twain, visited the area in 1861. He wrote in his best seller *Roughing It*: "The lake burst upon us—a noble sheet of blue water lifted six thousand three hundred feet above the level of the sea, and walled in by a rim of snow-clad mountain peaks....I thought it must surely be the fairest picture the whole earth affords."

The mining era's history was not all so rosy. The silver rush decimated the forests of the Tahoe Basin between 1860 and 1900, with entire stands stripped to stumps and shipped via flumes and narrow gauge railroads to Virginia City for mine timbers and building construction and for firewood to drive machinery. More than two billion board feet of timber was cut in the Tahoe Basin by 1881. By the turn of the century the land was so over-logged that one Bureau of Forestry official wrote, "...the forest is much reduced in density...the sugar pine has disappeared almost entirely...the finest of Jeffrey and yellow pine and white fir has been removed." Today, a second-generation forest coats the mountain slopes above Lake Tahoe. The common trees include Jeffrey, ponderosa, sugar, lodgepole, and pinyon pines, incense cedar, Sierra juniper, white fir, quaking aspen, willow, and alder.

Wildlife abounds in the woodlands along the drive, particularly on the lake's west shore, which butts up against the Desolation Wilderness. Beavers dam creeks that meander across meadows. Mule deer, which migrate down to the warmer Carson Valley in winter, often graze in the early evening near Baldwin Beach. Black bears roam the highlands, dropping down to forage in residential areas and campgrounds. As with other areas in the Sierras, store all food in your car or hang it from a tree to avoid bear problems. Other animals include the ubiquitous coyote, raccoon, porcupine, pine marten, marmot, and golden-mantled ground squirrel. Commonly seen birds are the mountain chickadee, Canada goose, western tanager, yellow-head blackbird, Steller's jay, and hairy woodpecker. Bald eagles occasionally winter at the lake. California gulls scavenge along Tahoe's beaches.

Lake Tahoe, contrary to what early visitors thought, is not the interior of a collapsed volcano like Crater Lake. Rather, the lake lies in a down-faulted basin, which lies between two uplifted fault blocks that form the Sierra Nevada on the west and the Carson Range on the east. Lava later spilled from Mount Pluto, a volcano north of the lake, and blocked the path of the ancestral Truckee River. Streams and rivers swollen with runoff, especially in postglacial periods, filled the basin. Today's Lower Truckee River eventually wore an outlet through the lava dam and dropped down steep canyons to Reno and the Carson Sink in the Nevada desert.

The narrow, winding highway runs north around Emerald Bay and into D.L. Bliss State Park. The 1,237-acre park offers almost four miles of mostly pristine coastline, a swim area at Lester Beach, four miles of trails, a picnic area, and a 168-site campground. A short nature trail winds through the forest and passes a huge balanced boulder.

Continuing north, the road passes through Meeks Bay, a popular summer recreation area managed by the Forest Service. Visitors flock to the bay's huge white sand beach to sunbathe, swim, and boat. Nearby is a forty-site forest campground. Just north of Meeks Bay lies Sugar Pine Point State Park, a 2,000-acre park with hiking trails, picnicking, and 175-site General Creek Campground. The park is named for a stand of towering sugar pines that were not logged on a 160-acre homestead here. The historic Ehrman Mansion, built by banker I.W. Hellman, was acquired by the state in 1965. In summer, tours explore the three-story estate. From Meeks Bay to Tahoe City, a distance of about fifteen miles, the drive meanders along the lake shore. Views of its blue water glimmer through open pine woodlands. This road section is lined with summer cabins and rustic retreats. Also, many homes line the lake's shore with piers jutting into the water. Homewood Ski Area offers great views and many intermediate ski runs. It sits north of Meeks Bay. Just past Tahoe Pines and Eagle Rock lies Kaspian Recreation Area, with a ten-site campground, a pier, and public beach. Eagle Rock, lying alongside the road, is also worth a stop. Scramble up the west side for a spectacular view of Lake Tahoe and the surrounding Sierra peaks. William Kent Campground has ninety-five sites and is reached just before Tahoe City.

The drive turns away from the lake at Tahoe City, the largest town on the lake's north shore. For the next thirteen miles, the highway runs alongside the Lower Truckee River to Truckee. Three national forest campgrounds—twenty-seven-site Silver Creek, twenty-four-site Goose Meadows, and seventy-five-site Granite Flat—scatter through this placid gorge. Rafting, once a popular activity, has declined because the river is low after many drought years. The river, however, offers excellent trout fishing in its deep clear pools. A four-mile bike path runs along the river from Tahoe City to Midway Bridge, offering a gentle, but scenic ride. Rock climbers are steadily exploring the volcanic crags above the river, putting in many excellent sport routes.

The Truckee Canyon is best known for its two world-class ski resorts—Alpine Meadows and Squaw Valley—tucked into side-canyons west of the

Fannette Island, in Emerald Bay, is Lake Tahoe's only island.

river. Alpine Meadows offers excellent skiing in steep gullies and chutes with names like Our Father and Promised Land. The area usually remains open until July Fourth. Squaw Valley, site of the 1960 Winter Olympics, is justly famous. It boasts 8,300 acres of ski terrain serviced by twenty-seven lifts.

Truckee lies astride Interstate 80 at the end of the scenic drive. The town grew up along the tracks of the transcontinental railroad at the east base of Donner Pass and Donner Lake. Donner Lake is the site of one of the greatest Gold Rush tragedies. In the harsh winter of 1846-47, a number of families en route to California, including George and Jacob Donner, were caught by winter storms at the foot of the pass. The travelers constructed rough lean-tos, including one against a granite boulder where the smoke marks are still visible. Severe winter weather stranded them. Food ran out, and one by one the Emigrants perished. A relief party that arrived in March found survivors lying among half-eaten human remains. Donner Memorial State Park, just west of Truckee, interprets the party's tragic story and the construction of the Central Pacific Railroad through the Sierras in the park's Emigrant Trail Museum. The park also offers camping, fishing, hiking, and boating.

General description: A seventy-five-mile highway that climbs over 8,573-foot Carson Pass in the central Sierra Nevada.

Special attractions: Carson Pass, Emigrant Trail, Hope Valley, Silver Lake, Caples Lake, Mokelumne Wilderness Area, Indian Grinding Rocks State Historic Park, scenic views, fishing, camping, hiking, backpacking, cross country skiing.

Location: East-central California. The highway runs from Jackson on California 49 east over Carson Pass to Woodfords, six miles from the Nevada border.

Drive route name: California Highway 88.

Travel season: Year-round. The road's upper elevations receive heavy winter snowfall, be prepared for adverse conditions by checking weather reports and carrying chains and survival equipment. The road may be closed or chains may be required in winter.

Camping: Eleven Eldorado and Toiyabe national forest campgrounds are found on or just off the drive.

Services: All services, including food, lodging, and gas, are found along the drive at Jackson and several resort areas.

Nearby attractions: Grover Hot Springs State Park, Lake Tahoe, Yosemite National Park, Mono Lake, Ebbetts Pass, Sonora Pass, Desolation Wilderness Area, Donner Summit, Tahoe ski areas, Placerville, Calaveras Big Trees State Park.

For more information: Eldorado National Forest, 100 Forni Road, Placerville, CA 95667, (916) 621-5265. Toiyabe National Forest, 1200 Franklin Way, Sparks, NV, (702) 331-6444. Amador County Chamber of Commerce, 30 S. Hwy. 49, P.O. Box 596, Jackson, CA 95642, (209) 223-0350.

The drive: The seventy-five-mile-long Carson Pass drive ascends the gentle western slope of the Sierra Nevada from Jackson, crosses 8,573-foot Carson Pass on the range crest, and drops steeply through Hope Valley and Carson Canyon to Woodfords near the Nevada border. The drive traverses diverse terrain, including oak-shrouded foothills, dense forests, rocky peaks, and a deep canyon. Marvelous views unfold along the highway, particularly in the upper elevations. The two-lane, paved highway also offers interesting historical sites from an Indian grinding area and Gold Rush towns to the path of John C. Fremont's ill-fated 1844 expedition and the Emigrant Trail over Carson Pass.

Expect a variety of climates along the drive. As the road ascends to higher elevations, the temperature cools and precipitation increases. Summer offers the mildest weather. Expect hot temperatures above ninety degrees in the

The Mokelumne Wilderness Area lies south of the Carson Pass drive.

western foothills. Above 5,000 feet, temperatures are more moderate with warm days and cool nights. Occasional severe thunderstorms occur on summer afternoons. Autumns are delightful, with warm Indian summer days and cloudless skies. Winter is generally frigid in the high elevations, with heavy snowfall and below-freezing temperatures. Be prepared for adverse conditions by carrying tire chains and adequate clothing.

The scenic drive, following California Highway 88, begins in the historic town of Jackson at the highway's junction with California 49. Jackson is an old Gold Rush town that was originally named Bottileas, a misspelling of the Spanish "botellas" or bottles, by Chilean miners who noted many bottles left around a nearby spring. The town was later renamed for Indian fighter Colonel Alden Jackson. Much of Jackson's wealth came from the hard-rock Kennedy and Argonaut mines, both famed gold producers. The Kennedy mine operated from 1850 to 1942 and boasted a straight-down shaft of 4,600 feet, more than 150 miles of tunnels, and yielded more than thirty-two million dollars in gold. The Argonaut Mine, west of town, was the site of one of California's worst mine disasters. Forty-seven men died from poisonous gas during a 1922 fire. The Amador County Museum that is housed in an 1850s brick house details Jackson's colorful history and explains local gold mining operations. Jackson, with its historic buildings, narrow streets, and wooden sidewalks, is a perfect place to explore on foot. The chamber of commerce offers a walking tour map.

The highway runs northeast from Jackson up Jackson Creek past undulating foothills covered with grass and open oak woodlands. After nine miles, the road climbs onto a ridge and the small hamlet of Pine Grove. A side trip here leads a few miles north on Pine Grove-Volcano Road to a couple interesting sites—Volcano and Indian Grinding Rocks State Historic Park.

The sleepy village of Volcano is worth visiting today because it was once one of the Gold Rush country's richest towns. Volcano sits in a cup-shaped crater rimmed by forested hills mistaken for a volcanic crater. In 1848, General John Sutter mined on Sutters Creek here. The following year Colonel J.D. Stevenson's New York Volunteer Regiment found rich gold deposits in Soldier's Gulch and a town of 5,000 instantly arose. By 1850, Volcano was a leading California city, producing millions of dollars in gold annually. The town also became a cultural haven, with the state's first public library, first astronomical observatory with a three-inch refractor telescope on nearby Observatory Hill, and first literary and debating society. It also boasted seventeen hotels, three breweries, four bakeries, thirty-five saloons, two temperance societies, and a Chinatown.

Indian Grinding Rocks State Historic Park lies 1.5 miles north of Pine Grove and the highway on the road to Volcano. The park preserves a grassy meadow broken by flat outcrops of limestone and groves of oaks. The bedrock is covered with 1,185 "chaw'ses" or mortar cups, shallow holes used by Miwok Indian women to grind acorns and seeds into flour. This grinding site is California's largest. The acorns, ground with stone pestles, yielded a palatable meal that was eaten as mush or baked as small cakes on hot rocks.

Petroglyphs or stone carvings cover the main grinding rock. A reconstructed Miwok village with a roundhouse, bark tepees, and ball field help visitors understand and experience village life. The Chaw'se Regional Indian Museum displays Miwok and other local Indian artifacts. The park has two short hiking trails and a twenty-one site campground.

The drive follows rounded ridge lines coated with dense forest northeastward, slowly climbing up the gentle western slope of the Sierra fault block. The roadside forest changes as the road gains elevation from oak woodlands to mixed conifer forests filled with towering ponderosa and sugar pines, Douglas and white fir, and incense cedar. Azalea and California dogwood add colorful blossoms to the forest in springtime. By thirty-two miles, the road is at 6,000 feet and enters Eldorado National Forest, a 586,000-acre mountain playground that spreads north from the North Fork of the Mokelumne River to Lake Tahoe. The forest includes little-used Mokelumne Wilderness Area and Desolation Wilderness Area west of Lake Tahoe, the nation's most visited wilderness.

Lumberyard Campground, with eight sites, sits at the turn to Salt Springs Reservoir, a popular recreation site on the Mokelumne River. A nineteen-mile paved road leads to the lake. Three campgrounds, Mokelumne, Moore Creek, and White Azalea, are found along the road on the river's North Fork below the dam. Two miles further up the highway is the turn to Bear River Reservoir, a long lake surrounded by forest that lies in the broad valley south of the road. South Shore Campground sits on the lake shore. The lake offers good fishing as well as water-skiing and swimming before the water level drops in late summer and fall.

Past the reservoir turn, the drive edges across Peddler Hillon a high ridge that separates the Mokelumne and American rivers. An overlook here gives one of the road's best vistas. The Sierra crest spreads across the eastern skyline with high peaks poking above glistening snowfields. Granite domes and crags break the dense green forest that spreads southward into the Mokelumne River drainage.

Almost seven miles later, the highway joins the Mormon Emigrant Trail. This was the first wagon road to traverse the lofty Sierras. The original trail ran up the divide between the American and Consumnes rivers from Placerville and climbed over Carson Pass, sometimes called Mormon Pass. Men in the Mormon Battalion, soldiers organized by Brigham Young to fight in the Mexican War, axed the road out of the thick forest on their way home to Utah in 1848. Much of the early gold rush traffic followed this route in 1849 and the early 1850s. It became a toll road in the 1860s and is roughly paralleled today by California Highway 88. In the late 1850s, much of the road's business was usurped by the Placerville Road over Echo Summit to the north.

After the road junction, the highway enters the high Sierra country. An uplifted block of granite some 350 miles long and fifty miles wide forms the Sierra bedrock. Above that lies dark volcanic deposits of mud and ash left by violent eruptions twenty million years ago. The deep volcanic deposits sit

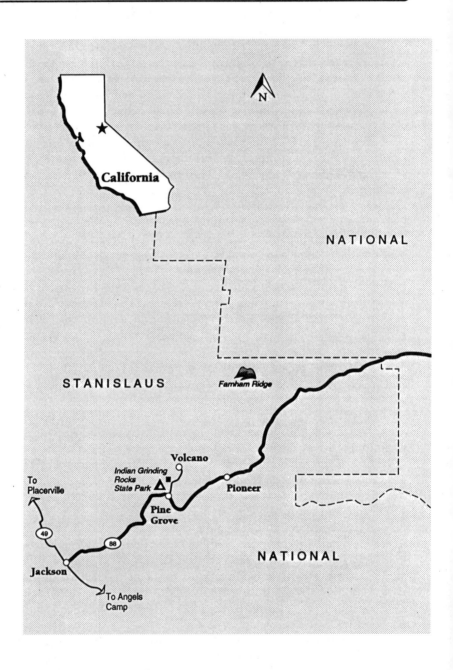

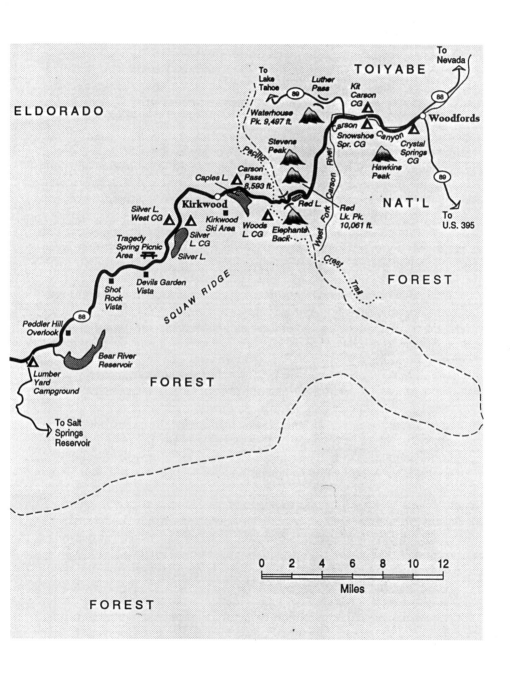

ELDORADO

TOIYABE

To Nevada

To Lake Tahoe

Luther Pass

89

Kit Carson CG

Woodfords

Waterhouse Pk. 9,497 ft.

Carson Canyon

Snowshoe Spr. CG

88

Stevens Peak

Crystal Springs CG

Hawkins Peak

89

Caples L.

Carson Pass 8,593 ft.

Pacific

West Fork Carson River

NAT'L

To U.S. 395

Silver L. West CG

Kirkwood

Kirkwood Ski Area

Red L.

Red Lk. Pk. 10,061 ft.

Silver L. CG

Woods L. CG

Elephants Back

Tragedy Spring Picnic Area

Silver L.

Crest

FOREST

Devils Garden Vista

SQUAW RIDGE

Trail

Shot Rock Vista

88

Peddler Hill Overlook

Bear River Reservoir

FOREST

Lumber Yard Campground

To Salt Springs Reservoir

0 2 4 6 8 10 12

Miles

FOREST

atop the range crest above Carson Pass and California 88. Glaciation did the final sculpting of the range, gouging deep U-shaped valleys, sharpening peaks and aretes, and leaving crystal lakes nestled behind moraines left by melting glaciers. The Sierra's geology is visible from a couple good overlooks—Shot Rock Vista and Devil's Garden Vista Point—beyond the intersection with the Mormon Emigrant Trail.

Tragedy Spring sits a little more than a mile past Devil's Garden Vista. This lovely spot hides a sad history. In 1848 as the Mormon Battalion hacked their way up the western slope of Carson Pass, an advance party of three men was sent ahead to scout the trail. On July 18, party member Henry William Bigler told of a gruesome discovery: "As we were returning to camp we found the place where we supposed our three pioneers had camped by a large spring. Near where they had their fire, was the appearance of a fresh grave. Some of us thought it might be an Indian grave...but the more we looked at it, the more we felt there lay our three men. Determining to satisfy ourselves, it was soon opened. We were shocked at the sight. There lay the three murdered men robbed of every stitch of clothing, lying promiscuously in one hole about two feet deep...We called this place Tragedy Spring." The massacre was blamed on Indians, but further investigations revealed the perpetrators were probably white men seeking gold. A three-site picnic area sits among the firs and pines near the spring.

The highway drops from Tragedy Springs to Silver Lake Recreation Area, a popular boating, fishing, and camping spot in a broad valley above the Silver Fork of the American River. Silver Lake and Silver Lake West campgrounds lie on the lake's northern edge. Plasse's Resort is a private campground operated here since 1853; several other resorts nearby offer additional accommodation choices. A sub-alpine forest of lodgepole pine, Jeffrey pine, mountain hemlock, and California juniper spreads a green mantle over surrounding mountain ridges.

The drive swings north and then east above Caples Creek and climbs into an alpine valley with Kirkwood Ski Area and Caple Lake Recreation Area. In spring and summer, this serene valley's meadows are clad with wildflowers. The area's forests of pine and aspen and the snowy peaks of the high Sierra offer popular getaways. The lake, one of the largest in the central Sierras, bustles with activity. Fishing here is superb for rainbow, cutthroat, and brook trout, as well as trophy-sized mackinaw and brown trout. Boaters, swimmers, and wind surfers enjoy the mountain water. Kirkwood Campground at tiny Kirkwood Lake offers thirteen campsites, while nearby Caples Lake Campground has thirty-five sites and a boat ramp. A few miles south of the lake is Kirkwood Ski Area and Kirkwood Cross Country with eighty kilometers of groomed track.

The highway runs along the north shore of Caples Lake and then begins its final ascent to Carson Pass up Woods Creek. A turn leads to Woods Lake Recreation Area and a fourteen-site forest campground. The Pacific Crest National Scenic Trail passes the lake, crosses the highway, and runs north toward Echo Summit. It offers excellent day hikes and backpacking trips to

Elephants Back dominates the southern end of Hope Valley on the east slope of Carson Pass.

a number of alpine lakes like Round Top, Winnemucca, and Upper Blue and into the popular northern section of the Mokelumne Wilderness Area.

The summit of 8,573-foot Carson Pass lies almost two miles east of the turn to Woods Lake. A monument atop the pass honors famed scout Kit Carson, who, with celebrated pathfinder and gold and land speculator John C. Fremont, blazed a trail over this pass in February 1844. Fremont was an officer in the army's Topographical Engineers and was charged with exploring possible rail and overland routes to California. His detailed geographic information was later used in the conquest of California. Fremont's party had floundered through deep snow up the East Carson River and then over the pass where they encountered even deeper drifts. Scanty food and frigid temperatures forced the men to eat their mules and pet dog Tlamath. Fremont and Charles Preuss, the expedition cartographer, climbed Red Lake Peak north of the pass and became the first Anglo-Americans to see Lake Tahoe. That same day Kit Carson carved the only words he could spell—his name—into a tree trunk atop the pass named after him. A replica of his engraving is on the pass summit today. Another monument atop the pass honors Snowshoe Thompson, a skiing mailman who carried mail over the Sierra in the 1850s and 1860s. A national forest information station is maintained on the pass during the summer.

From Carson Pass, the drive drops down the abrupt east face of the Sierra escarpment on a steep eight percent grade, swinging north around Red Lake nestled in a valley below. Red Lake Vista Point provides great views of the lake, 10,061-foot Red Lake Peak to the north, and 9,635-foot Elephant's Back to the south. The route of the old Mormon Emigrant Trail is visible on the steep slopes above the lake. This abrupt section, called Devil's Ladder, was the final steep pull to the Sierra crest for California-bound Forty-niners. Ropes and chains along with triple-teamed oxen and mules pulled the pioneer's wagons up the rocky trail. A careful examination of rocks and trees along the pitch reveal marks left by their efforts.

The highway quickly loses elevation and enters Hope Valley, a broad, grassy valley carved by the meandering West Fork of the Carson River. This 7,000-foot-high valley is one of the prettiest in all the Sierras and was named by the Mormon road builders. Emigrant chronicler Bigler wrote, "...camped at the head of what we called Hope Valley, as we began to have hope." The handsome valley, edged by lodgepole pine and aspen forest, blazes with wildflower colors in summer. On the valley's east end, the drive intersects with California Highway 89, which runs north over Luther Pass to Lake Tahoe. Just east of the road junction sit twelve-site Kit Carson and thirteen-site Snowshoe Springs campgrounds in Toiyabe National Forest.

The river and the highway make a mad dash down steep Carson Canyon east of Hope Valley. The river through here offers Class II and III runs in May and June. The rocky canyon slopes are studded with granite crags and sharp boulders. As the highway drops, the climate dries and the plant communities change from the Sierran forest to the scrubby Great Basin flora. A forest fire decimated the lower canyon's slopes in 1987, but the area was reforested in 1988. Near the canyon's east mouth, the drive passes twenty-site Crystal Springs Campground, a pleasant overnight spot along the river sheltered by sugar and Jeffrey pines.

Woodfords, the end of the scenic drive, sits at the yawning canyon mouth. Steep, rock-ribbed slopes tower above and the broad Diamond Valley stretches northwest into Nevada. Woodford was a stop on the old Emigrant Trail named for Daniel Woodford, who opened the Sign of the Elephant Hotel here in 1849. A small monument commemorates the town's Pony Express Trail station. Limited services are available. California 89 turns south at Woodfords and goes to Markleeville and over Monitor Pass. California 88 continues northeast across gravel benches above the Carson River, past hayfields and paddocks filled with grazing cattle before turning north and entering Nevada and the wide Carson Valley.

General description: An eighty-mile-long paved highway between Sonora and U.S. 395 that climbs the gradual western slope of the Sierra Nevada to the summit of 9,624-foot Sonora Pass.

Special attractions: Sonora Pass, Stanislaus National Forest, Toiyabe National Forest, Columns of the Giants, Donnell Vista, Strawberry, Emigrant Wilderness Area, Carson-Iceberg Wilderness Area, Sonora, camping, hiking, fishing, winter sports, scenic views.

Location: East-central California. The highway runs between Sonora, off California Highway 49, to U.S. 395 seventeen miles north of Bridgeport near the Nevada border.

Drive route name: California Highway 108.

Travel season: The highway closes in winter past Pinecrest, generally from November to early May. Call the forest service office for information on road closure.

Camping: Fourteen national forest campgrounds are found on or just off the highway. The two at Pinecrest Lake—100-site Meadow View and 200-site Pinecrest—are very popular. Reservations are needed through MISTIX. The campgrounds along the Middle Fork of the Stanislaus River are deservedly popular. The scenery and fishing are magnificent.

Services: All services are at Sonora and Bridgeport. Limited services are found at Pinecrest and Strawberry.

Nearby attractions: Ebbetts Pass, Carson Pass National Scenic Byway, Yosemite National Park, Moaning Caves, Columbia State Historic Park, Railtown 1897 State Historic Park, Calaveras Big Trees State Park, Hoover Wilderness Area, Mono Lake.

For more information: Stanislaus National Forest, 19777 Greenley Road, Sonora, CA 95370, (209) 644-6048. Toiyabe National Forest, 1200 Franklin Way, Sparks, NV 89431, (702) 355-5300. Tuolumne County Visitors Bureau, 55 W. Stockton Road, P.O. Box 4020, Sonora, CA 95370, (209) 532-4212.

The drive: The eighty-mile-long Sonora Pass scenic drive twists up forested ridges on the gentle western slope of California's mountain backbone, the Sierra Nevada, to the airy summit of 9,624-foot Sonora Pass, one of the highest automobile roads in the state. The drive follows paved California Highway 108 and offers a wealth of scenic vistas and recreational opportunities. The road's upper reaches from Kennedy Meadows on the west to Leavitt Meadow on the east is unsuitable for large RVs and trailers. The winding road has no shoulder, narrow lanes, and grades as steep as fifteen percent.

The drive, like other Sierra routes, boasts a wide variety of climates. The elevation difference between 1,826-foot-high Sonora and 9,624-foot Sonora

Pass is almost 8,000 feet. The area experiences relatively dry summers and wet, snowy winters. Summers in the foothills around Sonora are hot and dry, with temperatures often above ninety degrees. As the highway climbs, temperatures decrease, and precipitation increases. Summer days along the drive's upper elevations are usually between sixty and seventy degrees with occasional afternoon thunderstorms. Winters can be severe, closing the highway beyond Pinecrest. As much as thirty feet of snow falls in the high valleys along the range crest. Deep snow drifts remain well into the summer in sheltered ravines along the highway edge.

The drive begins in downtown Sonora at the intersection of California highways 49 and 108. Head south and then east on route 108 via Washington Street (town's main street) and then Mono Way. Sonora is an old, picturesque mining town that was originally built on seven rounded hills in 1848 by Mexican miners from the state of Sonora in northern Mexico. A year later, the town boasted a population of more than 5,000, but in 1850 the town government slapped a twenty dollar tax on all foreign-born miners. Almost overnight the town's population dropped to 2,000. In 1851 the tax was repealed and Sonora again began to prosper. Millions of dollars worth of gold was extracted from the ore-rich gravels under Sonora and Columbia to the north. One of the richest lodes was Big Bonanza discovered by Chilean miners in 1851. Besides its impressive old buildings, Sonora's Tuolumne County Museum, which is housed in an old jailhouse, displays the area's colorful history.

Columbia was Sonora's main rival in the 1850s and lies just to the north. Columbia, once nicknamed "Gem of the Southern Mines," is perhaps the best-preserved gold country town in California. The entire downtown district is preserved in Columbia State Historic Park. The town lost the state capital to Sacramento by just two votes in 1854. Columbia is a good place to investigate history. Through its buildings and artifacts the roaring 1850s come alive. Visitors can step backwards in time here to a place where every day is yesterday.

The highway heads northeast from Sonora and immediately begins climbing high ridges covered with oak groves and grass, and then a thick mixed Sierra forest. By six miles, the four-lane road is at 3,000 feet and a couple miles later passes the turn to Twain-Harte, a small suburban town named in the 1920s for the Gold Country's two most famous writers—Mark Twain and Bret Harte. Past Twain-Harte, the highway drops back to two-lanes and reaches Mi-Wok Ranger Station on the edge of Stanislaus National Forest.

The ranger station is a good place to get camping and visitor information. The forest stretches across 1,090,543 acres between the Merced and Mokelumne rivers on the western slope of the Sierra Nevada. The Stanislaus River and the forest are named for Estanisalo, a Miwok Indian leader who resisted Spanish efforts to capture and colonize the Indians. The river's name was anglicized to its present spelling. It's three forks drain most of the land in the Stanislaus forest.

Donnell Lake is encased by granite walls below Donnell Vista on the Sonora Pass drive.

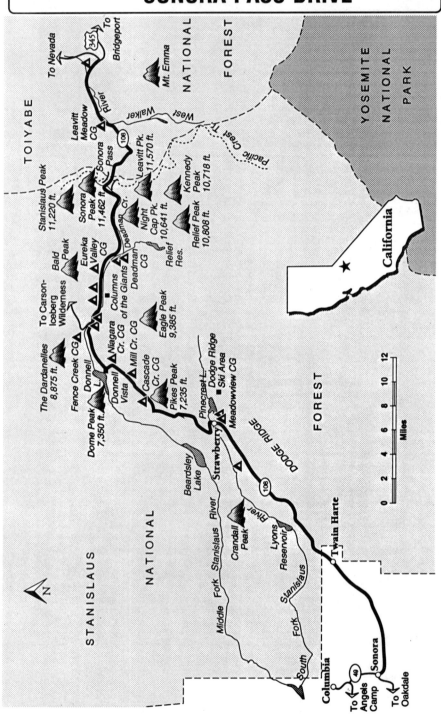

The road continues climbing along ridgelines, with occasional views through breaks in the thick forest. Twenty-six miles from Sonora the drive reaches Summit Ranger Station and the turnoff to Pinecrest Lake, a popular summer boating, fishing, and swimming reservoir on the South Fork of the Stanislaus River. Two large national forest campgrounds, Pinecrest and Meadowview, sit on the lake's south shore. The Shadow of the Miwok Trail begins at Summit Ranger Station. The quarter-mile walk offers interpretations of Miwok Indian life and traditions. The easy Pinecrest Lake National Recreation Trail encircles the lake, offering good views of the lake nestled in its shallow granite basin. A thick forest of ponderosa pine and red fir lines the trail along the south shore. The Forest Service offers a variety of interpretative walks, tours, and campfire programs in summer. Dodge Ridge Ski Resort, with downhill skiing from beginner to advanced, sits on the hills east of the lake.

From the ranger station, the highway drops down to Strawberry, crosses the South Fork of the Stanislaus River, and winds northeast onto high forested ridges. Nine miles from Strawberry the drive passes Cascade Creek Campground. Three miles further lies primitive twelve-site Mill Creek Campground. Acorn grinding holes left by summering Miwok Indians are found on flat boulders alongside the creek. Small five-site Niagara Creek Campground sits two miles up the road in a stand of tall Jeffrey pines. Nearby is the quarter-mile-long Trail of the Ancient Dwarfs. This excellent path explores a dwarf tree grove stunted by poor soil. A ten-mile dirt road, Forest Road 5N01, threads up Niagara Creek and across Eagle Creek to the gnarled Bennett juniper, the largest known western juniper. The tree is named for naturalist Clarence Bennett. It stands eighty feet tall and is thought to be over 3,000 years old.

Donnell Vista, one of the road's best viewpoints, is just past the campground. A short trail drops down from the parking lot through granite bedrock to the lofty 6,400-foot viewpoint. Donnell Lake is a long reservoir along the Middle Fork of the Stanislaus River that tucks into the steep canyon far below. Rock buttresses and cliffs soar above the glassy water. The reservoir was built for electricity generation and irrigation diversion. There is no public access or recreational development. The Dardenelles, named by the Whitney Survey party for some Turkish mountains, lift their craggy volcanic summits above the river to the north. These flat-topped buttes were formed when 1,000-foot-thick lava flows spread across the land over nine million years ago. This 8,875-foot mountain stands above the forested 77,993-acre Carson-Iceberg Wilderness Area.

The road drops away from Donnell Vista, skirting the north flank of Double Dome Rock, and reaches the Middle Fork of the Stanislaus River after four miles. A side road heads north up the river's Clark Fork, allowing access to the Carson-Iceberg Wilderness, The Dardenelles, excellent trout fishing, and several placid campgrounds.

For the next ten miles, the highway parallels the Stanislaus River as it tumbles over worn boulders in the bottom of a deep, glaciated valley. Seven campgrounds—Boulder Flat, Brightman Flat, Dardanelle, Pigeon Flat, Eureka Valley, Baker, and Deadman—scatter along the river banks. The campgrounds, deservedly popular with Californians escaping summer heat in the lowlands, usually fill up early in the day.

Some good stops lie along this scenic road stretch. The world's largest Jeffrey pine sits at the end of a one-mile hike that begins at Brightman Flat. At Dardanelle is a store, gas, lodging, and RV park. A sign claims the town's population is two. The Columns of the Giants geologic site, reached by a 0.25-mile trail from Pigeon Flat Campground, is a miniature replica of famed Devils Postpile. Fluted basalt columns, deposited by ancient lava flows, tower above the river's south bank. Eureka Flat was the site of an early stage stop on the old Sonora and Mono Toll Road. A roadside marker tells of Dave Hays' log roadhouse. A few posts, fallen logs, and foundation pieces are all that remain.

Kennedy Meadows spreads across the far eastern end of the canyon. Steep forested slopes climb away from the river, broken by granite crags. A side road passes Baker and Deadman campgrounds and ends at the northern trailhead for the 112,277-acre Emigrant Wilderness Area. The popular trail wends south across the grassy meadows toward Relief Reservoir and the wilderness backcountry. Soaring Sierra mountains—Leavitt Peak, Relief Peak, and Granite Dome—lift their snowy ridges high above the trail. A rustic resort lures visitors to Kennedy Meadows to enjoy horseback riding and fishing.

The drive effectively ends at Kennedy Meadows for large RVs or vehicles pulling trailers. Beyond the meadows, the highway climbs steeply away from the river valley, winding shelf-like across boulder-strewn slopes. For the next twenty miles, the road twists, turns, switchbacks, and ascends grades as steep as fifteen percent. The road climbs over 3,000 feet in ten miles from Kennedy Meadows to the crest of Sonora Pass. A shoulder is lacking along most of the way. Drive carefully, stay in your lane, and pull off to enjoy the scenery.

As the road climbs, it bends east into Deadman Canyon. A couple viewpoints, Que de Porka and East Flange, offer majestic views south into the Emigrant Wilderness. The original pioneer road is visible below the second overlook. Past East Flange, the highway climbs into Deadman Canyon. This deep U-shaped valley was excavated by ancient glaciers. It is now thinly forested with cedars, white fir, and stream-side willows. A spectacular waterfall slices through granite bedrock just past Chipmunk Flat. A small primitive campground is located here. South of the road, granite aretes and buttresses, separated by steep snow couloirs, sweep up to the 10,641-foot summit of Night Cap Peak. Glacier-polished slabs, broken by vertical cracks, north of the drive are popular with rock climbers.

The drive follows Deadman Creek to the pass summit, paralleling the old Sonora-Mono Toll Road. When gold was discovered near Mono Lake in 1860, a road was needed to haul supplies and equipment from the bustling Sonora area to the new mines. The wagon road was completed in 1865. A round-trip

A waterfall along Deadman Creek plunges over a worn granite bench on the Sonora Pass drive.

from Sonora to Bridgeport by six mule team took up to three weeks. That same year the road was completed, Deadman Creek received its morbid name. In early spring, a man attempted to cross the snowbound Sierras on snowshoes. Trapped by a storm, he froze to death just west of the pass summit. The owners of Douglas Station found his rigid corpse the next day and named the valley. Traces of the old road can be seen past Chipmunk Flat.

After a couple more miles, the drive climbs out of the granite gorge and enters a gentle, shallow valley surrounded by peaks. Two miles later the highway crests the summit of 9,624-foot Sonora Pass, the second-highest road crossing of the Sierras. A small picnic area among stunted pines lies on the ridge. A panorama of peaks and valleys surrounds the pass. Northward looms broad 11,463-foot Sonora Peak and to the south towers 11,570-foot Leavitt Peak. The Pacific Crest Trail, accessed by a trailhead on Sonora Pass, closely follows the range crest here.

Sonora Pass is one of the oldest trans-Sierra emigrant trails. The Bartleson-Bidwell party, the first pioneers to follow an overland route to California, crossed the pass on October 18, 1841. The pass was not attempted by wagons again until 1852. Grizzly Adams traversed it in April of 1854 and noted, "On all sides lay old axle trees and wheels...melancholy evidence of the last season's disasters."

From the pass summit, the highway plunges down a fifteen percent grade for one mile. The road loses 2,500 feet in the next seven miles in a series of steep grades, curves, and switchbacks. Great views unfold from the drive

Nightcap Peak towers above the Sonora Pass drive in the Sierra Nevada.

southward to the rugged heart of the Emigrant Wilderness. As the road drops, the flora changes from the high Sierra fir forest to the pine forest and sagebrush typical of the upper Great Basin Desert.

The road eventually reaches broad, grassy 7,200-foot-high Leavitt Meadow. The West Walker River uncoils across the wide valley. Leavitt Meadows Campground, with sixteen sites, sits on the river's bank among boulders and pines. A side road leads south to a trailhead. The trail goes south from here, following the historic Emigrant Trail up the river, past a string of high mountain lakes that offer excellent trout fishing.

Running northeast above the river, the highway continues losing elevation and drops into sagebrush-covered Pickel Meadow, the site of the U.S. Marine Corps Mountain Warfare Training Center. The road swings around 8,084-foot Pickel Mountain, enters the Walker River Canyon, and passes Sonora Bridge Campground. Three miles later in grassy meadows and beaver ponds the drive deadends at U.S. 395. A right turn leads to Bridgeport and a left heads north to Nevada and Carson City.

15 CALIFORNIA 120
Tioga Pass Road

General description: A fifty-five-mile highway that climbs from the high sagebrush desert at Lee Vining on the east slope of the Sierra Nevada over 9,945-foot Tioga Pass into Yosemite National Park. It passes glaciated domes and wide meadows before dropping through dense forest to Big Oak Flat Road west of Yosemite Valley.

Special attractions: Tioga Pass, Ellery Lake, Tioga Lake, Yosemite National Park, Tuolumne Meadows, Tenaya Lake, Olmsted Point, sequoia grove, hiking, backpacking, camping, fishing, rock climbing, scenic views.

Location: East-central California. The drive runs from U.S. 395 west to the Big Oak Flat Road, California Highway 120, just west of Yosemite Valley.

Drive route name and number: California Highway 120, Tioga Pass Road.

Travel season: May or June through October. The highway usually opens sometime in late May and is closed after the first severe snowstorm around November 1. Check with Yosemite National Park or Inyo National Forest for information on road closure.

Camping: Four national forest campgrounds—Big Bend, Tioga Junction, Ellery Lake, and Tioga Lake—sit alongside the highway on the east side of Tioga Pass. Saddlebag and Sawmill campgrounds lie just north of the road at Saddlebag Lake. Yosemite campgrounds include 314-site Tuolumne Meadows, fifty-two-site Porcupine Flat, seventy-five-site Tamarack Flat, and 166-site Crane Flat. Reservations are needed for Crane Flat and Tuolumne Meadows through MISTIX at (800) 365-2267. The others are first-come, first-served.

Services: All services are in Lee Vining. Limited services, including gas and food, are in Tuolumne Meadows.

Nearby attractions: Yosemite Valley, Half Dome, Merced River, Glacier Point, Badger Pass, Mono Lake, Ansel Adams Wilderness Area, Hoover Wilderness Area, Devil's Postpile National Monument.

For more information: Yosemite National Park, P.O. Box 577, Yosemite National Park, CA 95387, (209) 372-0201. Inyo National Forest, 873 N. Main Street, Bishop, CA 93514, (702) 873-2400.

The drive: The fifty-five-mile-long Tioga Pass scenic drive twists across the southern Sierra Nevada mountains in Yosemite National Park and Inyo National Forest. The highway climbs through steep canyons, crosses grassy Tuolumne Meadows, passes under soaring granite domes etched by glaciers, offers one of California's best views at Olmsted Point, and drops through a thick forest to Yosemite Valley.

The Sierra Nevada, called "the range of light" by pioneer naturalist John Muir, forms California's backbone. This immense sawtooth escarpment stretches 430 miles from Bakersfield to Lassen Peak. It is a range of awesome beauty that includes three national parks, eight national forests, and eleven 14,000-foot peaks. The Sierra Nevada, a fault-block range, is a tilted, and uplifted block of granite with a steep east face and a gentle western slope. Giant glaciers a mile thick gouged out the mountains, excavating deep valleys and carving sharp peaks as recently as 12,000 years ago. Small glaciers still nestle in north-facing cirques, echoes of the great Ice Age glaciers.

Temperatures along the drive vary greatly from the sagebrush desert at Lee Vining to the summit of Tioga Pass, a 3,200-foot elevation difference. Summer daytime temperatures reach into the nineties in the lower elevations, while temperatures in the sub-alpine zone at Tuolumne Meadows seldom climb above eighty degrees. Nights are cooler, sometimes dropping into the thirties. Afternoon thunderstorms occur in July and August, while snow can line the road in any month. Fall is chilly in the upper elevations, while the climate is more moderate around Lee Vining and the drive's west end. The highway closes after the first heavy snowfall, which occurs anytime from mid-October to early December. The road seldom opens before mid-May.

The Tioga Pass Road follows California Highway 120. It turns north at Crane Flat off the Big Oak Flat Road between Big Oak Flat Entrance Station and Yosemite Valley in western Yosemite National Park. The big Oak Flat Road, which drops west into the Central Valley, was completed in 1874; it was the second road built into Yosemite Valley. Just past the Tioga Pass Road's intersection with Big Oak Flat Road is a junction with the Old Big Oak Flat Road, a steep, one-way road that runs west to the entrance station. A short drive down this one-way, spur road leads to the Tuolumne Grove, one of Yosemite's three groves of giant sequoia trees. Travelers will return back to the Tioga Pass Road via the Big Oak Flat Road. A self-guiding nature trail loops through the grove. Hikers should stay on the trail to protect fragile sequoia roots.

Fairview Dome looms over the Tioga Pass Road.

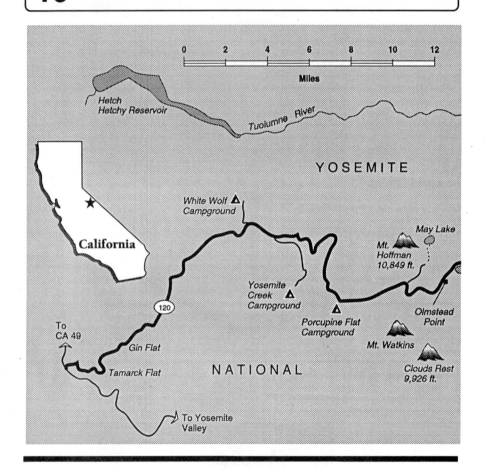

Historians believe this grove of twenty-five sequoia or the nearby Merced Grove were the first big trees discovered by Anglo-Americans. In 1833, a party of trappers led by Joseph Walker crossed the Sierra crest somewhere north of Tioga Pass and followed this high forested ridge between the Merced and Tuolumne rivers west to the San Joaquin Valley. En route they happened upon these forest giants. On October 30, trapper Zenas Leonard noted in his journal, "...we have found some trees of the Redwood species, incredibly large." *Sequoia gigantea* lives 3,000 years, weighs more than two million pounds, and is the world's largest living thing. The trees have thick cinnamon-colored bark and grow in isolated groves on the western slopes of the central and southern Sierra Nevada. A walk among these immense trees is a fitting start to one of California's best scenic drives.

The highway threads east from the meadows at 6,200-foot Crane Flat, climbing along the high divide between the Merced and Tuolumne rivers. A

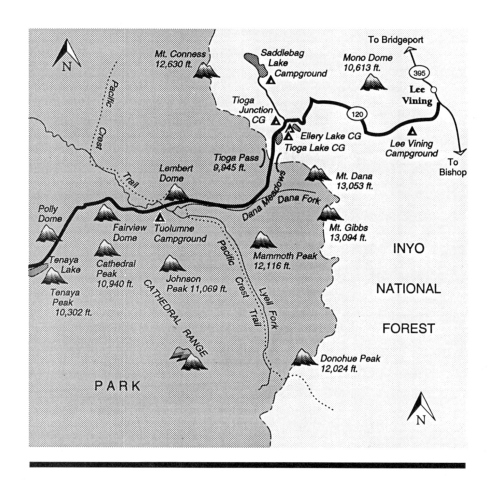

dense forest of mixed conifer—incense cedar (not a true cedar), ponderosa pine, and sugar pine—hems in the road. After a few miles, the drive runs northeast and climbs up along the South Fork of the Tuolumne River. As the road ascends, the forest changes and becomes an almost pure stand of California red fir. This handsome tree, growing to heights of 120 feet, thrives along the Sierra's west slope between 6,000 and 9,000 feet elevation with its dry summers and heavy snows. Here, as in most Sierra stands, lodgepole pine mingles with the red fir. Lodgepole pine is perhaps the most ubiquitous tree of the Yosemite highlands. It grows straight in thick stands as well as twisted and bent over at timberline.

After thirteen miles, the road passes Siesta Lake, a lake that formed when a terminal moraine at the end of a small glacier south of the lake blocked the stream's course. White Wolf, supposedly named for an Indian chief, lies a mile north of the highway on the Old Tioga Road. The original road was built by Chinese laborers in 1883 by the Great Sierra Consolidated Silver Company to haul ore from the old Tioga Mine on the east side of the pass. Facilities here include eighty-seven-site White Wolf Campground (first-come, first-served), dining, lodging in tent cabins, and stables. A popular hike goes north to Harden Lake.

Past White Wolf, the drive swings into the Yosemite Creek drainage and the white granite characteristic of the high Sierra peaks. Yosemite Creek, fed by melting snow on Mount Hoffman and Tuolumne Peak, tumbles southward over boulders and glacier-polished slabs before dropping 2,425 feet into Yosemite Valley as three-tiered Yosemite Falls (North America's highest waterfall). A five-mile spur road, not suitable for trailers and large vehicles, drops down to pleasant seventy-five-site Yosemite Creek Campground. A six-mile-long trail follows the creek down to the waterfall, and switchbacks another 3.6 miles to the valley floor.

The drive turns south above Yosemite Creek and bends east around the forested shoulder of 10,850-foot Mount Hoffman, a rocky peak at the geographic center of Yosemite National Park. Past Porcupine Flat Campground, the road enters the magical world of the upper Sierras. Views begin opening around every corner; the Clark Range lifts its ragged crest to the southeast. Ancient granite, chiseled and smoothed by glaciers, dominates the roadside. Hardy western junipers nestle among the rock outcrops. These gnarled evergreens reach ages of 2,000 years and trunk diameters of sixteen feet. John Muir described them as, "...a sturdy storm-enduring mountaineer of a tree, living on sunshine and snow, maintaining tough health on this diet."

The North Dome Trail begins about a mile east of Porcupine Flat. This 3.7-mile path drops south from the road and climbs to the rounded summit of North Dome perched above Yosemite Valley. Further east a spur road leads north toward May Lake, site of one of Yosemite's five High Sierra camps. A 1.2-mile trail heads up to this backcountry camp that offers meals and rustic accommodations. Reservations are required. Mount Hoffman towers above May Lake to the west.

Olmsted Point is the next stop that offers a superlative view. This overlook provides an unsurpassed panorama of the Sierra crest and the upper reaches of Yosemite Valley. The point is named for Frederick Law Olmsted who chaired the Board of Commissioners that managed the Yosemite Grant as the world's first natural park land. To the south above glacier-polished slabs towers 9,926-foot Clouds Rest, a rocky peak often wreathed in gray clouds. Beyond looms the rounded granite bulk of 8,842-foot Half Dome, one of Yosemite's most famous and beloved landmarks. Half Dome's sheer 2,000-foot-high northwest face was quarried by the thick Tenaya Branch of the Tuolumne Glacier, which spread from the Sierra crest into today's Yosemite Valley. A short walk south from the parking lot to a low dome yields a spectacular view down Tenaya Canyon to Half Dome.

Tenaya Lake nestles east of Olmsted Point in a broad trough surrounded by massive granite domes. This glorious alpine lake is named for Chief Tenaya of the Yosemite Indians. State militiamen captured the Indians at the

The Tioga Pass Road threads past Tenaya Lake, past granite domes, and into Tuolumne Meadows in Yosemite National Park.

picturesque lake in June of 1851. A few years later John Muir wrote, "A fine monument the old man has in this bright lake, and likely to last a long time, though lakes die as well as Indians." The Indians called the lake "Pywiak" or shining rocks, a more fitting name. The highway wends down over granite benches to Tenaya Lake and skirts its northern shore. Picnic sites lie along the road. Trout fishing and boating (motors not permitted) are popular lake uses. A strenuous seven-mile hike begins at Tenaya Lake and scales Clouds Rest, offering lofty views of the Yosemite backcountry.

Superb rock climbs scale the grey granite domes surrounding Tenaya Lake. Most popular are Stately Pleasure Dome's gentle slabs north of the lake and Pywiak Dome just east of the lake. A roadside pulloff allows visitors to watch climbers edge their way up Pywiak Dome, including the classic Dike Route. The climbing here and at Tuolumne Meadows to the east is among the best in the United States, with steep, glacier-polished slabs, knobby bolt-protected faces, and long crack routes up Fairview Dome, Lembert Dome, Daff Dome, and others. The Yosemite Mountaineering School at Tuolumne Meadows provides daily lessons and guided climbs for novices.

The drive climbs away from Tenaya Lake through upper Tenaya Canyon, crossing a low divide into the Cathedral Creek drainage and running east past soaring granite domes. Geologists note that Tuolumne Meadows boasts the largest concentration of granite domes in the world. Fairview Dome, the largest, towers almost 2,000 feet south of the highway. Daff Dome, its initials spelling "Dome across from Fairview," squats north of the forest-lined drive.

The domes formed when glacial ice buried and scoured the rock. Exfoliation of granite slabs gives the unique dome shape when surface rock peels off like thick onion layers. Also note the shiny glacial polish on domes where ice scraped the featureless rock surface smooth.

The road threads through the domes, their roadside flanks coated in hemlocks and pines, and enters Tuolumne Meadows. The meadows form the largest subalpine meadow in the Sierras, sprawling along the meandering course of the upper Tuolumne River at 8,600 feet. The Dana and Lyell forks of the river arise from deep snows along the range crest and flow down through the Grand Canyon of the Tuolumne River into Hetch Hetchy Reservoir where much of the river's water is diverted to the San Francisco area.

The drive runs across the meadows with an open panorama of jagged peaks poking above snowbound cirques to the east. The pastoral meadows are one of Yosemite's best scenic features. The rolling grassland spreads eastward to the mountain wall, broken by forested hump-backed ridges and rounded rock domes. An immense 2000-foot-thick glacier once divided in the meadows; one branch dropped into Yosemite Valley and the other down the Grand Canyon of the Tuolumne River. The last glacier melted away some 10,000 years ago, leaving a damp bog studded with shallow ponds. The meadows are covered with short grasses such as beaked sedges, Sierra ricegrass, tufted hairgrass, and shorthair reedgrass. Summer brings wildflowers that carpet the ground with blazes of color. The meadow's wetness halts an advancing forest of lodgepole pine along the flattened valley edges. The pines, preferring a drier mineral soil, are slowly encroaching on the meadows, particularly on the south edge where the highway blocks runoff.

John Muir described the meadows on his first visit in 1869 as "...the most spacious and delightful high pleasure-ground I have yet seen. The air is keen and bracing, yet warm during the day; and though lying high in the sky, the surrounding mountains are so much higher, one feels protected as if in a grand hall." Most visitors today agree with Muir's assessment. The meadows, besides being a place of great beauty, are a recreational playground.

A network of excellent trails fan out from the Tuolumne Meadows Visitors Center. The Pacific Crest Trail runs across the meadows from Lyell Canyon and down to the High Sierra camp of Glen Aulin. Other good paths include the trail to Elizabeth Lake and the John Muir Trail to Cathedral Lakes. Climbers, besides scaling the polished slabs of Lembert Dome north of the campground, ascend the sharp horn of 10,940-foot Cathedral Peak. An excellent 314-site campground (half reservations and half first-come, first-serve) hides in a thick lodgepole pine forest. A small museum with interpretative exhibits, grocery store, and gas station completes the meadow's visitor services.

Past bulky Lembert Dome, the road ascends through glacial moraines, huge boulder piles left by retreating glaciers, above the Dana Fork of the Tuolumne River. Lembert Dome is a water-streaked granite crag named for 1885 homesteader Jean Baptiste Lembert. After a few more miles, the drive turns northeast into Dana Meadows, a broad swath of grassland broken by

Above: The Redwood Coast drive is lined with soaring redwood trees and plunges through dense fog in Del Norte Redwoods State Park.

At right: Fern Canyon, nestled in Prairie Creek Redwoods State Park on the Redwood Coast, is one of northern California's most beautiful and secluded spots.

Top: *Clouds wreath the Santa Lucia Mountains above the wave-battered Big Sur Coast.*

Bottom: *Deadman Creek cascades like filmy lace over polished granite alongside the Sonora Pass drive. The creek received its name after a traveler froze to death near the pass summit in the spring of 1865.*

Steep granite ramparts on Nightcap Peak tower over California Highway 108 just west of the Sonora Pass summit in the Sierra Nevada. Sonora Pass was first crossed in 1841 by the Bartleson-Bidwell party.

The Merced River plunges 317 feet over Vernal Falls in the Little Yosemite Valley. Seven of the ten highest waterfalls in the United States lie in Yosemite National Park.

Top: *The panorama from Glacier Point is one of Yosemite National Park's best views, encompassing monolithic Half Dome, the snowy Sierra crest, and Nevada and Vernal falls in Little Yosemite Valley.*

Bottom: *Fairview Dome, etched and smoothed by ancient glaciers, lifts its granite brow high above the Tioga Pass Road.*

The Kings Canyon Highway swings around rocky Horseshoe Bend, an abrupt canyon of broken crags carved by the rushing Kings River. The bend sits just west of Kings Canyon National Park, an immense landscape of snowcapped peaks and precipitous gorges in the Sierra Nevada.

The Angeles Crest Highway ascends to the lofty crest of the San Gabriel Mountains north of Los Angeles. The twisting highway offers distant views, chaparral-covered mountains, pine forests and hidden glades filled with ferns, tumbling creeks, and serenity.

Above: Gangly Joshua trees spread across flat valleys tucked between broken granite ridges in Joshua Tree National Monument. The tree, a huge yucca, grows as tall; as forty feet, lives for 800 years, and provides food and shelter to numerous birds and animals.

At right: Keys View yields a spectacular vista of the broad Coachella Valley, the distant Santa Rosa Mountains and the Salton Sea. The viewpoint sits atop the Joshua tree-studded Little San Bernardino Mountains in Joshua Tree National Monument.

Half Dome lies beyond Olmsted Point on the Tioga Pass Road.

islands of granite and small tarns that mirror the rounded ridges of 13,053-foot Mount Dana and 12,764-foot Mount Gibbs. James Dana was a 19th century Yale geologist and Wolcott Gibbs a Harvard chemist.

Eight miles from Tuolumne Meadows, the highway crosses 9,945-foot Tioga Pass, the highest highway pass in the Sierra Nevada. Yosemite National Park's east entrance station sits on the pass summit. A forest of whitebark pine stretches beyond the meadow edge atop the pass and climbs to timberline on surrounding peaks. Whitebark pine is a characteristic high-altitude tree in the Sierra. Timberline, the uppermost limit of the subalpine forest, occurs at about 10,500 feet in Yosemite. The high mountains along the range crest lie in the Arctic-Alpine life zone, a windswept, barren land of harsh winters, rock fields and talus slopes, dwarfed shrubs, and delicate tundra flowers—alpine sorrel, elephant's head, saxifrage, rock primrose, and alpine paintbrush.

A mile-long trail climbs north from the pass summit to Gaylor Lakes on the west flank of Gaylor Peak and the derelict site of the Tioga Mine. Another short, rough trail at the end of the old Tioga Pass Road begins on the east side of the pass and leads to the ghost town of Bennettville, headquarters of the Great Sierra Consolidated Silver Company. The company tunneled into the mountain in search of the Sheepherder Lode, a supposedly wealthy silver vein. The old Tioga Road reached the town in 1883 before the company and Bennettville closed down. Tioga, an Iroquois word meaning "where it forks," was probably attached by a pioneer from New York's Tioga County.

From the Tioga Pass summit, the highway begins dropping eastward. A couple good fishing lakes, Tioga and Ellery, lie along the roadside. Three Inyo National Forest Campgrounds—Tioga Lake, Junction, and Ellery Lake—offer first-come, first-served sites. They fill up early in summer. A side trip heads up Forest Road 1N04 to two more campgrounds and Saddlebag Lake, a large reservoir on the southern edge of the Hoover Wilderness Area.

Past Ellery Lake, the road sweeps around 11,513-foot Tioga Peak and begins spiraling down steep grades on rocky talus slopes above abrupt Lee Vining Canyon. The road falls almost 4,000 feet in less than six miles on the eastern escarpment of the Sierras from Tioga Pass to the sagebrush desert at Lee Vining. A huge glacier once spilled down this canyon, shoving its icy snout into an immense lake at the range base. The upper part of the canyon below the Tioga Pass summit is a hanging valley left by the glacier. Lateral moraines, rock ridges left by the retreating glacier, line the edges of the broad lower canyon.

Spectacular views spread out below the road as it descends. To the south looms the peaks and aretes of 228,500-acre Ansel Adams Wilderness Area, and to the east stretches the snowcapped Inyo and White ranges, glassy Mono Lake, and the dark volcanic plug domes of Mono Craters. Lee Vining Creek, offering trout fishing, meanders across the cobbled canyon floor. Lee Vining Campground has 100 sites. Seventeen-site Big Bend Campground sits just south of the drive. Forests of Jeffrey pine sprinkled with intermittent aspen groves blanket the hillsides above the creek.

An Inyo National Forest ranger station sits at the drive's eastern terminus, with national forest information, maps, and wilderness area permits. Beyond the station, the drive ends at U.S. 395, the major north-south highway on the eastern slope of the Sierra Nevada. Lee Vining is a small town named for an 1852 prospector. It's immediately north of the junction and has all traveler services.

Ancient Mono Lake, one of California's most unusual natural features, straddles the wide basin to the northwest. The million-year-old lake, surrounded by volcanic domes, lava flows, and sagebrush-covered benches, is the drying remnant of what was in glacial times a 900-foot-deep lake. The lake is known for the bizarre and exquisite tufa formations that scatter along the shoreline. Mono Lake is also alive with birds. About eighty-five percent of the California gull population nests here in spring, while more than 300 other bird species have been identified. But the lake has come under siege by water-hungry Los Angeles. Water is taken from Mono Lake's four feeder streams in the Sierra, leaving nothing to replenish water that disappears through evaporation. Since 1941 when water was first diverted from Mono Lake, the lake's level has dropped forty-five feet or an average of eighteen inches a year.

16 YOSEMITE NATIONAL PARK SCENIC DRIVE
Oakhurst to Yosemite to Mariposa

General description: Two California highways form this 105-mile-long scenic loop between Oakhurst, Yosemite Valley, and Mariposa. The drive crosses high ridges cloaked in mixed Sierra forests, traverses the incomparable Yosemite Valley, and drops down the abrupt Merced River Gorge.

Special attractions: Yosemite National Park, Yosemite Valley, Glacier Point Road, Glacier Point, Taft Point, Bridalveil Falls, Sentinel Rock, Half Dome, Yosemite Falls, El Capitan, Merced Wild and Scenic River and gorge, Mariposa Grove Big Trees, Pioneer Yosemite History Center, Wawona, Badger Pass Ski Area, Sierra National Forest, Yosemite Mountain-Sugar Pine Railroad, historic Mariposa, California Mineral Exhibit (Mariposa), scenic views, camping, hiking, rafting, rock climbing, photography, wildlife.

Location: East-central California. The drive lies on the western flank of the Sierra Nevada range east of Merced and the Central Valley.

Drive route names and numbers: California highways 41 and 140, Glacier Point Road, Wawona Road, Merced Road.

Travel season: Year-round. Winter driving can be hazardous, especially on the Wawona Road; use snow tires or carry tire chains. The Glacier Point Road closes in winter.

Camping: Seven campgrounds with 817 sites are in Yosemite Valley—North

Pines, Upper Pines, Lower Pines, Upper River, Sunnyside Walk-in, and Backpackers Walk-in. Camping is available year-round, but many main campgrounds are only open April through October or November. Reservations through DESTINET at (800) 365-2267 are required. Sunnyside and Backpackers campgrounds are available on a first-come, first-served basis at $2 a person. Sunnyside is a popular rock climbers campground. Wawona Campground, with 100 sites, on California 41 at Wawona, and 110-site Bridalveil Creek Campground on the Glacier Point Road, are on a first-come, first-served basis. Seven other campgrounds are scattered across the national park. A couple Sierra National Forest campgrounds are on the drive—Redbud on the Merced River and Summerdale at Fish Camp on the park's southern boundary. Private campgrounds are found in the Oakhurst and Mariposa areas.

Services: All services are available in Yosemite Valley, Oakhurst, and Mariposa.

Nearby attractions: Tioga Pass scenic drive, Tuolumne Meadows, Sierra Nevada crest, Pacific Crest Trail, Sequoia-Kings Canyon national parks, Millerton Lake State Recreation Area, Wassama Round House State Historic Park, Sonora, Columbia State Historic Park, Railtown 1897 State Historic Park.

For more information: Yosemite National Park, P.O. Box 577, Yosemite National Park, CA 95389, (209) 372-0201. Sierra National Forest, 1130 O Street, #3017, Fresno, CA 93721, (209) 297-0706. Mariposa County Chamber of Commerce, 5158 Hwy. 40, P.O. Box 425, Mariposa, CA 95338, (209) 966-2456.

The drive: Yosemite Valley, one of the world's most beautiful places, is an astounding spectacle. It's a place of exquisite beauty and grandeur, a place that inspires reverence and awe. John Muir, its poet laureate and ardent admirer, wrote: "God always seems to be doing his best here." The dramatic valley, molded and sculpted by great rivers of ice, sits like a giant, open-air cathedral on the western slope of the Sierra Nevada. It's granite walls soar upward to merge with a roof of turquoise sky and diaphanous clouds. In spring and early summer, waterfalls plunge in frothy veils over the valley rim. Thick forests and verdant meadows cloak the valley floor and line the gravel banks of the Merced River. Yosemite Valley, the centerpiece of 748,542-acre Yosemite National Park, remains the enduring heart of California. It remains, despite its popularity, a place touched with the timeless magic and mystery of planet Earth.

The Yosemite scenic drive, following California highways 41 and 140, makes an open 105-mile loop that begins in Oakhurst in the Sierran foothills, climbs into Yosemite National Park, makes a side-trip to Glacier Point, explores Yosemite Valley's floor, and follows the Merced River down a deep gorge to Mariposa. Every California visitor and resident needs to drive this route—it's simply the best the state has to offer.

This is a land of distinct seasons, with each bringing its own voice to the year's rhythm. Summers are hot on the valley floor and along the drive, with daily high temperatures often climbing into the 90s and even to 100 degrees.

The Merced River plunges down steep Merced Gorge in Yosemite National Park.

July and August highs average eighty-nine degrees on the valley floor, with an average low of fifty. Cooler weather is found on the higher elevations along the Glacier Point Road. It's generally dry, but occasional thunderstorms dampen the mountains. Hikers should wear a hat and use suntan lotion. Autumn is crisp and clear, with warm days and chilly nights. Early snows whiten the peaks and provide contrast to colorful fall foliage, which climaxes in late October. Winters are generally mild in the lower foothills and the valley floor. As much as ninety percent, however, of the valley's annual thirty-seven inches of precipitation falls between November and March. December, the wettest month, averages 7.10 inches of precipitation and an average high of forty-nine degrees. Be prepared for snowy road conditions in winter. Carry chains and warm clothing. The Glacier Point Road closes in winter. The lower elevations are mild and rainy in winter. Spring, a season of transition, brings both warm and cool days as well as extended wet periods. The park's famous waterfalls peak in May and early June as the high country's blanket of snow melts away.

The drive begins at the intersection of California highways 41 and 49 in 2,290-foot Oakhurst, forty-seven miles north of Fresno. Oakhurst lies in the bottom of a broad valley called Fresno Flats along the Fresno River. The town, originally named Fresno Flats, was renamed for the luxuriant groves of oaks that scatter across the scrubby foothills above town. Oakhurst, Yosemite's southern gateway, offers all visitor services as well as the Fresno Flats Historical Park with several historic buildings and nearby Bass Lake, a popular fishing, motor boating, and water-skiing reservoir southeast of

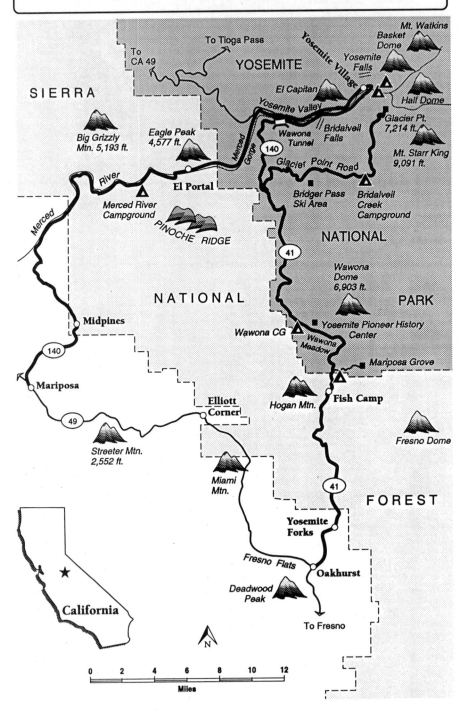

town. Five forest campgrounds lie along its shores. Wassama Round House State Historic Site, a ceremonial round house maintained by the local Miwok Indian tribe, sits northwest of town off route 49.

Head north on California 41 from Oakhurst. This drive section, from Oakhurst to its junction with route 140 in Yosemite Valley, is forty-five miles long. The road begins climbing immediately, winding up grass and oak-covered hillsides above the Lewis Fork of the Fresno River. The Oakhurst Ranger Station for Sierra National Forest provides information and maps. It sits just over a mile up the highway. The road enters the national forest 4.5 miles north of Oakhurst. As the highway ascends, the surrounding woodland changes to a mixed Sierra forest dominated by pine, oak, manzanita, and incense cedar. The rounded foothills here form a transition zone between the oak, gray or "digger" pine, and chaparral woodland on the east side of the Central Valley and the pine belt of the lower Sierra Nevada.

At six miles the highway reaches an elevation of 4,000 feet. West Fall Picnic Area, three miles farther, sits along the roadside in a shady cedar and pine forest with a thick fern understory. The Yosemite Mountain Sugar Pine Railroad, operating from mid-April through October, makes a delightful stop. The forty-five-minute ride twists down a four-percent grade into Lewis Creek Canyon on the narrow gauge tracks of the old Madera Sugar Pine Lumber Company Railroad. The railroad operated from 1899 to 1931, hauling some 1.5 billion board feet of lumber from the surrounding forests. Two massive Lima Shay locomotives transport tourists on old logging cars with sectioned log benches around the tracks now instead of timber and logging crews.

Past the railroad the highway climbs to 5,000 feet, crosses a divide, and drops into Fish Camp. This small town, a popular summer stop, offers food and lodging. A mile up the road sits thirty-site Summerdale Campground. It makes a good overnight stop for visitors touring southern Yosemite.

Fourteen miles from Oakhurst the drive enters Yosemite National Park. An entrance fee of $20 per vehicle is required. Just past the entrance, a two-mile side road wiggles east to the Mariposa Grove of Giant Sequoias. This grove, Yosemite's largest, contains more than 500 mature sequoias on a 250-acre tract that ranges from 5,500 to 7,000 feet in elevation. The giant sequoia, *Sequoiadendron giganateum*, is the world's largest living thing. The trees are found only in isolated stands on the western slope of California's Sierra Nevada and grow as tall as 310 feet, measure more than forty feet in diameter, and live as long as 3,000 years. These giants grow from tiny seeds that are the size of an oat flake. The trees scatter billions of seeds on the forest floor, yet few sprout. As John Muir wrote, "...not one seed in a million shall germinate at all, and of those that do perhaps not one in ten thousand is suffered to live through the vicissitudes of storm, drought, fire and snow-crushing that beset their youth." The Mariposa Grove, discovered in 1849, is explored by a tram system that runs through the grove to the Mariposa Grove Museum and by a loop trail. The Grizzly Giant, the grove's largest sequoia, grows about a half mile back. The huge tree is the largest in Yosemite and fifth largest in the world; it is at least 2,700 years old. Note its side limbs—some are bigger than most other tree species. The Mariposa Grove was protected by the 1864 act signed by President Abraham Lincoln along with Yosemite Valley.

The drive twists north from the Mariposa Grove and drops to Wawona Meadow in the broad valley of the South Fork of the Merced River. Wawona, an Indian word meaning "big tree," is a surprising oasis of civilization in the wild Sierran forest. Wawona, originally called Clark's Station after Yosemite pioneer Galen Clark, was a popular stopover on the old stage route to Yosemite. Today, manicured lawns spread up from the highway to the elegant Wawona Hotel, a gleaming white, two-story structure built in the 1800s for wealthy visitors. The hotel offers a spacious veranda, swimming pool, and tennis courts. A nine-hole golf course stretches alongside the road across from the hotel. Make reservations through the Curry Company, the park's concessionaire.

Wawona is also home to the Pioneer Yosemite History Center, an interesting living history program that recreates historic Yosemite National Park and its horse era. The area includes furnished buildings and cabins, a 1858 covered bridge, and educational exhibits. A stagecoach ride gives greater appreciation for the ease of today's transportation. The 100-site Wawona Campground, open all year on a first-come basis, is nestled among pine trees above the Merced River just up the drive. The site was originally used by the U.S. Army, who administered the park, as a camp and headquarters from 1981 to 1906.

Past Wawona, the highway leaves the Merced River, swings around Turner Ridge and begins contouring across steep, forested hillsides and crossing shallow, tumbling creeks. Ten miles later the road climbs to 6,000 feet and a mile later reaches Chinquapin, the junction of route 41 and the Glacier Point Road. The site is named for the common evergreen chinquapin, a low shrub that scatters across the dry hillsides here. The sixteen-mile-long Glacier Point Road begins here. Turn east on it for some of the scenic drive's most spectacular views.

The two-lane, paved Glacier Point Road climbs east from Wawona Road, crossing steep slopes densely forested with red fir, lodgepole pine, and sugar pine. At three miles the El Portal View offers a view westward down the Merced River gorge to the chaparral-covered Sierra foothills and beyond to the San Joaquin Valley, California's agricultural breadbasket. On clear days, look for the hazy outline of the coastal ranges 125 miles away. Badger Pass Ski Area is two miles farther up the drive. It offers 900 feet of vertical drop and great beginning and intermediate skiing on the state's first ski slopes. The area opened in 1935. In winter, the Glacier Point Road is only open to the ski area. Beyond lies a white wilderness that beckons cross-country skiers. This backcountry yields fabulous skiing. Most popular is the long, groomed track out to Glacier Point itself. The park offers more than 350 miles of signed cross-country ski trails. The Yosemite Cross-Country Ski School is based at Badger Pass. Skiers are advised to take a free shuttle from the valley floor to the ski area, especially on weekends, to avoid the parking crunch, to save gas,

Yosemite Falls, one of the world's tallest waterfalls, plunges over a sheer granite cliff into Yosemite Valley.

and to limit air pollution in the area.

The road crests a hill just past the ski area and descends to meadows, which are sprinkled with wildflowers in summer. Deer often graze along the forest edge. Just before crossing Bridalveil Creek, a side road that is a quarter mile long leads to the 110-site Bridalveil Creek Campground. This campground is open June through September on a first-come basis; it lies at a cool 7,200 feet. At Mono Meadow, the drive bends north and alternately plunges through dense forests and crosses open meadows. At Sentinel Dome, a short trail scrambles over bedrock to its rounded 8,122-foot summit. Jeffrey pines, stunted by fierce winds, twist out of granite fissures. The rocky top gives a splendid view into Yosemite Valley. Three-tiered Yosemite Falls and the sweeping nose of El Capitan lies opposite. Another rewarding trail begins at the parking area and goes one mile to Taft Point, an isolated lookout with another marvelous view.

For the last two miles the narrow road switchbacks steeply down to Glacier Point. A short walk from the parking lot leads to the 7,214-foot overlook. This viewpoint, some 3,000 feet above the valley floor, yields one of the premier views in a park of superlative views. Immediately below the railing is a thousand-foot vertical cliff atop the sloping Glacier Point Apron. The floor of Yosemite Valley, broken by forests and meadows and laced with roads, stretches out below. Half Dome's vertical face lifts a rocky brow to the east. Little Yosemite Valley, Vernal Falls, and Nevada Falls are nestled south of Half Dome. The lofty crest of the Sierra Nevada rims the eastern horizon; its tall peaks—11,522-foot Mount Clark, 13,114-foot Mount Lyell, and 10,850- foot Mount Hoffman—pierce the sky. Facilities at Glacier Point include restrooms, limited food service, and ranger-led activities. Retrace the road back to the Wawona Road.

From Chinquapin, Highway 41 edges north across wooded slopes that dip into shallow ravines. Six miles later the drive crosses exfoliated granite layers on Turtleback Dome and enters Wawona Tunnel, a 0.8-mile-long passage chiseled in granite to avoid an unsightly roadcut. The traveler's first dramatic view of Yosemite Valley lies on the other side. Watch for the pull off on the road's north side; but it may be full of vehicles in summer. This is the classic Yosemite view. Towering cliffs of white granite form the wall around the flat valley floor, with 8,842-foot Half Dome lording over the rocky domain. The white plume of Bridalveil Falls plunges 620 feet from a hanging valley between Cathedral Rocks and the Leaning Tower. A 1.25-mile trail climbs south to Inspiration Point, a lookout on the old road into Yosemite. Be careful pulling on and off the highway; be wary of heavy traffic during summer months.

The road descends steeply down the valley's south slope and 1.5 miles later reaches a parking area with a short trail that leads to a view of Bridalveil Falls. The falls is particularly spectacular in late spring when snow melts and swells its stream. The water leaps off the rim, exploding into filmy mists and draperies at its base. The area below the falls is treacherous, with slick boulders and a roaring creek. Just past the parking area the route joins the one-way Southside Drive on the valley floor. Continue east on the road into Yosemite Valley.

Some legends say Yosemite was named from the southern Miwok Indian word "yo'hem-iteh" meaning grizzly bear by members of the Mariposa Battalion, a rag-tag band of militia who in 1851 found the valley while searching for its native inhabitants. The Indians had raided several stores in retribution for incursions by miners into their territory. The Indians called themselves "Ahwahneechee" or dwellers in Ahwahnee, their name for the magnificent valley.

The valley is truly one of the world's beauty spots. Writers and visitors have sung its glories since its discovery. Philosopher Ralph Waldo Emerson called it "the only place that comes up to the brag about it, and exceeds it." Horace Greeley wrote in the New York Tribune in 1859 that Yosemite was "the greatest marvel of the continent." In 1860 travel writer Thomas Starr King proclaimed, "Great is granite, and the Yo-Semite is its prophet." Lafayette Bunnell, a doctor with the Mariposa Battalion and among the first whites to enter the valley, wrote that on seeing the spectacle for the first time

Clouds wash against El Capitan, the largest granite monolith in Yosemite Valley.

"...a peculiar exalted sensation seemed to fill my whole being, and I found my eyes in tears with emotion."

John Muir, however, was the greatest chronicler of Yosemite's wonders. In his classic book *The Yosemite* he wrote: "No temple made with hands can compare with Yosemite. Every rock in its walls seems to glow with life. Some lean back in majestic repose; others, absolutely sheer or nearly so for thousands of feet, advance beyond their companions in thoughtful attitudes, giving welcome to storms and calms alike, seemingly conscious, yet heedless of everything going on about them. Awful in stern, immovable majesty, how softly these mountain rocks are adorned and how fine and reassuring the company they keep."

Yosemite Valley, as John Muir ascertained through his ramblings in the high Sierra, formed not from earthquakes and uplifts but by massive glaciers that gouged and excavated the deep Merced River canyon, beginning about one million years ago. Several glacial advances filled the valley to the brim and chiseled the park's familiar topographic features—Half Dome, El Capitan, and Sentinel Dome—from the valley's granite walls during this long era of periodic glaciation. By 10,000 years ago, the last glacier retreated from the valley, leaving a long lake dammed by a terminal moraine or pile of eroded glacial debris near El Capitan's base. Sediments eventually filled the lake, forming a flat floor.

The drive tours the loop road through Yosemite Valley, paralleling the serpentine Merced River and passing numerous visitor services scattered through what is called Yosemite Village. About 3.5 million annual visitors flood the valley. In summer, crowded trails, stressed interpretative services, full campgrounds, smog from auto emissions and campfires, and crunched parking lots await park visitors. To alleviate parking problems, the Park Service offers free shuttle buses around the valley's eastern end and eight miles of paved bike paths. Buses run to Glacier Point and Tuolumne Meadows in summer. The park is much less congested during the off season.

North Pines, Upper Pines, Lower Pines, Upper River, and Lower River campgrounds, with 757 total campsites, sit in the eastern valley. Reservations are required through MISTIX. Sunnyside Walk-in Campground, the old climber's Camp 4, still attracts climbers to its first-come, first-served sites. Campers need to be aware of black bears in the park. Keep a clean camp, do not leave food unattended, and cover all food, food containers, and ice-chests in unattended vehicles. The bears will recognize the food and break the car windows.

A wealth of outdoor adventures greet the Yosemite visitor. Many hiking trails lace the valley. Some of the best include the five-mile walk up Four-Mile Trail to Glacier Point, the one-mile round trip to Mirror Lake, the seven-mile round trip to Upper Yosemite Falls, and the hike up the rushing Merced River to Vernal and Nevada falls. Swimmers and tubers cool off in summer in the Merced's placid valley waters. Rock climbers scale all the cliffs. Climbs range from one-pitch sport routes near Sunnyside Campground and the Chapel Wall to difficult, multi-pitch free climbs like Astroman on Washington

Column to ascending the valley's famed big walls of Half Dome and El Capitan—most popular are the Nose and Salathe Walls on El Capitan and Half Dome's Northwest Face. At El Cap Meadows, visitors crane their necks and peer through binoculars and telescopes to spot climbers clinging to El Capitan's 3,000-foot-high face, the world's single largest piece of exposed granite. Numerous interpretative programs, including ranger-led hikes, evening programs, and nature talks are held daily. Inquire at the visitor center for information and schedules and consult the Yosemite Guide issued at the park entrances.

At the gas station just beyond the Yosemite Lodge, the drive turns onto one-way Northside Drive and runs west. Yosemite Falls, the world's third highest waterfall at 2,425 feet, plunges over the canyon rim, stair-stepping down over three separate falls to the valley floor. The Lower Falls itself is twice the height of Niagara Falls. The road bends through a pine forest, skirts the Three Brothers, and enters El Capitan Meadow. This broad grassland, flanked by towering oaks and tall pines, lies beneath El Capitan. Southward, in the shade, towers bulky Middle Cathedral Rock. Past the meadow the road crosses a low, hummocky ridge of glacial rubble, left as a terminal moraine at the far western edge of the Yosemite Valley. A pull off down the road gives the famed valley view through the portals of Yosemite. El Cap on the north and the Cathedral Rocks and Bridalveil Falls on the south frame this postcard-perfect view. A half-mile farther west is the junction with Southside Drive. Turn here to head back into the valley or take the Wawona Road out of the park to California Highway 41 and Wawona. The scenic drive continues west on El Portal Road. Another road junction lies just down river. The Big Oak Flat Road climbs up to Tuolumne Meadows and Tioga Pass on the scenic Tioga Road.

For the next seven miles the road descends sharply down the Merced River's abrupt V-shaped canyon, dropping from 4,000-foot Yosemite Valley to 2,100 feet at El Portal just outside the park. As the drive descends it passes from the mixed Sierra forest of conifers and deciduous trees through chaparral to the dry Upper Sonoran life zone with its blue oaks and gray pines. The highway passes several points of interest. Cascade Falls plunges through a granite-encased box canyon north of the road. Farther west the highway intersects the old Coulterville Road, an old wagon route that was used from 1874 until a landslide blocked it in 1982. The frothy river rushes over huge boulders alongside the highway, until reaching the Arch Rock Entrance Station five miles from the valley. The station is named for the two immense boulders that form an arch over the east-bound traffic lane. The park boundary is two miles west of Arch Rock.

El Portal sits just outside the park. This small community serves as home for many of Yosemite's employees. The town, once the terminal station on the Yosemite Valley Railroad, offers an informative train display that includes a locomotive and train cars. From here, early visitors climbed aboard stagecoaches for the journey's final leg to the fabled valley.

The drive edges the Merced River for the next eighteen miles to Briceburg.

The view from Glacier Point includes Half Dome, Little Yosemite Valley, and the distant Sierra Nevada crest.

The river begins at snowfields on the Sierra crest, tumbles clear and cold down Nevada and Vernal falls, meanders peacefully through Yosemite Valley, and foams fiercely through its canyon above El Portal. The river was named "El Rio Nuestra Senora de la Merced" or The River of Our Lady of Mercy by Mexican Army Lieutenant Gabriel Moraga after a hot, forty-mile march to its banks in 1806. Miners plied its banks in the 1850s, finding rich gold deposits. Between 1907 and 1945 the railroad toted passengers up the river canyon to El Portal. The level, abandoned railbed follows the north bank across the Merced from the highway. Much of the river, one of California's outstanding, free-flowing streams, is protected as a National Wild and Scenic River.

The Merced River, managed by the Bureau of Land Management and U.S. Forest Service, offers superb rafting and kayaking on its rough waters. Stand on its banks and listen to the flow. Its racing waves sing as they roar over boulders and churn through rapids. In spring when the river swells with runoff from melting snow, it is full of white-water dreams for the river runner. The Merced's first nine miles from Rosebud just west of El Portal to Emory boasts several difficult and scary Class III and IV rapids. Stark Reality and Ned's Gulch rapids can flip a sixteen-foot raft at high water levels. The seven-mile section from Emory to Split Rock below Briceburg is easier, with deep pools and shallow Class II and III riffles. Local outfitters offer Merced River trips. The best time to float the river's white water is spring and early summer.

Fishing is decent along the Merced also, with the section around Rosebud Picnic Area designated as wild trout water. Good hiking is also found in the canyon. The abandoned rail grade is popular. Two bridges allow access to the grade on the river's north bank. A superb hike follows the river's South Fork in Sierra National Forest west of El Portal. The wildflower display on the grassy hillsides above the sparkling river is simply breathtaking in April and May, when more than fifty flower species carpet the hills. Campers stay overnight at the fourteen-site Indian Flat Campground near El Portal, and three primitive BLM campgrounds—McCabe Flat, Willow Placer, and Railroad Flat—downriver from Briceburg. The Bureau of Land Management also manages an information station at 1,441-foot Briceburg, offering nature guides, maps, and river information.

The drive swings inland at Briceburg and leaves the Merced River behind. It climbs steeply up Bear Creek canyon, its slopes coated with brushy chaparral, and four miles later reaches a pine forest in Midpines at 2,962 feet. Mariposa straddles oak-covered hills a couple miles farther west. Mariposa is near the southern tip of California's gold country and was named by Spanish explorers in 1806 for the area's multitude of butterflies. The town was established by trailblazer and mapmaker John C. Fremont who acquired some 40,000 acres of seemingly worthless land here. Gold was later discovered and his Las Mariposas Land Grant was worth a fortune. Mariposa offers California's oldest courthouse, built in 1854, and the excellent Mariposa County History Center with mining and Miwok displays. The California State Mining and Mineral Museum exhibits one of the nation's best rock collections, including placer gold nuggets, meteorites, gems, and stunning minerals.

17 CALIFORNIA 180 & 198
The Kings Canyon Hwy. & the Generals Hwy.

General description: These two drives form a 160-mile open loop drive that begins in Minkler on the eastern edge of the San Joaquin Valley, climbs into the western Sierra, visits the spectacular gorge at Kings Canyon National Park, traverses towering stands of giant sequoia trees in Sequoia National Park, and descends sharply down the Kaweah River to Lemon Cove.

Special attractions: Kings Canyon National Park, General Grant Tree and Grove, Kings Canyon, Zumwalt Meadow, Boyden Cave, Redwood Canyon, Sequoia National Park, Giant Forest, General Sherman Tree, Moro Rock, Crystal Cave, Kaweah River, Sequoia National Forest, camping, hiking, backpacking, rock climbing, nature study, wildlife, scenic views, photography.

Location: East-central California. The Kings Canyon drive begins about twenty miles east of Fresno, following California Highway 180, and ends at

Cedar Grove. The Generals Highway Drive begins in Kings Canyon's General Grant Grove at the intersection of CA 180 and CA 198 and ends at Lemon Cove on route 198 about twenty miles east of Visalia.

Drive route name and numbers: California highways 180 and 198, Kings Canyon Highway, Generals Highway.

Travel season: Most of the route is open year-round. The section on route 180 from Grant Grove to Cedar Grove in Kings Canyon National Park closes in winter from November until May. Check with the park office for information. The Generals Highway is open in winter, although it may temporarily be closed during periods of heavy snow and for plowing. Be prepared for adverse conditions by carrying adequate clothing and food. Have proper snow tires, carry chains, and drive with extra care.

Camping: Ten excellent National Park campgrounds lie along the drives. Kings Canyon National Park offers three campgrounds in the Grant Grove area—118-site Azalea, 184-site Sunset, and sixty-seven-site Crystal Springs. Azalea is open year-round. The other two are closed from mid-September to Memorial Day. The park's Cedar Grove area has three campgrounds—eighty-three-site Sentinel, 120-site Moraine, and 111-site Sheep Creek—near the Kings River. They are closed from mid-October to mid-May. Sequoia National Park's campgrounds include 218-site Dorst and 260-site Lodgepole in the Giant Forest area, and forty-four-site Potwisha and twenty-eight-site Buckeye Flat near the Ash Mountain entrance. Potwisha and Lodgepole are open year-round, although limited services are available at Lodgepole in winter. Other park campgrounds are at South Fork and Mineral King areas. Reservations are necessary for Lodgepole through MISTIX at (800) 365-2267 from mid-May through Labor Day.

Services: All services are found at Fresno, Visalia, and surrounding towns. Services on the drive include gas, food service, lodging, showers, and supplies at Grant Grove, Cedar Grove, and Lodgepole.

Nearby attractions: Kings Canyon and Sequoia national parks backcountry, Mount Whitney, Sierra crest, Kern Canyon, Mineral King area, Lake Kaweah, Fresno, Yosemite National Park, John Muir Wilderness Area.

For more information: Sequoia and Kings Canyon national parks, Three Rivers, CA 93271, (209) 565-3101. Road and weather conditions: (209) 565-3351.

The drive: The Kings Canyon Highway and Generals Highway drives form a 160-mile-long open loop across the western foothills and mountains of the southern Sierra Nevada. The highways traverse both Sequoia and Kings Canyon national parks, passing groves of huge sequoia trees and dipping into deep canyons. The scenery along the drive is on a grand scale. Here lies evidence of the power and complexity of the changing earth, the raising and erosion of a great mountain range, and the passage of different lives. Along the drive grow the largest groves of giant sequoias, the world's biggest living things, and Kings Canyon, one of North America's deepest canyons.

The weather along the highway, as with most mountain areas, is unpre-

A spectacular viewpoint on the Kings Canyon Highway overlooks the confluence of the Middle and South Forks of the Kings River in one of North America's deepest gorges.

dictable and variable. Temperatures generally fall about one degree for every 300 feet gained in elevation. Summer temperatures in the western part of the San Joaquin Valley and the low foothills are often in the 90s occasionally over 100 degrees, while in the Giant Forest at 6,500 feet the daily high ranges from 50 to 80 degrees, with a July average of seventy-six degrees. Summers are generally dry, although occasional thunderstorms drop a curtain of rain across the high country. Autumns are pleasant, with warm days and cool nights. Snow can fall in the upper elevations as early as October. More than 250 inches of snow seal the parks by late November. Most of the area's forty or so inches of precipitation falls as rain in the lowlands and snow in the mountains between October and May. Expect heavy snow that may temporarily close the Generals Highway. The Kings Canyon Highway closes because of rock slides and doesn't reopen until late spring. Carry chains and warm clothing when traveling the drive in winter. In the lowlands, spring begins in December when luxuriant greenery coats the foothills and lasts until May. On the drive's upper elevations, however, spring doesn't arrive until April when the snow melts away.

The Kings Canyon Highway scenic drive, following California 180, begins in Minkler twenty miles east of Fresno, the "Raisin Capital of the World," on the eastern edge of the broad San Joaquin Valley. The Kings River drains out of the mountains north of Minkler, feeding irrigation ditches and watering the vast fields of California's salad bowl. The gentle western slope of the

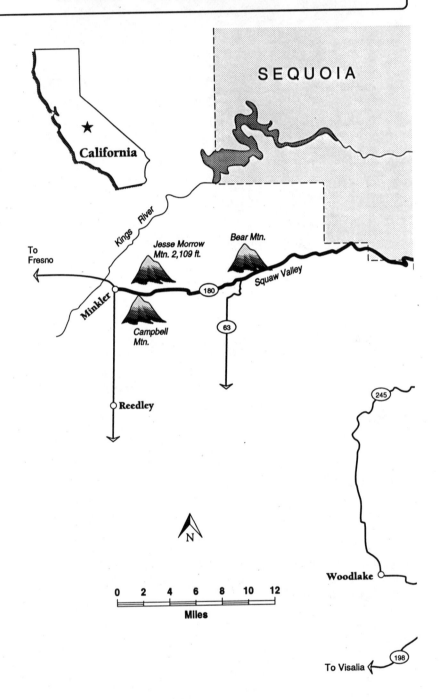

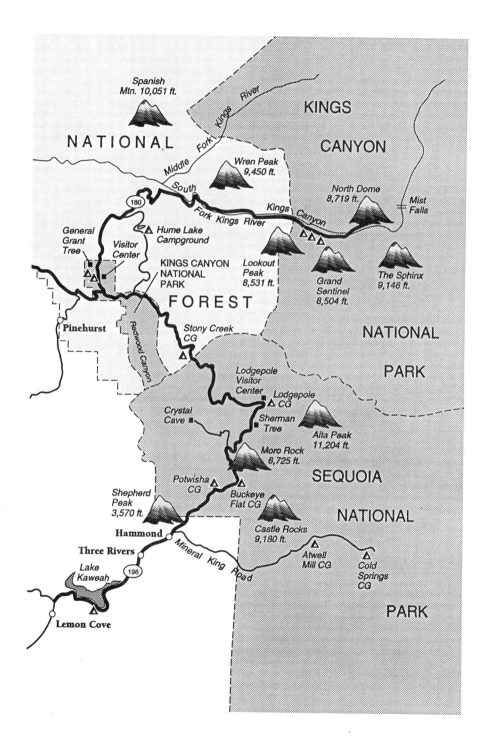

Sierra Nevada, the state's mountainous backbone, stair steps up from the valley here through rounded grassy foothills to steep forested ridges. Beyond and out of sight lies the sawtooth crest of the middle Sierras, a wild range of cirques and peaks that includes Mount Whitney, the highest point in the lower forty-eight states.

Minkler, a pleasant little farm town, sits along the Blossom Trail, which is a Fresno County back road tour that explores verdant fruit orchards. The scenic drive heads east on route 180 from Minkler through a broad gap between rounded Jesse Morrow Mountain on the north and Campbell Mountain on the south. Orange and plum orchards and irrigated fields line the Frant-Kern Canal along the valley floor, while wavering grass among dark boulders blankets the smooth hillsides. After six miles, the drive enters low foothills and climbs above 1,000 feet. Granite crags, oak trees, and golden grass spread over the hills. The highway crests a ridge line below Bear Mountain and drops into broad Squaw Valley. The city of Squaw Valley lies on the valley's northern edge at 1,700 feet. Sequoia National Forest's Hume Lake Ranger Station dispenses visitor information and maps five miles up the road.

Past the ranger station, the drive begins seriously climbing upward, edging shelf-like above Mill Creek and its broad valley to the south. At twenty-one miles, the road enters Sequoia National Forest and reaches 3,000 feet. The road, as it ascends, crosses a foothills transition zone from what is left of the great open savannas of the San Joaquin Valley to the Sierran forests in the national parks. This terrain ranges from the valley edge to about 5,000 feet in elevation. It is a two-season land of mild winters with moderate rainfall and dry, hot summers. The plants that clothe the slopes have correspondingly adapted to these conditions by growing vigorously in the wet season and lying dormant during the dry periods. Chaparral, a stunted drought-resistant forest, covers the driest slopes with a dense, ragged brush that includes manzanita and chamise. Oak groves interspersed with grassland and stands of California buckeye range across moist hillsides. At twenty-five miles, the road passes the 4,000-foot level and ponderosa pines and incense cedars appear in the forest. Precipitation on the Sierra's western slope increases eight to ten inches for every 1,000 feet of elevation up to about 7,000 feet. As the drive continues edging upward, great views of the rolling foothills, the San Joaquin Valley, and the Coast Ranges unfold to the west. At thirty miles, the elevation is over 5,000 feet, and the drive intersects California Highway 245. Three miles later, it leaves the national forest and enters Kings Canyon National Park.

Kings Canyon and Sequoia national parks together preserve more than 863,000 acres of the pristine southern Sierra Nevada. The two parks harbor an incredible diversity of life zones, plants, and topography. The elevation range itself begins at 1,700 feet at Sequoia's park headquarters at Ash Mountain and tops out on 14,494-foot Mount Whitney. The rugged parks are seamed by abrupt river canyons, lorded over by glacier-carved peaks, and blanketed by the world's most unique forest.

After a couple more miles, route 180 intersects the Generals Highway.

Turn north on 180, the Kings Canyon Highway. The highway is a twisting, narrow ribbon that ends thirty-nine miles ahead at Copper Creek in Kings Canyon. A couple miles up from the highway junction, the drive reaches General Grant Grove Village. The 6,500-acre area, once the headquarters of former General Grant National Park, offers numerous visitor services including a visitor center, lodging, food service, and gas. The small Grant Grove section of Kings Canyon National Park became a national park in 1890, one week after Sequoia National Park was established. The park status preserves the area's pristine sequoia forests from logging. In 1940 the grove was combined with Kings Canyon and the rugged Sierra wilderness to form Kings Canyon National Park. Three campgrounds are found at Grant Grove—118-site Azalea, 184-site Sunset, and sixty-seven-site Crystal Springs.

The Grant Grove is a spectacular forest of giant sequoias perched atop a broad ridge. A side road drops down to the General Grant tree, the third largest tree in the world. The tree is a designated National Shrine honoring American servicemen and the nation's Christmas Tree. It towers 267 feet above the forest floor, boasts a base diameter of forty feet, and is as old as 2,000 years. Another side road begins opposite the General Grant road and winds 2.3 miles to Panoramic Point. The view overlooks a maze of canyons and high peaks in the high Sierra.

Numerous trails wend through the Grant Grove section. An excellent path begins near the General Grant tree and threads among the North Grove's mature sequoias. The mile-long Big Stump Basin Trail, near the park entrance, loops through a sequoia grove destroyed by 1880s lumbering. Sequoia cutting here and north of Grant Grove led to the rapid protection of remaining sequoia stands throughout the Sierras. Timber companies in the late nineteenth century dreamed of huge profits from these forest giants, but, fortunately for the sequoia, the wood was brittle and tended to splinter when the tree toppled. More than sixty percent of virgin sequoia forest remains scattered in some seventy-five groves on the western flank of the Sierra Nevada today, whereas over ninety-five percent of the original coast redwood forest has been harvested.

The Kings Canyon Highway runs north from Grant Grove and enters Sequoia National Forest, a 1.1-million-acre forest that includes more than 264,000 acres of designated wilderness and 135 National Wild and Scenic River miles. The next twenty-five miles of highway cross national forest lands. McGee Vista Point lies a couple miles up the road at 6,800-foot Cherry Gap on Park Ridge. A major forest fire devastated this area in the summer of 1955 when a rancher lost control of a fire in the foothills below. The fire, fanned by dry winds, engulfed the forest. More than four million trees were later planted on the burned hillsides. The point offers good views west across the foothills to the San Joaquin Valley.

Past the overlook, the highway begins steeply descending down the east side of Park Ridge, passing the remains of the Indian Basin and Converse Basin sequoia groves. A lumber company decimated both groves 100 years ago. The Converse Basin was reputed to be the largest sequoia grove in the

The Kings Canyon Highway uncoils through an abrupt gorge carved by the Kings River.

Sierra. All that remains of its majesty are immense stumps and the solitary Boole Tree, ironically named for the timber foreman who oversaw the forest's destruction. A two-mile loop trail hikes out to the tree through a maze of stumps.

The drive descends through a dry forest of ponderosa pine and incense cedar. A side road runs three miles east to eighty-seven-acre Hume Lake, a popular forest recreation site with fishing, boating, and a seventy-four-site campground. A couple miles past the Hume Lake turnoff, the highway swings around a corner and enters the abrupt defile of Kings Canyon. The road edges the steep mountainside and three miles later reaches Junction View at 4,500 feet. This view is one of California's grandest sights. It overlooks deep gorges carved by the Middle and South forks of the Kings River. The Middle Fork originates high on 13,361-foot Mount Powell and plunges down steep canyons, including Tehipite Valley, before draining into the South Fork far below the overlook. The South Fork begins with melting snow on Taboose Pass on the Sierra Crest and empties down Paradise Valley into Kings Canyon. The canyon below Junction Overlook reaches its greatest depth with a vertical relief of 7,891 feet from the river bottom just west of the two forks confluence to the summit of 10,051-foot Spanish Mountain north of the gorge. The canyon's depth exceeds both Idaho's Hells Canyon and Arizona's Grand Canyon. The canyon was chiseled out of bedrock by the relentless cutting force of the river and eons of time. The river was named in 1805 when Spaniard Gabriel Moraga and an exploratory force encamped by the river's foothill mouth. Since the day was Epiphany, he dubbed it "El Rio de los Santos Reyes" or River of the Holy Kings for the Christmas Magi.

The narrow road was built by convict labor in the 1930s. It turns away from the river and traverses steep ridges ragged with chaparral and broken by rocky crags. After a few switchbacks, the drive crosses Ten-Mile Creek, a tumbling stream locked in a shallow granite canyon. A mile after crossing the creek the highway reaches Yucca Point and enters the inner gorge of South Fork Canyon. A thousand feet below this point lies the two great river forks. A one-mile path descends rocky slopes to the river. The highway turns east and creeps shelf-like across the steep canyon walls. The canyon slowly narrows, with the river rushing over boulders below.

Four miles from Yucca Point the road swings around Horseshoe Bend. A scenic pullout lies on the bend's apex. Soaring cliffs of metamorphosed ocean sediments tower overhead, while the Kings River, just a couple hundred feet below the overlook, roars and foams through boulder-choked rapids. This is a place of savage beauty, a marvelous page of geological history that is ever-changing yet somehow eternal. Be careful pulling off the highway, especially coming from the west, for the road curve is sharp and blind. After another mile, the drive, now alongside the river, cuts through an abrupt gap called the Portals of the Kings where more cliffs stair step away from the road. Boyden's Cave, a private grotto, lies on the river's south bank in a tall gray cliff of marble. The cliff is composed of an ancient limestone that metamorphosed into marble by underground heat and pressure. Guided tours are offered daily from spring through fall.

The road snakes along the river's north bank as it runs eastward. The river is a strong, commanding presence. Its untamed waters, filled with spring runoff, are a raging, frothy torrent hemmed in by granite boulders. The canyon here is a classic V-shaped gorge excavated by millions of years of running water. The river's steep gradient coupled with prodigious amounts of water, especially in spring and while the Sierra's great glaciers melted, form a sharp tool that slowly deepens the canyon. Grizzly Creek Falls tumbles over granite bedrock partway up the canyon. A national forest picnic ground sits under nearby shade trees.

The drive reenters Kings Canyon National Park a couple miles farther upstream. Just after the road enters the park, the topography changes abruptly. The V-shaped river gorge broadens and assumes the classic U-shape of a glacier-carved valley. Four gorgeous granite valleys grace the western slope of the Sierra Nevada—famed Yosemite Valley, dammed Hetch Hetchy, remote Tehipite on the Kings River's Middle Fork, and Kings Canyon. John Muir, the famed pioneer naturalist, called it "a rival to Yosemite," and wrote in 1891, "In the vast Sierra wilderness far to the southward of the famous Yosemite Valley, there is a yet grander valley of the same kind." Muir's century-old words still ring true. Kings Canyon is indeed grand, and unlike its famed northern counterpart, it is virtually pristine and almost unvisited.

As the road climbs, the valley broadens; and tall pines and incense cedars (not a true cedar) tower over river benches. Just up the highway at 4,600 feet sits Cedar Grove. The site, named for the shaggy cedars along the river flat, is the human focus of the canyon. Here sits the old Cedar Grove Ranger Station with maps, information, and displays on the park. Nearby, spread along the river, are three spacious campgrounds—eighty-three-site Sentinel, 120-site Moraine, and 111-site Sheep Creek. Other visitor services include a small motel, diner, laundromat, showers, and service station. Several good trails begin here, including the Cedar Grove Overlook Trail, which climbs to a viewpoint on the valley's north slope.

The Kings Canyon Highway traverses the valley floor for six miles more to the road's end at Copper Creek. A short trail climbs up from the drive to Roaring River Falls, a gushing waterfall that plunges down a cliff-locked granite canyon to an emerald pool. This tributary is an actual river that drains some of the park's most inaccessible backcountry. The three-mile-long Motor Nature Trail begins just past the falls and parallels the river's north bank down to Cedar Grove along a dirt road. This is a good side-trip on your return journey.

Zumwalt Meadows sits another mile up the drive. This spacious grassland is rimmed with tall pines and traversed by the meandering Kings River, with its deep, cold currents riffling over boulders. A 1.5-mile nature trail loops through the meadow, making a superb hike. The trail crosses the river on a bridge, threads through tall grass and silent forest before emerging on a broken talus slope. North Dome lifts its craggy 8,717-foot summit to the north, while the vertical cliffs of Grand Sentinel soar southward. The drive ends a mile past Zumwalt Meadows. Beyond lies the great wilderness of Kings Canyon, a wild, untrammeled region of peaks, meadows, canyons, and cirques that comprises over ninety percent of the park's total area. The wilderness, coupled with Sequoia's wilderness, composes California's largest wilderness area. Numerous trails fan out from here into the backcountry. A good day hike climbs four miles to Mist Falls, one of the park's largest waterfalls. Other trails roam up Bubbs Creek and Paradise Valley to the Pacific Crest Trail below the serpentine Sierra crest. Highway travelers must turn around at road's end and retrace the King's Highway back to Grant Grove and its intersection with the Generals Highway.

The Generals Highway scenic drive heads east from its intersection with the Kings Canyon Highway, edging along a ridge top. Redwood Canyon Overlook is reached after four miles. This scenic view looks south into the 3,400-acre Redwood Mountain Grove, the largest remaining stand of sequoias in the world. More than 15,000 sequoias larger than a foot in diameter and many thousands more younger trees grow in moist Redwood Canyon and on Redwood Mountain.

Quail Flat lies just down the highway. A left turn on a forest road descends to Hume Lake in Sequoia National Forest, while a right turn leads 1.5 miles down a rough road to Redwood Saddle and the Redwood Canyon Trailhead. Sixteen miles of trail explore the ancient Sequoia forest, passing Barton's Post Camp, an old logging camp, the Hart Tree, and the Fallen Goliath. A mile down the drive lies 7,100-foot Kings Canyon Overlook with marvelous views into the deep gorges of the Middle and South forks of the Kings River. The next viewpoint is on the border of Kings Canyon National Park and Sequoia National Forest at Big Baldy Saddle, the high point on the Generals Highway at 7,600 feet. An excellent four-mile, round-trip trail traverses Big Baldy Ridge to Big Baldy's 8,209-foot granite-domed summit. Sequoias stud Redwood Canyon to the west, their lacy canopies towering over surrounding trees. The drive meanders southeast from here, dipping in and out of shallow ravines to Stony Creek Resort, which offers groceries and lodging but no gas. The national forest's forty-nine-site Stony Creek Campground sits a half-mile beyond on the wooded banks of trickling Stony Creek. The drive enters 403,023-acre Sequoia National Park a mile later.

Sequoia National Park is the cradle of the giant sequoia. Here, on high rounded ridges that catch Pacific moisture, the sequoia still flourishes in immense groves. This is a place that startles the imagination and forces the visitor to step back and contemplate important questions like time and space. Mature sequoias are so massive and so old that it confounds the senses. To stand in the shadow of these forest giants is to stand in a shadow that fell when Sir Francis Drake, the first European to see California, sailed the *Golden Hinde* up the coast in 1579. These forest sentinels have stood for more than ninety human generations, taking the dictionary's definition of a human generation as thirty years. Sequoias, next to the venerable bristlecone pine, are the world's second oldest living trees.

Sequoias grow from tiny seeds the size and weight of oat flakes bundled in egg-sized cones that hang as long as twenty years on the tree's upper branches. Soil and moisture conditions must be just right for the seeds to germinate. The trees have few enemies besides the saw. John Muir wrote, "Most of the Sierra trees die of disease, fungi, etc., but nothing hurts the Big Tree. Barring accidents, it seems to be immortal." The tree's thick, cinnamon-red bark is resistant to fire and insect damage. The trees continue growing until death, which usually comes during severe windstorms that topple them. Sequoias have shallow, spreading root systems with no main tap root to anchor it. The trees grow in excess of 300 feet, live to 3,200 years, weigh as much as 1.4 million pounds, and boast base diameters as thick as forty feet. Sequoias once spread across North America, but over the last ten million years climatic changes isolated the species to the range's western slopes of the Sierra Nevada's. Today, they grow only in seventy-five groves scattered across a 260-mile range between 5,000 and 7,000 feet. Thirty of the groves lie in Kings Canyon and Sequoia national parks. Their close relatives are the coast redwood in California and the rare dawn redwood in a remote Chinese valley. Sequoias were named by an Austrian botanist for Sequoyah, the Cherokee Indian who devised an alphabet for his people's language.

The drive, after entering the park, swings through fifty-acre Lost Grove, a stand of 200 mature sequoias. A couple short trails explore the grove. The road crosses Dorst Creek, named for the park's first superintendent Army Captain Joseph Dorst. Dorst Campground, with 218 sites, nestles in a thick forest of white and red firs. Muir Grove is an almost pure stand of more than 1,000 mature sequoias and lies at the end of a two-mile path that begins here.

The highway climbs to 7,335-foot Little Baldy Saddle and then drops south and east seven miles around Little Baldy, an 8,044-foot granite dome. Then the drive continues on to Lodgepole on the Marble Fork of the Kaweah River. En route the road passes Halstead Meadow and runs through a mixed conifer forest of pine, fir, incense cedar, and occasional western juniper.

Lodgepole, the logistic center of Sequoia National Park, tucks into a steep glacier-carved valley below the tall, craggy peaks of the Silliman Crest. A large visitor center details the park's unique natural history, geology, and history, as well as dispenses essential information on camping, hiking, and backcountry exploring. Nearby is 260-site Lodgepole Campground, showers, food service, and gas; campground reservations are necessary in summer. A trail climbs almost two miles up the river to gushing Tokopah Falls.

The highway bends away from Lodgepole and traverses a rounded ridge blanketed with sequoias—the Giant Forest. The forest was named by John Muir and offers an unforgettable look at several pristine sequoia groves. John Muir described the majestic sight: "Advancing southward the giants become more and more irrepressibly exuberant, heaving their massive crowns into the sky from every ridge and slope, and waving onward in graceful compliance with the complicated topography of the region." The grove was first seen by Anglo-Americans when Yokut Indians guided farmer Hale Tharp to the forest in 1858.

Almost three miles from Lodgepole, the road reaches the General Sherman Tree, the world's largest living organism. This huge patriarch is a marvel, dwarfing even the surrounding sequoias. The 2,700-year-old tree towers 274.9 feet above its 36.5-foot-thick trunk and boasts a volume of 52,500 square feet of wood. All the events and inventions that made western civilization possible have occurred during this giant's lifetime—from the Greek philosophers and the birth of Christ to the automobile and the invention of printing and paper. The excellent nature trail called Congress Trail begins here and loops through the sequoia woods for two miles, passing numerous other tall trees, including the President, McKinley, and Chief Sequoyah trees, and the House and Senate tree groups.

The Giant Forest is lined with sequoias, the only way to really begin to fathom the sequoia's sheer size and regal beauty is by parking the car and walking into the cathedral groves. An age-old hush envelopes the towering trees, with only an occasional call from a woodpecker or Steller's jay and a whisper of wind in the high branches breaking the silence. Ponderosa, sugar pine, and white fir mingle with the sequoias, but even these trees, giants of their own species, are dwarfed by the mighty cinnamon-barked sequoias. Under the giants, Pacific dogwood, western azalea, and California hazelnut scatters about the forest floor. Occasional meadows, resplendent with summer wildflowers, break the forest shade.

More than forty miles of trail lace the Giant Forest. Many begin at the Giant Forest Village a couple miles south of the General Sherman Tree, including the Trail for all People around Round Meadow and the Hazelwood Nature Trail, which is accessible to the physically challenged. Several visitor

Fire-scarred Sequoia trees dominate the forest in the General Grant Grove of Kings Canyon National Park along the Kings Canyon Highway.

facilities cluster here—a visitor information kiosk as well as the Giant Forest Lodge. The three-mile Crescent Meadow Road begins at the village and winds out to Moro Rock and Crescent Meadow. This spectacular road explores some of Sequoia's best roadside scenery. Moro Rock, two miles from the village, is an abrupt 6,725-foot granite precipice that overlooks the Kaweah River gorge and the sawtooth skyline of peaks along the Great Western Divide. The airy summit is reached by a short trail and a 400-step staircase. Crescent Meadow is surrounded by sequoias and sits at the road's end. Several trails roam the meadow and woods including one to Tharp's Log, a hollowed-out log used as a camp by early rancher Hale Tharp, and the seventy-one-mile High Sierra Trail that ends atop Mount Whitney.

Past the Crescent Meadow turn-off, the drive begins losing elevation, and after a mile the highway passes the Four Guardsmen—four sequoias guarding the Giant Forest's western gates. At Commissary Curve, a narrow, winding side road drops down 6.4 miles to Crystal Cave. Guided summer tours explore the cave, the only one open in the park. No trailers, RVs, or buses are allowed on the cave entrance road.

163

The drive begins falling steeply past Crystal Cave Road, uncoiling like an asphalt serpent down steep slopes into the deep canyon of the Kaweah River's Middle Fork. In the next eight miles, the road loses more than 3,000 feet in elevation, passing from the damp sequoia forest to dry oak woodlands to chaparral-studded foothills. The temperature rises as the road drops into the lowlands. Amphitheater Point is a great overlook a couple miles downhill. Moro Rock looms overhead and snowy peaks punctuate the eastern horizon. Big Fern Springs makes a good stop on a hot day, with thick oak shade and huge chain ferns. The chain ferns are California's largest native ferns, with six-foot-long fronds. Hospital Rock is on a bench above the Kaweah River and offers numerous Indian sites including pictographs and bedrock mortars for grinding seeds. Nearby at 2,820 feet lies twenty-eight-site Buckeye Campground.

The drive runs west down dry slopes above the river, passing forty-four-site Potwisha Campground. The site is named for a tribe of Monache Indians who often camped here. The Marble Fork joins the Middle Fork of the Kaweah River near the campground. The Kaweah River, with three other forks, drains most of Sequoia National Park. It's waters, fed by melting snow, gush into the San Joaquin Valley and feed lush fruit orchards and fields. The river is named for the Kaweah Indians. The road passes under Tunnel Rock farther down the canyon and reaches the park's Foothills Visitor Center and headquarters. Near the entrance station sits a massive hand-carved sign in the shape of an Indian head that has welcomed visitors to the park since the 1930s.

Past the park boundary, the highway picks up the designation of California 198 continues west down the Kaweah River. As the road and river drop, the surrounding mountains lower into foothills and the canyon broadens into a valley. The road runs through Hammond and Three Rivers, passing the twenty-five-mile Mineral King Road, which follows the Kaweah's East Fork to a pretty mountain-locked basin. Seven miles later the drive skirts the south shore of Lake Kaweah, a wide reservoir. Horsecreek Recreation Area, with a campground, boat ramp, and picnic area, scatters along the lake shore. Past the dam, the road drops through grass and oak-covered hills into fertile orchards on the eastern edge of the San Joaquin Valley. The drive ends at Lemon Cove. Continue west on California 198 through croplands to Visalia and California 99.

General description: A sixty-six-mile-long highway that climbs from La Canada to the lofty, forested crest of the San Gabriel Mountains north of Los Angeles.

Special attractions: Angeles National Forest, Pacific Crest Trail, Mount Wilson Observatory, San Gabriel Wilderness Area, Sheep Mountain Wilderness Area, San Andreas Rift Zone, Mount Wilson Viewpoint, Devil's Canyon Overlook, skiing, camping, hiking, scenic views, cool summer temperatures.

Drive route name and number: California Highway 2, Angeles Crest Highway.

Travel season: May through October. The road closes after the first snow and reopens when conditions permit. In 1992 the entire highway opened on June 12. The road is open, however, to the ski areas along the route.

Camping: Four Angeles National Forest campgrounds are spread along the drive—Buckhorn with forty sites, Chilao with 110 sites, Grassy Hollow with fifteen sites, and Table Mountain with 115 sites. Jackson Flat has five group sites. Many other forest campgrounds lie just off the main highway. Check a forest map for their locations.

Services: No services are found along the drive. Services are at either end of the road at La Canada and Wrightwood.

Nearby attractions: Rim of the World Scenic Byway, San Bernardino National Forest, Big Bear Lake, Los Angeles attractions and museums, Cucamonga Wilderness Area, Placerita Canyon State Park, Silverwood Lake State Recreation Area.

For more information: Angeles National Forest, 701 N. Santa Anita Ave., Arcadia, CA 91006, (818) 574-1613.

The drive: The sixty-six-mile Angeles Crest Highway is simply breathtaking. It's one of southern California's best scenic drives. The two-lane, paved road ascends to the twisting crest of the San Gabriel Mountains north of the Los Angeles Basin. The spectacular road, far removed from the hustle, smog, and traffic of nearby cities, accesses startling landscapes that seem out of character with the usual conceptions of southern California.

A rare peace is found atop these mountains. The wind, sweeping off the ocean, whispers through ancient limber pines at timberline; long views of other snowcapped ranges, dusty desert basins, and distant city streets stretch out beyond abrupt ridges; and the elemental earth seems unchanging and almost unmarked by the passage of man. The mountains are chaotic, shaped and changed by faults, uplifts, and earthquakes. Its ecosystems include dense chaparral-covered hillsides, windy boreal forests, and woody glades filled with wildflowers and ferns.

Like southern California's other mountain ranges, elevations and climates vary dramatically from mountain base to summit. Elevations range from 1,200 feet at the drive's west end to 7,901 feet at Dawson Saddle. Annual precipitation changes with elevation. Pasadena, on the range's southern front, averages twenty inches of rain yearly, while Mount Wilson, only six miles north, is doused with thirty-five inches. Summer temperatures are usually in the nineties in the lowland valleys, but as the road climbs the temperature drops with daily highs in the seventies or low eighties. Occasional thunderstorms darken summer afternoons. Spring and fall are cooler. Winters are cold atop the peaks with freezing temperatures and snow from November through March. The highway is closed and unplowed from Islip Saddle to Big Pines, providing a good cross-country ski track. It closes with the first snow and opens when the last snow melts. In 1992, the road was closed until June 12. Be prepared in winter for icy roads, particularly on shaded corners, by using snow tires or chains.

The drive begins at the intersection of California Highway 2 with Interstate 210 in La Canada just northwest of Pasadena. Turn north on Highway 2. The road leaves the city suburbs behind after two miles and at 2.6 miles enters Angeles National Forest. The drive, a national forest Scenic Byway, edges onto the precipitous western slope of Arroyo Seco. Angeles National Forest covers 693,454 acres that includes the San Gabriel Mountains north of Los Angeles. The forest boasts a wide range of plant communities from chaparral to pine and fir forests, offers more than 100 campgrounds and picnic areas, and is threaded by more than 550 miles of hiking trails, including 145 miles of the Pacific Crest Trail. Mount San Antonio, known locally as "Old Baldy," is the 10,064-foot high point in both the national forest and the San Gabriel Mountains. Angeles National Forest, originally called the San Gabriel Forest Reserve, was created in 1892.

The twisting road steadily climbs above the canyon and after eight miles passes Clear Creek Vista. Another mile up the highway on the south slope of 5,557-foot Josephine Peak is Clear Creek Ranger Station. Nearby is Switzer Picnic Area with twenty-two tables. This site was an 1880s public camp, accessible by pack train and run by Commodore Perry Switzer. The highway also intersects the Angeles Forest Highway (Forest Road FH59) just west of the picnic area, providing access to the western section of the San Gabriels.

The warm south-facing mountain slopes above the drive here are densely covered with chaparral, including sagebrush, manzanita, whitethorn, and chamise. Chaparral climbs to elevations of 5,000 feet and covers sixty-five percent of Angeles National Forest. The moist, cool north-facing slopes are blanketed by forests of pine, fir, and oak. As the highway ascends eastward, the chaparral fades out and coniferous forests dominate.

By twelve miles, the highway rises to 4,000 feet, and two miles later reaches Red Box Gap and the Mount Wilson Road. This five-mile-long road (Forest Road 2N52) makes a good side trip to the top of 5,710-foot Mount Wilson, a local landmark, and the famed Mount Wilson Observatory with its 100-inch telescope. A picnic area, scenic overlook, small museum, and

The Angeles Crest Highway climbs serpentine fashion out of narrow canyons of the San Gabriel Mountains.

weekend tours of the observatory are found atop the mountain. The peak is named for pioneer settler Benjamin D. Wilson, who, with Mexican and Indian labor, built a trail to the summit in 1864 to bring needed lumber to the valley below. The mountain's clear air led Harvard professor W. H. Pickering to build a telescope atop the summit in 1889. Shortly afterward the Pasadena and Mount Wilson Toll Road Company built a ten-foot-wide road up the peak.

Past the Mount Wilson turn, the road runs east above the thickly wooded canyon of the West Fork of the San Gabriel River. Past Shortcut Picnic Area and Shortcut Saddle, it turns away from the canyon and follows a high ridge crest east and then north through pine forests. The road swings around 5,908-foot Vetter Mountain. A good 1.5-mile-long hike begins at Charlton Flat Picnic Area and climbs up a shallow valley to the fire lookout atop the peak. Another easy hike starts at the picnic ground and climbs east to Mount Mooney and Devil's Peak. Both offer great views into the 36,000-acre San Gabriel Wilderness Area, a rugged land of peaks and canyons bounded on the south by the San Gabriel River and on the north by the Angeles Crest Highway. The region, one of the nation's first established wilderness areas, was protected as a primitive area in 1932.

Devils Canyon Overlook is the next road stop. It sits on the edge of the San Gabriel Wilderness Area and deep Devils Canyon. The high crest of the San Gabriel Mountains runs east from here, forming an open, south-facing horseshoe. The San Gabriels are one of California's Transverse Ranges. These sierras trend east-west, instead of the north-south orientation of other California ranges. The Transverse Ranges, along with the Uinta Mountains in Utah, are the only east-west ranges in the continental United States. The ranges run from Santa Barbara on the coast to San Gorgonio Pass and have long separated Northern California from Southern California.

The looming San Gabriels are young mountains, composed primarily of granites and ancient metamorphic rocks, which, says geologist H. C. Storey, have "... been as intensively faulted and fractured as probably any other region in the world." The range is laced with faults, including the San Gabriel Fault and the famed San Andreas Fault, which runs through Swarthout Valley on the east end of the highway and below the range's northern escarpment. The mountains are still growing, as much as five inches each century.

The drive reaches Chilao Visitor Center and campground just beyond the overlook. The visitor center offers displays on the forest's history, natural history, and geology, as well as books and hiking information. Ranger-led nature hikes and self-guided trails help introduce visitors to the San Gabriel Mountains. The nearby 110-site Chilao Campground, at 5,300 feet elevation, is surrounded by grassy meadows and an open woodland of Jeffrey, Coulter, sugar, and ponderosa pine. Several excellent trails roam the country above the campground. Timbered Chilao Flat was used in the 1870s to pasture livestock stolen by rustler Tiburcio Vasquez. An unconfirmed local legend says Jose Gonzales, one of Vasquez's herders, killed a bear here with a knife earning him the nickname "Chillia" or Hot Stuff. The spelling was later bastardized to Chilao.

The drive climbs away from Chilao and seven miles later reaches Three Points. This lofty pass is a major trailhead for the Pacific Crest Trail, a 2,500-mile path that runs from Mexico to Canada. The trail parallels the highway from here east to Wrightwood and offers many excellent day hikes and short backpacking trips in Angeles National Forest.

The highway swings onto the north side of the range crest at 7,018-foot Cloudburst Summit and drops down through a pine forest on the north slope of 8,038-foot Waterman Mountain and the Kratka Ridge. Two ski areas—Mount Waterman and Kratka Ridge—are found along this road stretch. Buckhorn Campground, with forty sites, also nestles in a shallow canyon just north of the drive. This beautiful spot amid incense cedars and evergreens lies along fern-lined Little Rock Creek. Three picnic areas sit alongside the road, offering spectacular views northward to the Mojave Desert. Jarvi Memorial Vista, a lookout named for a former Forest Supervisor at the head of Bear Creek, gives a spectacular view down canyon. Short Sierra Alta Trail loops down from the overlook.

Endangered Nelson's bighorn sheep are sometimes spotted on the steep mountain slopes above the highway. More than 700 bighorns thrive in Angeles National Forest. Other wildlife in the range includes black bear, mule deer, bobcat, mountain lion, gray fox, Pacific rattlesnake, Mojave green rattlesnake, pinyon mouse, and kangaroo rat. A great variety of birds frequent the forests—including crows, quail, woodpeckers, and jays.

Past Jarvi Vista, the highway crosses Windy Gap, sweeps around the north side of Mount Islip, and winds northeast to 7,901-foot Dawson Saddle. The road edges around more high peaks and reaches Vincent Gap where the Pacific Crest Trail crosses the drive. A popular four-mile-long hike climbs from here to the summit of rocky 9,399-foot Mount Baden-Powell, a sharp peak named for the founder of the Boy Scouts. Near the summit, the trail winds through 2,000-year-old, wind-stunted limber pines.

Grassy Hollow Campground, with fifteen sites shaded by towering ponderosa pines, lies three miles beyond Vincent Gap on Blue Ridge. The Pacific Crest Trail skirts this excellent campground. Inspiration Point lies just east of the campground atop the ridge crest at 7,386 feet. Marvelous views spread out below this lofty overlook. On clear days, the Catalina Islands are visible off shore. The rugged 44,000-acre Sheep Mountain Wilderness Area, cleaved by deep canyons and lorded over by abrupt peaks, stretches southward above the headwaters of the San Gabriel River. To the southeast towers the range high point, snowcapped 10,064-foot Mount San Antonio, also known as Old Baldy. The peak's alpine summit can be reached from Blue Ridge via a ten-mile-long trail.

The highway begins dropping at Inspiration Point, spiraling down the north slope of Blue Ridge. After two miles from Inspiration Point, the drive reaches Big Pines Visitor Center on the San Andreas Fault. Displays here explain the fault, and a self-guided auto tour brochure, available at the center,

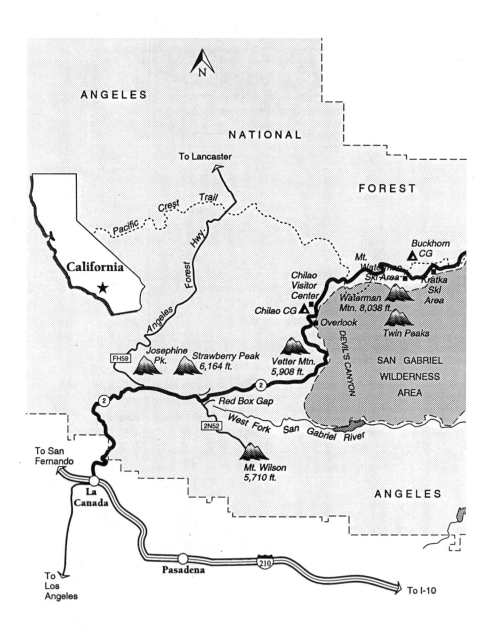

ANGELES

NATIONAL

To Lancaster

FOREST

Pacific Crest Trail

California

Buckhorn CG

Mt. Waterman Ski Area

Kratka Ski Area

Chilao Visitor Center

Waterman Mtn. 8,038 ft.

Chilao CG

Overlook

Twin Peaks

Josephine Pk.

Strawberry Peak 6,164 ft.

Vetter Mtn. 5,908 ft.

FH59

DEVIL'S CANYON

SAN GABRIEL WILDERNESS AREA

Red Box Gap

West Fork San Gabriel River

2N52

Mt. Wilson 5,710 ft.

To San Fernando

ANGELES

La Canada

Pasadena

210

To Los Angeles

To I-10

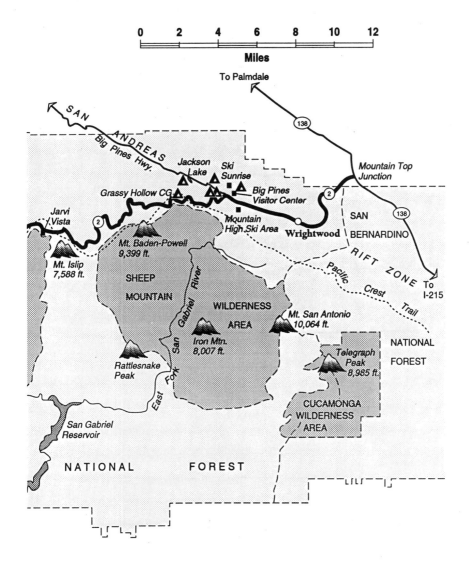

The Angeles Crest Highway winds along the lofty ridges of the San Gabriel Mountains.

explores the surrounding earthquake features. Other summer interpretative programs and short nature trails detail the area's natural history and geology. The San Andreas Rift Zone runs southeast to northwest through the pine-covered valley here. Note the differing rock types on either side of the valley, evidence of the fault's lateral movement.

Two downhill ski areas—Mountain High East and West and Ski Sunrise—are found above Big Pines. Five national forest campgrounds, including 115-site Table Mountain Campground, are popular summer getaways from the heat of surrounding lowland valleys. Just north of the drive on Big Pines Highway is Jackson Lake, one of the forest's few trout fishing lakes. Further north lies stunning Devil's Punchbowl County Park, a jumble of upturned, tilted sandstone slabs eroded into bizarre shapes.

The scenic drive turns southeast from Big Pines and drops down Swarthout Valley along the San Andreas Fault to the mountain community of Wrightwood. Past the town, the road dips steeply on six percent grades and rapidly drops away from the ponderosa pine forest into a strange woodland of sagebrush, western juniper, and Joshua trees. A mile after leaving Angeles National Forest, the drive ends at Mountain Top Junction, the intersection of California highways 2 and 138. A right turn heads nine miles down Cajon Canyon to Interstate 15 northwest of San Bernardino.

General description: An eighty-seven-mile-long, open-loop drive that climbs from San Bernardino to the forested crest of the San Bernardino Mountains, winds along the mountain rim to the resort town of Big Bear Lake, and drops down through thick forests and deep canyons to Redlands.

Special attractions: Rim of the World Scenic Byway, San Bernardino National Forest, Lake Arrowhead, Big Bear Lake, San Gorgonio Wilderness Area, San Andreas Rift Zone, camping, hiking, fishing, boating, scenic views, skiing.

Location: Southern California. The drive, east of Los Angeles, makes an open loop between San Bernardino and Redlands.

Drive route name and numbers: California highways 18 and 38, Rim of the World Drive.

Travel season: Year-round. Temperatures in the higher elevations are cooler than in the surrounding basins. Snow falls in the winter. Expect icy road conditions and use chains or adequate snow tires.

Camping: Six National Forest Campgrounds—Dogwood, Serrano, Heartbar, South Fork, San Gorgonio, and Barton Flats—scatter along the drive. Many other forest campgrounds, including group sites, lie close to the drive in the national forest. Most open in May and close in October.

Services: Services are available along the drive in the many resort communities, including Crestline, Lake Arrowhead, Running Springs, Big Bear City, and Big Bear Lake. All services are found in San Bernardino and Redlands.

Nearby attractions: Angeles Crest Scenic Byway, Angeles National Forest, Cucamonga Wilderness Area, Silverwood Lake State Recreation Area, Joshua Tree National Park, San Jacinto Mountains, Los Angeles attractions.

For more information: San Bernardino National Forest, 1824 S. Commercenter Circle, San Bernardino, CA 92408-3430, (909) 383-5588. San Bernardino Visitors Bureau, 440 W. Court St., Suite 108, P.O. Box 920, San Bernardino, CA 92402, (909) 889-3980. Big Bear Lake Visitors Bureau, 41091 Big Bear Blvd., P.O. Box 3050, Big Bear Lake, CA 92315, (909) 866-7008.

The drive: The Rim of the World Scenic Drive follows California highways 18 and 38 and travels eight-seven miles from San Bernardino to the Mill Creek Ranger Station on the east side of Redlands. The road, a National Scenic Byway, traverses the forested crest of the San Bernardino Mountains, southern California's highest mountain range, and offers spectacular views of surrounding ranges and the Los Angeles Basin below. The drive passes several resort communities, notably Big Bear Lake, five ski areas, and 59,000-acre San Gorgonio Wilderness Area with 11,499-foot San Gorgonio Mountain, southern California's tallest peak.

Elevations along the drive vary from just over 1,000 feet at San Bernardino to over 8,000 feet, offering a diverse range of temperatures and climates.

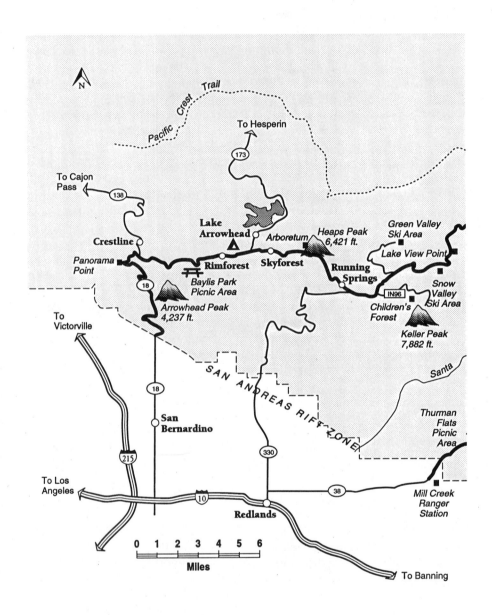

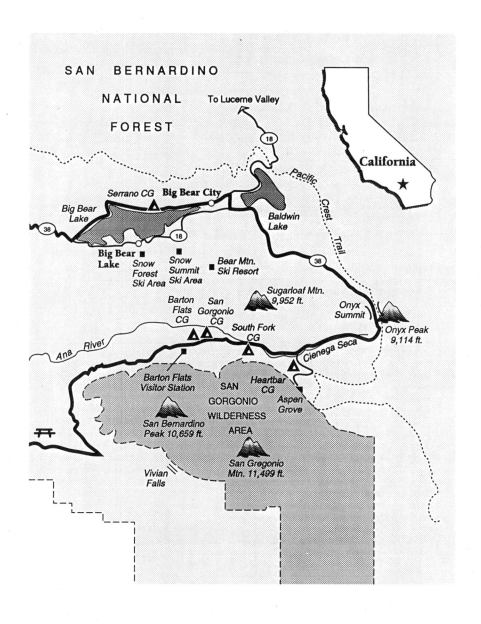

Summer temperatures can be in the nineties at the drive's start and in the cool seventies atop the mountains. Expect night temperatures as low as fifty degrees. Afternoon thunderstorms are frequent in late summer. Spring and fall offer brisk, but mild weather, while winters are cold and snowy from November to March. Snowfall totals reach forty-five to fifty inches each winter. Be prepared for icy roads during or after winter storms by using snow tires or carrying chains.

The drive begins at the national forest boundary on the north side of San Bernardino. Travel north on Waterman Avenue (California 18) from Interstate 10 to the forest boundary. Waterman Avenue is a north-south street and also can be reached by driving east from Interstate 215. The highway, as it enters the national forest, crosses the famed San Andreas Fault at the base of the San Bernardino Mountains.

The San Andreas Fault or Rift Zone stretches some 650 miles from the Mexican border to Cape Mendocino north of San Francisco and is one of the world's longest and most active faults. The fault zone, varying from 100 yards to a mile wide, separates the enormous Pacific and North American crustal plates. The two plates have been creeping past each other for the last thirty million years at an rate of about two inches annually. Geologists call the slippage along the horizontal fault a strike-slip fault. It creates frequent earthquakes, but tremors, occurring almost daily, are generally unnoticed. Most movement along the fault occurs in large, sudden jumps. The plates become locked against each other, and strain builds until a quick release creates an earthquake. The greatest movement recorded in historic times was the twenty-one feet the fault slipped at Point Reyes in the 1906 San Francisco earthquake. Big Bear Lake was the epicenter of a June 1992 quake along a branch fault of the San Andreas. The San Andreas Fault runs through San Gorgonio Pass between the San Bernardino and San Jacinto mountains along the southern base of the San Bernardinos then northwest through Cajon Pass and along the northern edge of the San Gabriel Mountains.

After entering the national forest, the drive begins climbing steeply up the western, chaparral-covered slopes of Waterman Canyon. The four-lane road rapidly gains elevation, reaching 4,000 feet after only eight miles. Two overlooks, Inspiration and Panorama points, provide excellent views. After nine miles, the highway narrows to two lanes and joins California 138 and the national forest Rim of the World Scenic Byway. By twelve miles, the road levels out and begins winding east along the mountain crest.

Baylis Park Picnic Area sits along the granite rim surrounded by a shady forest of pine, oak, and cedar. Marvelous views of San Bernardino and the lofty San Jacinto Mountains lie to the south. The area is named for John Baylis, who was instrumental in having the drive built in the early 1900s.

At nearby Rimforest, a two-mile drive up Bear Springs Road leads to 6,153-foot-high Strawberry Peak Lookout. The fire lookout is staffed during the fire season from May to November and offers great views of the surrounding forest including Lake Arrowhead. Dogwood Campground, with ninety sites, lies north off the highway.

A lone hiker in the San Bernardino Mountains along the Rim of the World Drive.

The drive runs east along the mountain rim and passes California 173. This short highway runs north two miles to Lake Arrowhead, an attractive lake lined with summer cabins. Unfortunately for recreationists, most of the lake's shoreline is private property, and only landowners can launch boats. Get information and maps of San Bernardino National Forest at the Arrowhead Ranger District office, which is just before Skyforest and past the turn to Lake Arrowhead. The 650,000-acre forest, including both the San Bernardino and San Jacinto ranges, is America's most used national forest. Lying within two hours of some ten million people, the forest records more than six million visitor-use days annually. Switzer Park Picnic Area is near the ranger station.

Heaps Peak Arboretum, at 5,996 feet, offers a good, short nature hike that introduces visitors to the area's plant life. This site was devastated by a 1922 forest fire. Trees were replanted beginning in 1928 until World War II. In 1982 the Rim of the World Interpretative Association, in cooperation with the U.S. Forest Service, began to develop the area into an arboretum. The easy 0.7-mile-long trail loops through the forest, passing a variety of native trees including Coulter, ponderosa, Jeffrey, and sugar pines, California black oak, incense cedar, white fir, Pacific willow, and Pacific dogwood. A small grove of giant sequoias, planted in 1930, already lift their stately crowns high above the forest floor. When they mature in another thousand years or so, they will take their place as some of the world's largest living things.

Past Heaps Peak, the drive turns away from the rim and passes through Running Springs and Arrowbear Lake, both small resort towns with food and lodging. A good side trip turns east on Forest Road 1N96 at Deer Lick Ranger Station just past Running Springs to reach the National Children's Forest. Three miles up the road is a forest that burned in 1970. Contributions by concerned school children helped replant the area in 1971. A handicapped-accessible trail, with interpretive signs in Braille, meanders through the forest. The forest road continues to 7,882-foot Keller Peak Lookout.

The drive runs east up shallow Snow Valley, past Snow Valley Ski Area, Ski Green Valley, and Rim Nordic Ski Area. This high area is studded with granite boulders and coated with an open forest of oaks and pines. It is popular with cross-country skiers in winter. The established ski areas here and at Big Bear Lake pile up lots of man-made snow and offer skiing until late March.

Past Snow Valley, the road climbs to a divide that separates the Pacific and Great Basin drainages. An overlook here, Lake View Point, offers glimpses of azure Big Bear Lake and beyond to the rugged snowcapped peaks in the San Gorgonio Wilderness Area. The drive twists east under the windy, fir-clad summits of Crafts and Butler peaks to Big Bear Lake. California highways 18 and 38 join here at the stone dam. Go north or left on route 38 around the lake's north shore. The south side of the lake, including the town of Big Bear Lake, is a residential and business area.

Seven-mile-long, 3,000-acre Big Bear Lake was formed by an arch dam completed in 1911. This and an earlier dam built in 1884 provided cities in the San Bernardino Valley with water. This dam on the Bear Creek branch of the Santa Ana River often released most of the lake's water for downstream irrigation until the 1970s when agreements between land owners and water users stabilized the lake level. The small, original lake here was given its present name in 1845 when a posse of ranchers searching for Indian cattle rustlers shot twenty-two bears in the area.

The placid lake is now lined with resort facilities and the towns of Big Bear Lake and Big Bear City, offering a wide range of outdoor recreation. Campers use Colbrook and Pineknot campgrounds on the south shore and 132-site Serrano Campground on the north shore. Fishermen angle for trophy-sized rainbow and brown trout, large channel catfish, both large-and small-mouthed bass, panfish, and crappie. Three ski areas—Snow Summit, Bear Mountain, and Snow Forest—adorn the wooded slopes south of the lake.

The drive skirts the lake's north shoreline, winding through pine woodlands and open meadows. Grout Bay Picnic Area, on a spit of land south of the town of Fawnskin, is a good spot to see bald eagles in winter. The Big Bear area protects as many as thirty bald eagles, the largest winter population in southern California. Further down the lake past Serrano Campground is Meadow's Edge Picnic Area, a boat ramp, and Big Bear Ranger Station. A pamphlet is available here on the self-guided auto tour for the Gold Fever Trail. The tour meanders on gravel roads through Holcomb Valley north of the lake, past the remnants of an 1860s gold rush that includes abandoned mines, cabins, arrastres, and a solitary grave. Two-mile-long Cougar Crest Trail begins a half mile west of the ranger station at a parking area off the drive. The trail climbs north through a mixed conifer forest to the Pacific Crest National Scenic Trail. The Pacific Crest Trail offers easy day and overnight hikes in the Big Bear Lake region.

East of the lake, about three miles from the ranger station, California 38 rejoins route 18. Turn south on 38 and continue through Big Bear City and across the wooded Bear Valley. After a few miles, the drive leaves the summer cabins behind and rolls past shallow canyons filled with open areas of sagebrush and rabbitbrush and scattered woodlands of western juniper and Jeffrey pine. The road climbs onto the broad, east shoulder of Sugarloaf Mountain, thick with juniper and mountain mahogany, and then crests 8,443-foot Onyx Summit, the drive's high point.

Past the summit, the road drops south, swings west along Cienaga Seca Creek, and six miles later reaches ninety-four-site Heart Bar Campground. A rough forest road heads south from the campground's west end and climbs up to the Aspen Grove Trailhead on the edge of 59,969-acre San Gorgonio Wilderness Area. A short walk up Fish Creek leads to one of two known groves of quaking aspen in California's southern mountains. The other grove lies in a steep gully southeast of Big Bear Lake. Aspens, one of North America's most widely distributed trees, are commonly found in the Rockies, Canada, northeastern United States, as well as handsome groves alongside high Sierra meadows. The farthest south that aspens grow is atop the San Pedro Martir Mountains in Baja California. The wilderness area also harbors limber pines as old as 2,000 years, endangered Nelson bighorn sheep, mountain lions, coyotes, eagles, bobcats, raccoons, mule deer, and black bears.

The drive runs west, first along the Santa Ana River and then edging the forested slopes south of the river. Three more excellent campgrounds—South Fork, San Gorgonio, and Barton Flats—lie along this road section. These make wonderful overnight stops, with grassy meadows and towering Jeffrey and sugar pines. Jenks Lake near Barton Flat and the Santa Ana River both offer good trout fishing. These campgrounds also serve as jumping off points for backpackers heading into the San Gorgonio Wilderness. South Fork Trailhead is popular. The glacier-sculpted summit of 11,499-foot San Gorgonio Mountain looms in the south almost nine miles away. More than ninety-six miles of trails lace the wilderness area leading to deep canyons, meadows sprinkled with iris, lupine, and shooting star, and magnificent views of the surrounding deserts.

Barton Flats Visitor Center dispenses information on the San Bernardino National Forest and the San Gorgonio Wilderness Area, including maps, books, and free wilderness permits. Permits are required to enter the wilderness, protecting its delicate ecosystems from over-use. Daily quotas limit the number of backcountry travelers departing from trailheads and ensure a quality wilderness experience. Several good nature trails thread through the forest near the ranger station. The easy Ponderosa Nature Trail interprets the area's plant communities and wildlife, while the Whispering Pines Nature Trail uses Braille signs to introduce physically challenged visitors to the forest.

Past the visitor center, the drive winds west and then south for eleven miles around the densely forested flank of San Bernardino Peak. On the mountain's south side, the road quickly loses elevation, passing from the conifer forest into brushy chaparral. At the bottom of Mill Creek Canyon, a broad valley paved with rocky cobbles and boulders, the highway sharply swings west. A good side trip heads east here up Forest Home Road. At the road's end, a short trail crosses Mill Creek and climbs to the national forest's tallest waterfall on Vivian Creek. Monkeyface and Forest Falls are farther west down the canyon. All the falls are best seen in early spring when melting snow swells the otherwise trickling streams.

The highway drops west down Mill Creek Canyon, passing Thurman Flats Picnic Area. A mile later the scenic drive leaves the national forest and recrosses the San Andreas Fault. The drive ends a couple miles later at Mill Creek Ranger Station. Forest information, maps, and wilderness permits are available here. Highway 38 continues west into Redlands and joins Interstate 10.

20 CALIFORNIA 243 & 74
Palms to Pines Highway

General description: A sixty-six-mile-long, two-lane highway that climbs from Banning over the scenic San Jacinto Mountains and down into Palm Desert in the Coachella Valley.

Special attractions: San Bernardino National Forest, Mount San Jacinto State Park, San Jacinto Wilderness Area, Idyllwild, Lake Hemet, Santa Rosa Wilderness Area, Palm Springs Aerial Tramway, scenic overlooks, hiking, backpacking, camping, rock climbing, fishing, boating.

Location: Southern California. The drive begins in Banning off Interstate 10 about eighty miles east of Los Angeles and ends in Palm Desert thirteen miles southeast of Palm Springs on California Highway 111.

Drive route name and numbers: California highways 243 and 74, Palms to Pines Highway.

Travel season: Year-round. The upper reaches of the drive receive snow in the winter. Temperatures in the lower valleys, however, are mild with highs in the sixties and seventies. Expect hot weather in summer, particularly near Palm Desert, with highs in the 100s. Mountain weather is pleasant. Summer weekends can be very busy.

Camping: Many campgrounds scatter across the San Jacinto Mountains. Nine San Bernardino National Forest campgrounds are found. Pinyon Flat, on the drive's east end, is open year-round with eighteen sites. Many others lie on the cool mountain slopes north of Idyllwild, including Fern Basin, Dark Canyon, and Marion Mountain. Idyllwild County Park Campground, just west of Idyllwild, offers large RV sites and showers. Two state park

The San Jacinto Mountains flank the Warner Valley and Palms to Pines Highway.

campgrounds, Idyllwild and Stone Creek, are along the drive near Idyllwild. Hurkey Creek Campground sits across the road from Lake Hemet. Most are closed in the winter.

Services: All services, including gas, food, and lodging, are found in Banning, Idyllwild, and Palm Desert.

Nearby attractions: Rim of the World Scenic Byway, Palm Springs, Palm Springs Desert Museum, Living Desert Reserve, Joshua Tree National Park, Anza-Borrego State Park, Cleveland National Forest, Salton Sea, Mecca Hills County Park, Los Angeles area attractions.

For more information: San Bernardino National Forest, 1824 S. Commercenter Circle, San Bernardino, CA 92408-3430, (714) 383-5588. Palm Desert Chamber of Commerce, 72-990 Hwy. 111, Palm Desert, CA 92260, (619) 346-6111. Mount San Jacinto State Park, P.O. Box 308, 25905 State Highway 243, Idyllwild, CA 92349, (909) 659-2607.

The drive: The Palms to Pines Highway, following California highways 243 and 74, is exactly that—a sinuous sixty-six-mile-long highway that climbs from the palm-studded lowlands of the Coachella Valley and Palm Springs to lofty pine forests that cling to the steep, rocky slopes of the San Jacinto Mountains. The San Jacintos are the northernmost sierra in the Peninsular Range, a long chain of mountains that extends southward to the tip of Mexico's Baja California. The San Jacintos present an immense front to the east that forms one of North America's tallest mountain escarpments—over 10,000 vertical feet lies between 458-foot-high Palm Springs and the wind-swept summit of 10,804-foot San Jacinto Peak. This huge difference in elevation makes a drive into the San Jacintos a telescoped journey from Mexico's Sonoran Desert ecosystems to the subalpine forests and Arctic tundra of northern Canada perched along the range crest.

The differences in elevation make a marked difference in climate and temperature along the drive. While summer temperatures in Palm Desert regularly register above 110 degrees, the temperatures in Idyllwild rarely climb out of the eighties. Summer days are generally clear and calm, with occasional afternoon thunderstorms atop the mountains. Winters are very pleasant in the Coachella Valley with highs in the sixties and seventies. The weather is more unpredictable in the mountains with snow falling along the drive's upper elevations. Spring brings strong winds to San Gorgonio Pass on the drive's north end. The pass funnels powerful Pacific air currents down the Coachella Valley and sweeps clouds of dust and sand toward the Salton Sea. Annual precipitation ranges from six inches in Palm Springs to more than thirty-six inches in the mountains.

The scenic drive begins at the 8th Street Exit on Interstate 10 in Banning east of Los Angeles. Turn south from the interstate and follow California Highway 243. Banning, platted by stagecoach operator Phineas Banning in 1883, sits on broad San Gorgonio Pass. The pass separates the San Jacintos from the San Bernardino Mountains, part of the Transverse Ranges that run west to the Pacific Ocean. The heralded San Andreas Fault, a huge rift zone that marks the boundary between the North American and Pacific crustal plates, passes along the eastern margin of the San Jacinto Mountains and runs northwest through the 2,500-foot-high pass. The pass has long been a pathway between California's interior desert and the Los Angeles basin. Early Indian trails passed through it; and later it was a stage route followed by the Southern Pacific Railroad and Interstate 10.

The road winds sharply up steep mountain slopes south of Banning, crossing arid hillsides strewn with rounded granite boulders. After three miles, the road reaches 3,000 feet and enters a chaparral ecosystem. Chaparral dominates much of southern California, cloaking the region's hot, dry land with dense shrubbery up to fifteen feet high. The chaparral plants, including chamise, coffeeberrry, bear brush, quinine bush, scrub oak, and manzanita, survive with thick, woody trunks and small, leathery leaves that conserve precious moisture. Chaparral generally claims the middle range of mountain slopes, forming a transition zone between desert plants and mountain forests on warm, south-facing hillsides.

After twisting upward for seven miles, the grade levels out on McMullen

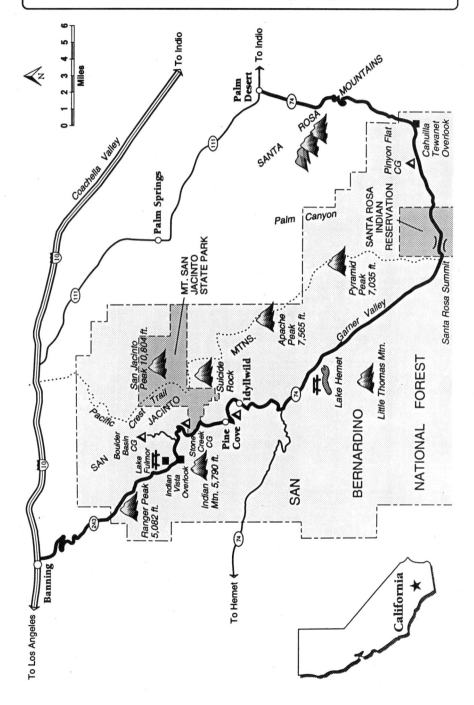

20

Flat and enters thick stands of oak and the San Bernardino National Forest. The 650,000-acre forest is America's most used national forest. It encompasses both the San Jacinto and San Bernardino mountains. By eleven miles, the drive reaches 5,000 feet and pines scatter among the oak woodland. The drive runs along the western edge of Black Mountain Scenic Area and passes two-acre Lake Fulmor. This small lake, backed up east of the highway, offers good trout fishing in spring, summer, and fall. A short nature trail threads through the surrounding Kellogg oak, pine, and manzanita forest.

Past the lake, the highway climbs onto a ridge and stops at Indian Vista Point. This overlook offers marvelous views to the west. The San Jacinto Valley, sprinkled with green farms and orderly towns, spreads out below. Further west towers the long ridge of the Santa Ana Mountains topped by 5,687-foot Santiago Peak above the glint of Lake Elsinore. The snowcapped crowns of the San Gabriel and San Bernardino mountains loom to the northwest, while Palomar Observatory's white dome atop forested Palomar Mountain rises in the southwest. Closer at hand lies chaparral-covered 5,790-foot Indian Mountain.

The drive winds east and then south into the heart of the San Jacinto Mountains. A mixture of black oak, sugar, Coulter, ponderosa, and Jeffrey pine woodland lines the highway, with a thick undergrowth of ferns and flowers in lush, well-watered side-canyons. Two forest roads leave the main highway and explore the mountains. Forest Road 4S01 climbs five miles to thirty-site Boulder Basin Campground, a great overnight spot shaded by pines, firs, and tall manzanitas. The road continues on to Fairview Point overlooking San Gorgonio Pass. Further down the drive, Forest Road 4S02 provides access to Fern Basin, Marion Mountain, and Dark Canyon forest campgrounds. Trout fishing is good in nearby streams. Fuller Mill Creek Picnic Area sits alongside the highway just past the Boulder Basin turnoff.

Just past the forest road turnoffs, the highway skirts the edge of 13,521-acre Mount San Jacinto State Wilderness and Park, a mostly wild park land that adjoins the national forest's San Jacinto Wilderness Area. The park, traversed by the Pacific Crest Trail, boasts fifty-four miles of trail and four peaks more than 10,000 feet, including 10,804-foot San Jacinto Peak, southern California's second highest summit. The peak is best climbed by ascending the strenuous 5.6-mile-long Marion Mountain Trail, which switchbacks up through thick forest to the bald, windswept mountaintop. The Palm Springs Aerial Tramway ascends the east flank of the park, climbing 4,000 feet from Chino Canyon near Palm Springs to a lofty vantage point at Mountain Station. The state park operates two campgrounds. Stone Creek Campground, off Forest Road 4S02 offers fifty sites; and Idyllwild Campground, next to park headquarters in Idyllwild, has thirty-three sites.

The drive meanders through the town of Pine Cove and drops down into Idyllwild, a picturesque resort community nestled in Strawberry Valley. The town was originally called Raynetta by George Hannah, its first postmaster, after his two children Raymond and Henrietta. Laura Rutledge, who managed a tuberculosis sanitarium here, called a second post office in a local hotel

Granite boulders scatter across steep hillsides above the Palms to Pines Highway.

Idyllwild and residents began using that name. The Idyllwild County Visitors Center, with displays on the area's history and natural history, lies just north of town along the highway.

The town offers lodging and dining and is surrounded by mountains. To the east towers 8,823-foot Tahquitz Peak. The Cahuilla Indians said the summit was the fearful home of a powerful medicine man who stalked through the canyons at night and made bad weather. Tahquitz and neighboring Suicide Rock are acclaimed rock climbing areas with hundreds of routes ascending their white granite slabs and buttresses. Idyllwild also makes a good base for hikers. Numerous trails roam the forests, canyons, and peaks above town. Good hikes include the Ernie Maxwell Scenic Trail, Devils Slide Trail, and Deer Springs Trail to the domed summit of Suicide Rock.

The road runs south from Idyllwild, descending gradually through a mixed pine and oak forest for a few miles to the junction of highways 243 and 74. The drive turns east on California 74. Palm Desert lies thirty-seven miles ahead. The drive quickly ascends to Keen Camp Summit between Keen Ridge on the east and Baldy Mountain on the west and then drops down into broad Garner Valley. The turn to Lake Hemet and Lake Hemet Picnic Area is almost two miles below the pass summit. The reservoir, tucked between forested ridges, offers good fishing for largemouth bass, channel catfish, bluegill, and rainbow trout. Boating is permitted at Lake Hemet, the largest body of water in the San Jacintos. Hurkey Creek Campground lies east of the highway at the lake turn.

The highway runs southeast through the wide Garner Valley. The trickling South Fork of the San Jacinto River meanders across the valley, passing sagebrush, open pine forests, and grazing cattle. The high ridge of Thomas Mountain dominates the western skyline, while the ragged crest of the southern San Jacinto Mountains marches across the eastern horizon. The Pacific Crest Trail traverses these peaks, which include 7,567-foot Apache Peak, Palm View Peak, and Lion Peak. The Butterfield Overland Mail Company route ran through this valley on its way to Los Angeles and San Francisco. Beginning in 1858, the Butterfield stages carried both mail and passengers. A stage station, now part of a private campground, once sat in Garner Valley.

The road slowly rises past vacation homes in Pine Meadow to the intersection with California Highway 371, and the Pacific Crest Trail. The highway swings east and crosses Santa Rosa Summit. This low pass separates the San Jacinto Mountains from the Santa Rosa Mountains, which are a steep, rugged range seamed by deep canyons with brush and boulder-covered slopes that reach south to Anza-Borrego Desert State Park.

Past the summit, the highway begins dropping toward the Coachella Valley. Pinyon Flats Campground sits seven miles east of the summit. This pretty eighteen-site campground, open year-round, is surrounded by pinyon pines, junipers, yucca, and sagebrush. The southern trailhead for scenic Palm Canyon is three miles west of the campground. The trail twists fourteen miles down the canyon to Palm Springs. The canyon's lower reaches, on the Agua Caliente Indian Reservation, harbor more than 3,000 California fan palms along its year-round stream.

Steep grades begin a mile past the campground as the highway bends around the south flank of conical 4,775-foot Sugarloaf Mountain. Cahuilla Tewanet Vista Point is an excellent overlook just off the highway here. The view is riveting, with the ragged, barren slopes of Deep Canyon falling away below. Southward stretches the Santa Rosa range, its forested peaks spotted with granite outcrops. Much of this land lies within the Santa Rosa Wilderness Area.

After the overlook, the drive leaves the national forest and enters the California Desert Conservation Area administered by the BLM. A viewpoint atop Seven-Level Hill provides a raven's-eye view of Palm Desert, the Coachella Valley, and beyond to the Little San Bernardino Mountains in Joshua Tree National Monument. The steep, dry mountainside below the vista is dotted with widely spaced creosote bushes, yellow-flowered brittlebushes, fleshy agaves topped with slender stalks, crimson-tipped ocotillos, and teddy-bear cholla cacti.

The highway spirals down precipitous slopes below the overlook and in four miles reaches the mountain base. The road passes barren hills and then runs straight into Palm Desert and California Highway 111. Palm Springs lies to the west, while Indio and Interstate 10 are immediately eastward. Besides its salubrious climate, Palm Springs offers several excellent attractions—the Palm Springs Desert Museum with exhibits on the California desert and the Living Desert Reserve, a unique park that displays native plants, animals, and birds in six desert habitats.

21 CALIFORNIA 94
El Cajon to Boulevard

General description: A forty-nine-mile drive that parallels the United States and Mexico border between El Cajon near San Diego and Boulevard on Interstate 10. The drive runs over rolling chaparral-covered mountains and broad valleys.

Special attractions: Tecate (Mexico), Potrero County Park, scenic views, hiking, bicycling.

Location: Far southern California. The drive runs along California 94 from its intersection with California 54 in south El Cajon off Interstate 10 to Boulevard on Interstate 10 in south-central California.

Drive route number and name: California Highway 94, Campo Road.

Travel season: Year-round.

Camping: Camping is available at Potrero and Lake Morena county parks as well as in adjoining Cleveland National Forest.

Services: All services are available in San Diego and El Cajon. Limited services are found in Tecate, Campo, and Boulevard.

Nearby attractions: San Diego attractions, Cabrillo National Monument, Tijuana, Hauser Wilderness Area, Pine Creek Wilderness Area, Cleveland National Forest, Laguna Recreation Area, Cuyamaca Rancho State Park, Anza-Borrego State Park.

For more information: El Cajon Chamber of Commerce, 109 Rea Avenue, El Cajon, CA 92020, (619) 440-6161. Cleveland National Forest, 10845 Rancho Bernardo Road, Rancho Bernardo, CA 92127-2107, (619) 673-6180.

The drive: This forty-nine-mile-long highway traverses rolling chaparral-covered hills and broad valleys in the southern Peninsular Ranges east of San Diego. The drive follows California Highway 94 along the United States and Mexico border between El Cajon and Boulevard and offers an excellent backroad adventure on a seldom traveled scenic route. The mountains separate the hilly country around San Diego from the hot, arid Colorado Desert that spreads eastward from the range base to the Imperial Valley and the Colorado River. The paved, two-lane highway has numerous pull-offs and side roads that explore the surrounding mountains. Traffic, generally local, is light to moderate.

The climate in San Diego and environs is just about perfect. Expect warm summer temperatures between seventy and ninety, with hotter weather in the lower valleys. Both spring and fall temperatures range from sixty to eighty, with cool nights, occasional clouds, and light rain showers. The fierce Santa Ana winds that blow across the desert to the northwest can rage through the mountains in autumn. Winters are mild and pleasant. Expect highs in the fifties and sixties, with chilly nights. Snow is a rarity, even on the higher peaks this far south, although heavy rains fall in February and March.

The drive starts at the intersection of Campo Road or California 94 and Jamacha Road or California 54 in Rancho San Diego just south of El Cajon. Jamacha Road runs south through El Cajon from Second Street and Interstate 8. California 94 begins in downtown San Diego, off Interstate 5, and runs northeast to its junction with route 54. Turn south on highway 94, also called the Campo Highway. The road crosses the usually dry Sweetwater River after a half mile and turns east up broad Steele Canyon. It climbs steadily up the brushy canyon, passing numerous residential areas including Indian Springs and Jamal. After five miles, the highway crosses a low divide and heads across a wide valley broken by hay fields, grazing horses, and small rancheros. Jamal Butte, a rounded cone, looms north of the drive and the low Jamul Mountains rise to the west. Oak and sycamore trees line shallow creeks that seam the undulating valley floor.

The drive descends through a thick oak forest and then follows Dulzura Creek to the small town of Dulzura at 1,240 feet. The road continues past the town along the tree-lined creek, passing small ranches with grassy meadows before reaching Dulzura Summit. White Mountain and Mother Grundy Peak tower to the north, their steep, rounded slopes littered with white granite boulders. The road then drops steeply down the summit's east slope and quickly reaches Cottonwood Creek, a placid stream that meanders through a broad valley. The road then winds up an abrupt, narrow canyon. A dense woodland of oak and sycamore lines Potrero Creek in the canyon alongside the highway. Brushy hillsides climb the steep slopes of 3,406-foot Potrero Peak to the north and Tecate Peak to the south.

Chaparral, which blankets most of the higher mountains along the drive, is a woodland of stunted scrubby trees adapted to the thin hillside soils and dry Mediterranean climate that prevails here. Chaparral plants typically have woody trunks and small, thick leaves that conserve precious winter and spring moisture for the hot, arid summer months. Chaparral covers about seven percent of California and is the dominant plant community of the state's southwestern corner from San Luis Obispo to the Mexican border. It generally thrives on steep mountainsides, while oak woodlands and grass-lands carpet the moister valley floors. Common chaparral species include scrub oak, chamise, and manzanita. One of California's rarest tree species— the Tecate cypress—grows in a few isolated stands on Otay Mountain and Tecate Peak southwest of the drive. The tree thrives on infertile soils that lessen competition from the surrounding chaparral. The trees are relict stands of more extensive cypress forests that flourished in wetter times. Two

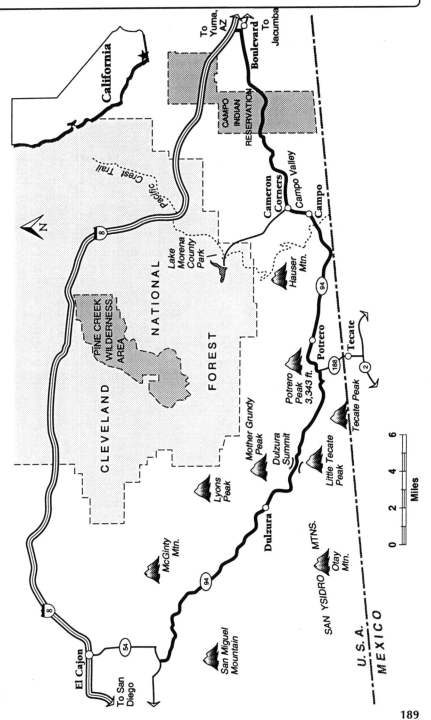

21

CALIFORNIA 94
EL CAJON TO BOULEVARD

To Yuma, AZ

Boulevard

To Jacumba

California

CAMPO INDIAN RESERVATION

Pacific Crest Trail

Cameron Corners

Campo Valley

Campo

N

Lake Morena County Park

Hauser Mtn.

8

94

NATIONAL

Tecate

PINE CREEK WILDERNESS AREA

FOREST

Potrero

188

2

Potrero Peak 3,343 ft.

Tecate Peak

CLEVELAND

Mother Grundy Peak

Dulzura Summit

Little Tecate Peak

Lyons Peak

Miles

6

4

2

McGinty Mtn.

SAN YSIDRO MTNS.

Otay Mtn.

0

Dulzura

94

8

San Miguel Mountain

U. S. A.

MEXICO

54

El Cajon

To San Diego

Tecate Peak straddles the U.S.-Mexico border along California 94 east of San Diego.

other endemic species also inhabit the mountains—Otay manzanita and Otay ceanothus, which is a member of the buckthorn family.

The road steadily climbs above Potrero Creek. White granite boulders, smooth and round from erosion are scattered across the green mountain slopes. In the midst of the canyon, a side road (California Highway 188) turns south and runs three miles south to the border with Mexico and the quaint Mexican village of Tecate, famed for its Tecate "cerveza" or beer. Tecate, unlike Tijuana thirty miles to the west, is a relatively quiet border town. Tecate also is known for its quality, rugged bricks, which are shipped across the border to grace southern California homes and patios. The local brewery and a colorful town fair held late in summer are the popular visitor attractions.

Past the Tecate turn, the drive swings around the southeast flank of brushy-shouldered Potrero Peak, leaves the creek, and enters the small town of Potrero at an elevation of 2,323 feet. Small ranches with open meadows and oak glades are scattered across a rolling basin here. After a couple more miles, the road drops into a wide canyon forested with oak; it then crosses Campo Creek at Canyon City and turns northeast along the stream. The Pacific Crest Trail, running from Mexico to Canada, begins just south of here on the border. The canyon quickly opens into a broad, grassy valley broken with hayfields and flanked by low granite hills. The town of Campo lies on the west end of the Campo Valley. This old town houses the San Diego Railroad Museum, with a good display of numerous old train cars and engines. The highway runs across the valley and then climbs a shallow canyon. A turn in the valley leads north to Lake Morena County Park, a popular fishing reservoir that is occasionally drawn down in summer.

The last nine miles of the drive from the east end of the Campo Valley to Boulevard runs through shallow canyons surrounded by rolling granite-studded hills, which are lightly coated with oaks and sagebrush. As the road runs east, the elevation drops, and the climate dries and warms. The drive ends in Boulevard. Turn north to Interstate 8. California 94 continues east, dropping down to the Mexican border and Jacumba. Eastward spreads the hot Colorado Desert and rows of barren mountain ranges and valleys.

22 JOSHUA TREE NATIONAL PARK SCENIC DRIVE

General description: A sixty-five-mile drive that crosses wide basins studded with creosote bushes and rough granite mountains in Joshua Tree National Park in south-central California.

Special attractions: Lost Palms Oasis, Lost Horse Valley, Hidden Valley, Queen Valley, Joshua trees, Joshua Tree Wilderness Area, hiking, camping, rock climbing, backpacking.

Location: South-central California. The drive's southern start is twenty miles east of Indio off Interstate 10. The road's northern end is at Joshua Tree on California 62, twenty-six miles northeast of Interstate 10. The national park lies 140 miles east of Los Angeles.

Drive route names: Cottonwood Springs Road, Eldorado Mine Road, Loop Road, Quail Springs Road.

Travel season: Year-round.

Camping: The national park has eight campgrounds and three group campgrounds. Black Rock Canyon and Cottonwood campgrounds have running water and flush toilets. Both charge a fee. The other campgrounds have no water and chemical toilets and are free. All are on a first-come, first-served basis, with a fourteen day limit from October to May. Reservations are accepted for Black Rock Canyon Campground and the group campgrounds at (800) 365-CAMP.

Services: All services are available at Indio and Palms Springs to the southwest and Joshua Tree, Yucca Valley, and Twentynine Palms to the north.

Nearby attractions: Palm Springs, Palm Springs Desert Museum, Living Desert Reserve, Anza-Borrego State Park, Salton Sea, East Mojave National Scenic Area, Palms to Pines Scenic Drive, Mount San Jacinto State Park, San Bernardino National Forest, Rim of the World Scenic Drive.

For more information: Joshua Tree National Park, 74485 National Monument Dr., Twentynine Palms, CA 92277, (619) 367-7511. Twentynine Palms Chamber of Commerce, 6136 Adobe Road, Twentynine Palms, CA 92277, (619) 367-3445.

The drive: The Joshua Tree National Park scenic drive wends across sixty-five miles of spectacular desert scenery in southern California. The road slices across wide Pinto Basin flanked by rock-strewn mountains, crosses the ecological boundary between the Colorado Desert and the Mojave Desert, and climbs into valleys studded with bizarre Joshua trees and granite buttresses and boulders. The national park, established in 1936, preserves 558,000 pristine acres of southern California's desert. Included here are extraordinary forests of Joshua trees, an odd yucca that is a member of the agave family. This windy, sunburnt landscape is a place of opposites—a place of parched water holes and palm-shrouded oases, a place of alluvial bajadas and stony mountains, a wild place full of sound and fury, yet a place of serenity and discovery.

The park offers excellent year-round weather. Winters are generally pleasant and dry, with high temperatures in the fifties and sixties. The lowland temperature around Twentynine Palms or Indio is as much as ten degrees warmer than the high desert in Queen Valley. Occasional snow falls in the upper elevations, and nights are chilly. Spring is warm and often windy. Summers can be very hot, although the park highlands are surprisingly cool compared with the inferno in the lower valleys. While Indio or Twentynine Palms roast under 100 degree weather, the park's upper reaches are in the 80s or low 90s. Nights at the higher elevations are also comfortably cool. Afternoon thunderstorms build up on occasional July and August afternoons, unleashing heavy downpours on the desert. The park receives 7.5 inches of rain annually, with forty percent of that falling from July through September. Watch for flooding in canyons and washes after these periodic storms. Autumn brings warm days and clear skies. The fierce Santa Ana winds, strong winds that sweep out of the northeast, often blow across the park in fall. Many of the campgrounds are surrounded by cliffs and boulders, offering some shelter from the gale.

The scenic drive begins on Interstate 10 twenty-four miles east of Indio. Exit the highway and turn north on Cottonwood Springs Road. The road climbs away from the interstate across a wide sloping "bajada" south of the Cottonwood Mountains, and enters Joshua Tree National Monument after one mile. A short distance further the road winds up broad Cottonwood Canyon, its dry wash littered with flood-strewn cobbles. The canyon separates the Cottonwood Mountains on the west from the Eagle Mountains to the east. After six miles, the drive climbs out of the canyon and onto a high bajada north of the mountains. Here, almost seven miles north of the interstate, sits Cottonwood Visitor Center. This small outpost and entrance station dispenses camping and hiking information, answers questions about the park, and offers a few informational displays, books, and maps. East down a short spur road lies the sixty-two-site Cottonwood Campground.

The Coachella Valley and Little San Bernardino Mountains lie below Keys View in Joshua Tree National Park.

An excellent one-mile trail begins in the campground and threads across the barren, rolling hills to lush Cottonwood Spring, an oasis of seeping water surrounded by towering cottonwoods and palms. The spring gushed as much as 3,000 gallons of precious water a day at the turn of the century, but today it is reduced to a meager trickle. The palms were apparently planted around 1920. Cottonwood Spring, like Joshua Tree's other four oases, is formed by faults related to the famed San Andreas Fault that runs along the monument's southwestern border. The faults permit underground water to percolate up along the fault line to the earth's surface where it flows out as a spring. Water in any desert spells relief. Shrubs and trees line the water here providing both a home and a watering hole for thirsty birds and animals. The spring is a good place to observe birds.

The road runs northeast across a gently sloping bajada, crosses Smoke Tree Wash, bends northwest around rough, stony ridges on the eastern end of the Hexie Mountains, and runs across broad Pinto Basin. This huge, barren basin is surrounded by the Pinto Mountains on the north, Coxcomb Mountains on the east, Eagle Mountains on the south, and the Hexie Mountains on the west. The basin encompasses much of the park's central and eastern portions is named for the "pinto" horse colors of 3,983-foot Pinto Mountain to the north. The area was not always so arid. Thousands of years ago during wet postglacial periods the basin was forested and traversed by a meandering river. Ancient peoples found the environment hospitable, with plentiful game and plants. Evidence of their long occupation was found in the 1930s by amateur archaeologist Elizabeth Crozier Campbell in the basin's remote eastern reaches. Spear points, scrapers, and other hunting artifacts of "Pinto Man" have since been uncovered in other parts of the basin and southern California's deserts.

Miners also left their mark on Pinto Basin. Numerous abandoned mines worked between 1880 and 1940 scatter along the basin's edge. The Golden Bell, Eldorado, Golden Bee, and Silver Bell mines lie just south of the drive on the basin's west end. In the 1920s, the basin was the site of a land scam. The Lake County Development Syndicate acquired several parcels in Pinto Basin and proclaimed the sere valley "ready for an attempt at development." Their sales letter promised "...to drill for water...so that in time to come we may see Pinto Basin changed from desert to highly developed ranches and farms." The speculation fell flat when little water was discovered.

Precipitation and temperature, coupled with elevation, determine the plant communities that inhabit a landscape. As one climbs in elevation, the temperature drops and precipitation increases. No where is this eco-maxim more apparent than in deserts. Joshua Tree's highest mountains are fringed with forests of pinyon pine and juniper, plants representative of the Great Basin Desert in Utah and Nevada. The low valleys, like Pinto Basin, are populated by scrubby plants adapted to an extreme climate. Summer temperatures regularly reach 110 degrees and less than four inches of rain falls in a year. Creosote bush, the basin's dominant plant, scatters across the ground. This shrub, with green waxy leaves and yellow flowers in spring, is

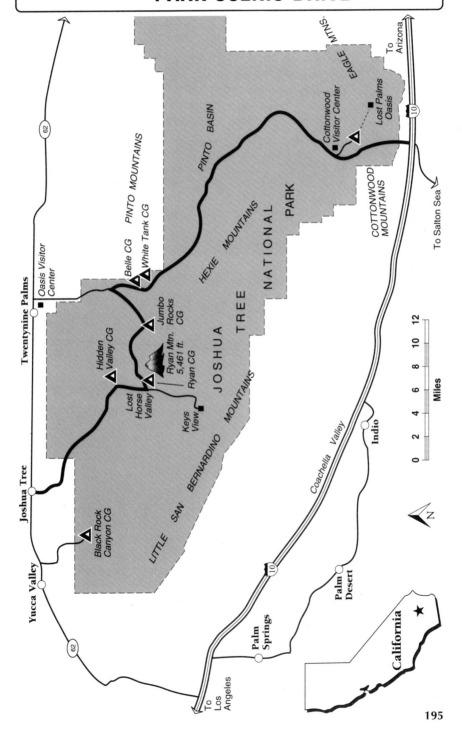

one of the desert's hardiest and oldest plants. The creosote, instead of growing in size as a single plant, sends out branches that root themselves as a clone of the original. Northwest of the park in Johnson Valley grows King Clone, a seventy-foot-long, twenty-five-foot ellipse that has thrived for more than 11,700 years—the world's oldest known living organism.

Joshua Tree National Park and Pinto Basin balance on the edge of two of North America's great deserts. The Colorado Desert subdivision of the vast, lowland Sonoran Desert lies to the south, while the higher Mojave Desert is to the north. The two deserts meet and mingle in the park. The transition zone where the two meet runs along the south and north sides of Pinto Basin. As the road heads west across the basin, it slowly climbs and leaves the Colorado Desert's characteristic plants—smoke tree, ocotillo, fan palm, palo verde, and cacti. A couple interesting stops explore these plants.

First, the road passes the Ocotillo Patch. The ocotillo is a strange plant of spindly arms studded with thorns. Rain brings a coat of leaves to the branches and bright crimson flowers on their tips. A mile and a half further lies the Cholla Cactus Garden. A short, self-guiding trail explores a dense stand of Bigelow cholla. This cactus, nicknamed "Teddy bear" and "jumping" cholla, is covered with a thick mat of long spines, each hooked with a microscopic barb. If the cactus is accidently brushed against, the spines attach onto the new host and the joint detaches itself from the cactus to be re-rooted elsewhere. Many people who frequent the desert carry pliers to remove the painful joint when hiking in cactus country. Other plants seen along the trail include: buckhorn and pencil cholla, calico cactus, climbing milkweed, and jojoba.

After the cholla garden, the drive ascends the western slope of the basin and after three miles enters a broad canyon. A couple miles later the road empties onto a high, rolling plain broken by rounded granite outcrops. Two campgrounds sit just east of the drive—fifteen-site White Tank and seventeen-site Belle. Both are peaceful overnight spots surrounded by eroded rocks. Short Arch Rock Trail explores the rock maze east of White Tank Campground, passing a unique granite arch. A short scramble south from the arch leads through a narrow, cliff-lined passage to the remains of White Tank, a small catchment built by early cattlemen to provide water for their stock. Farther east a couple miles hides Grand Tank, another stock dam with water up to twenty feet deep during wet seasons. A rough 1.25-mile path heads cross-country to this large water hole.

A couple miles past Belle Campground or thirty-seven miles from Interstate 10, the drive intersects the park's Sheep Pass Loop Road. Turn west on this road; it turns right and drops eight miles down Utah Trail to Twentynine Palms and the park headquarters and visitor center. The drive runs southwest and after two miles passes Live Oak and Split Rock picnic areas. A narrow dirt road twists south to Live Oak Tank, a small dam built by early cowboys. The large oak that gave the site its name towers against a rocky outcrop called Pope's Head. The unusual oak is a hybrid, a cross between the valley oak and the turbinella oak. Jumbo Rocks Campground, with 130

Joshua trees and granite boulders border the narrow Joshua Tree National Park scenic drive.

campsites, lies a mile and a half farther up the drive. This spacious campground nestles in a maze of jumbled granite—Jumbo Rocks—with each site well-spaced and private. Excellent 1.7-mile Skull Rock Trail begins at the campground's amphitheater and winds through the tors and boulders to rounded Skull Rock. Signs along the trail explain desert plants and geology. Past the rock the trail crosses the road and slices through bedrock canyons before looping back to the campground entrance.

After Jumbo Rocks, the drive enters Queen Valley and the heart of Joshua Tree National Park. This huge valley, bounded on the north by Queen Mountain, spreads its broad floor southward to a low divide separating it from Pleasant Valley. The road runs across the valley through a ragged forest of Joshua trees, a fanciful plant that resembles trees found in Dr. Suess books. The Joshua tree, one of California's most striking plants, has elicited strong reaction from travelers. Explorer John C. Fremont called them in 1844 "the most repulsive tree in the vegetable kingdom." J. Smeaton Chase wrote in

1919, "A landscape filled with Joshua trees has a nightmare effect even in broad daylight; at the witching hour it can be almost infernal." Forty-niner William Manly said they were "a brave little tree to live in such a barren land." While early pioneers called them "dagger trees," it was Mormon colonists en route to southern California who saw them as the Biblical prophet Joshua lifting spiked arms heavenward in supplication and prayer.

The Joshua tree, *Yucca brevifolia*, is the Mojave Desert's symbolic plant. The plant's range from southeastern California to southern Nevada and northwestern Arizona closely follows the desert's boundaries, occurring generally above 3,500 feet. Here in the park, the tree's southernmost limit, the Joshua tree grows in the higher, moister valleys in the monument's northern reaches. The tree, a huge yucca, grows as tall as forty feet with a diameter of four feet. It's difficult to ascertain the age of the monument's biggest Joshua trees, but with an annual growth rate of 1.5 centimeters the oldest are at least 800 years old. The Joshua tree forests harbor a wide array of animals that rely upon the tree for shelter and food. More than twenty-five bird species nest in the branches and feed on insects in the tree. Wood rats build nests using the tree's spiked leaves. Termites, night lizards, and snakes use fallen trees for shelter. But the most amazing relationship is between the Joshua tree and the pronuba yucca moth. It appears that the moth, in exchange for pollinating the yucca flowers, is allowed to lay its eggs in the tree's developing fruit. The moth larvae eat some of the yucca seeds before boring out of the fruit wall and start the process over again. The yucca was also the tree of life to area Serrano and Chemehuevi Indians, who ate the seeds and fruit, used the fibers for sandals and baskets and the roots for a laxative and shampoo.

Just after the drive enters Queen Valley, the dirt Geology Tour Road heads south. This self-guiding nature road is an eighteen-mile round trip that runs across Queen Valley. It then passes over a low divide and drops down to Pleasant Valley between the Hexie and Little San Bernardino mountains. The road is not always passable in a two-wheel drive vehicle; ask at the visitor center for road conditions. A road guide keyed to numbered posts is available at the road start and at the park visitor center.

The drive passes through Joshua tree forests in Queen Valley before crossing Sheep Pass and entering Lost Horse Valley. This spectacular valley is studded with bulging granite rock piles that scatter across the valley like an archipelago of islands. Much of the park's granite is 100-million-year-old monzogranite exposed on the earth's surface as the overlying gneiss eroded away. The dark gneiss still caps the park's high peaks, but the pink and white granite dominates the northern valleys. Groundwater etched out cracks in the granite along weak joints, and water erosion attacked the rock forming the jumbled rock piles. A good trail that overlooks Queen and Lost Horse valleys begins a half mile west of Sheep Pass Group Campground. The three-mile round-trip trail climbs 800 feet to the 5,461-foot summit of Ryan Mountain. Indian Cave, a rock shelter used by ancient Indians, lies just west of the trail parking area. Just down the road is twenty-nine-site Ryan

Campground and the site of the abandoned Ryan Ranch. Brothers Thomas and Jep Ryan had a small ranch here to provide water for their Lost Horse Mine. The ranch house burned in 1978. Nearby are eight graves, each ringed by boulders.

Beyond Ryan Campground, the drive turns sharply north at Cap Rock. An excellent side trip begins here and heads south six miles to Keys View, one of Joshua Tree's most spectacular views. The road traverses southern Lost Horse Valley, passing a thick stand of Joshua trees. A four-mile trail runs from the Keys View Road to Lost Horse Mine. This hike explores the park's gold mining legacy. The mine eked out $350,000 between 1896 to 1900. The mine closed after the rich lode met a fault and disappeared. Today, all that remains are building foundations, cyanide settling ponds, and a stamp mill that crushed and processed the gold ore. Be cautious when walking around the mine site, dangerous pits and tunnels remain.

Turning away from the valley, the road climbs into the Little San Bernardino Mountains and ends at 5,185-foot Keys View. The overlook takes in one of California's grandest scenes: to the south glimmers the Salton Sea, the state's lowest point; to the southwest spreads the Coachella Valley floor, adorned with Palm Springs and Indio; the huge escarpment of the San Jacinto Mountains towers almost 10,000 feet above the valley, the high ridges and basins coated with snow; and west lies San Gorgonio Pass, gateway to Los Angeles, Mount San Gorgonio, southern California's highest peak, and the forested San Bernardino Mountains. The viewpoint is named for pioneer rancher and miner Bill Keys, who lived here from the early 1900s to his death in 1969 at age eighty-nine. Keys' Desert Queen Ranch, in the park's northern part, preserves a slice of the old West. Tours are given almost every weekend from fall through spring; ask at a visitor center for a schedule.

The drive runs north from Cap Rock to thirty-nine-site Hidden Valley Campground. This area of rough granite domes and jumbled boulders is center stage for Joshua Tree National Park's rock climbers. More than 4,000 established climbing routes adorn the park's rocks. The mild winter and spring weather, coupled with diverse climbing challenges from easy beginner slabs to extreme bolted sport routes and vertical cracks, attract climbers from around the world. Some of the park's best and most accessible routes lie a stone's throw from Hidden Valley Campground. Intersection Rock at the campground entrance, The Old Woman and The Blob on the west side, and The Wall and Chimney Rock on the east all offer a plethora of excellent free climbs. Further afield lies the vast Wonderland of Rocks, Real Hidden Valley, Saddle Rock, and the classic Headstone Rock at Ryan Campground. Several excellent climbing guides are available.

Hidden Valley, west of the campground, is a good place to explore on foot. A good one-mile trail begins at the Hidden Valley Picnic Area and winds back to the hidden rock-rimmed valley once reportedly used by cattle and horse rustlers to hide their stolen stock.

The drive, following Quail Springs Road, runs northwest from Hidden Valley and passes valleys flanked by granite ridges and domes and covered with Joshua trees and creosote bushes. After a few more miles, the road begins to descend. The road crosses the park boundary almost nine miles from Hidden Valley. An entrance station here offers displays and visitor information. The drive drops down along Quail Wash, passing scattered homes and ends on California Highway 62 in the town of Joshua Tree. A turn west leads down the Twentynine Palms Highway to Yucca Valley and Interstate 10. A turn east leads fifteen miles to Twentynine Palms and the park's main visitor center. Two side roads along this stretch lead to Indian Cove Campground and lush Forty-nine Palm Oasis, where an excellent three-mile, round-trip hike climbs to a palm-lined desert water hole.

23 ANZA-BORREGO DESERT STATE PARK DRIVE

General description: A ninety-two-mile drive that runs through Anza-Borrego Desert State Park, passing remote canyons, eroded badlands, and sharp desert peaks.

Special attractions: Anza-Borrego Desert State Park, Southern Emigrant Trail, Box Canyon, California fan palm groves, Carrizo Badlands, Pacific Crest Trail, scenic views, hiking, camping, backpacking, four-wheel roads, spring wildflowers, historic sites, wildlife.

Location: Far southern California. The drive's southern start is eighty-five miles east of San Diego at Ocotillo on Interstate 8. The northern terminus is at the drive's junction with California 79 just south of Warner Springs.

Drive route numbers and names: Imperial County S2 (Imperial Highway), San Diego County S2 (Great South Overland Stage Route), California 78, San Diego County S3 (Yaqui Pass Road), San Diego County S22 (Montezuma Valley Road and San Felipe Road).

Travel season: Year-round. Expect hot temperatures in the summer, every day is usually over 100 degrees. Be prepared by carrying adequate water and supplies. Best travel season is October through May.

Camping: Two developed campgrounds—Borrego Palm Canyon Campground with fifty-two hookup sites, sixty-five non-hookup sites, and five group sites and Tamarisk Grove with twenty-seven sites. All have drinking water, showers, and restrooms. Make reservations for October through May, especially for weekends, through MISTIX at 1-800-444-7275. There are nine additional primitive campgrounds, with fees charged only at Bow Willow. The rest are dry, bring your own water. The park also has an open camping policy. Camp within one car length of a dirt road and not near developed campgrounds or water holes. Additional camping is at Agua Caliente County Park and Vallecito Stage Station County Park.

Services: All services, including gas, food, and lodging, at Borrego Springs.

The Anza-Borrego Desert State Park drive nears the summit of arid Yaqui Pass.

Limited services at Ocotillo.

Nearby attractions: Salton Sea (245 feet below sea level), Cuyamaca Rancho State Park, Julian, Cleveland National Forest, Sunrise Scenic Byway, Palomar Mountain State Park, Palomar Observatory.

For more information: Anza-Borrego Desert State Park, P.O. Box 299, Borrego Springs, CA 92004-0299, (619) 767-4684.

The drive: Anza-Borrego Desert State Park is a place of superlatives. California's largest state park stretches across a 600,000-acre wonderland of barren bajadas and alkali playas, broken badlands, abrupt canyons filled with graceful palms, and rock-rimmed mountain ranges. The park's diverse terrain, ranging from a high point of 6,193 feet on its western border to lowlands just above sea level near the Salton Sea, harbors an incredible diversity of wildlife habitats, plant communities, and climates. The park also boasts a colorful history that includes the 1774 route of Spanish explorer Juan Bautista de Anza, the 1849 Southern Emigrant Trail, and the famous Butterfield Overland Stage line of 1858. The park's name reflects its unique history and natural history—Anza honors its human exploration and Borrego, a Spanish term for bighorn sheep, symbolizes its wild desert heart. This ninety-one-mile-long scenic drive travels over four different paved roads, explores the park's wonders, offers spectacular scenery, excellent camping, numerous historic sites, and great hiking trails.

Anza-Borrego Desert State Park is best considered a three-season park land. Summers can be prohibitively hot. Expect daily high temperatures to be well above 100 degrees. Daytime temperatures in July, the warmest month, average 107 with nightime lows dropping to 75 degrees. August's average highs are 106 degrees. When traveling here in summer, make sure your vehicle is in good operating condition and carry lots of water. Five gallons is not too much for a morning drive. Be sure to carry water and wear a hat when hiking in summer. Cooler temperatures are found west of the park atop the coastal ranges. Fall, winter, and spring days are pleasant, with highs ranging between sixty and ninety degrees. Winter nights can be chilly. Annual precipitation at park headquarters is 6.7 inches. January is the wet month, receiving only 1.2 inches of precipitation; while June is the driest, receiving no precipitation.

The drive begins ninety miles east of San Diego at the Interstate 8 interchange at Ocotillo. Head north into Ocotillo on Imperial County Road S2. After two miles, the road heads northwest and leaves Ocotillo behind as it runs across a dry bajada. Cholla cacti and ocotillo scatter across the wide plain. Shell Canyon Road, offering an interesting side trip, begins on Ocotillo's outskirts. This road heads north into Fossil Canyon in the Coyote Mountains. The canyon boasts numerous fifty-million-year-old marine fossils, including coral and oysters in its rocks. This area is part of the Yuha Desert Recreation Area administered by the Bureau of Land Management.

After about eight miles, the road enters San Diego County and Anza-Borrego Desert State Park. The road follows a broad valley filled with detritus

ANZA-BORREGO DESERT STATE PARK DRIVE

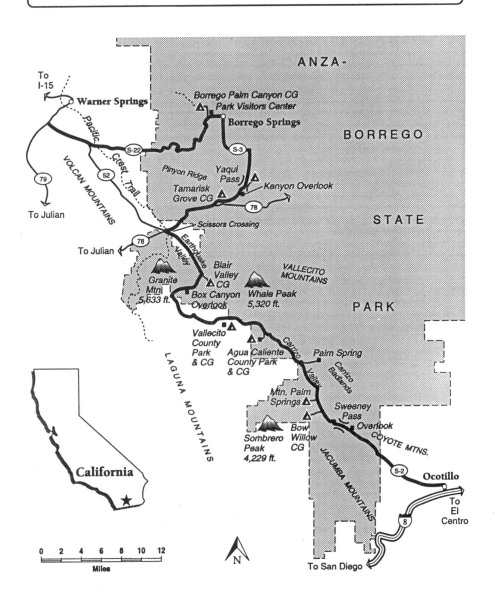

and flanked by the barren Coyote Mountains on the north and the Jacumba Mountains on the south. These ranges, a jumbled mass of uplifted granite and sedimentary layers, form intermediate steps between the below sea-level Salton Trough to the east and the 6,000-foot coastal ranges to the west.

After a few miles of slow climbing, the road passes Carrizo Badlands Overlook. This vista offers spectacular views into a badlands dissected by Carrizo Creek and its dry tributaries. A rainbow of colors—jade, yellow, white, rose, and cobalt—shade the twisted rock layers below. The sediments here have yielded a wealth of fossils, including saber tooth, mastodon, zebra, giant sloth, bison, llama, and camel that inhabited a fertile savanna over two million years ago. More than 170 species of marine shellfish have also been identified here in lake and sea deposits. The park is considered one of North America's greatest repositories of Pliocene and Pleistocene fossils. A jeep road winds down Canyon Sin Nombre just north of the overlook into the heart of the badlands.

Just past the viewpoint, the road crosses 1,065-foot Sweeney Pass and drops down Sweeney Canyon to Carrizo Creek. Three miles from the overlook a dirt road runs south to Bow Willow Campground and the entrance to Bow Willow Canyon. The primitive campground offers sixteen sites. A good hike meanders up the canyon, passing desert willows and California fan palms.

Just up the road lies Mountain Palm Springs, an interesting oasis tucked into the dry granitic Tierra Blanca Mountains west of the road. Ground water seeps along fault lines and waters six palm groves scattered along rock canyon floors. A half-mile hike up the north arm of Mountain Palm Springs Canyon leads to North Grove and Mary's Bowl Grove. Rare elephant trees are also found here. A half mile up the south canyon branch sits Pygmy Grove, with fifty palms, and further on lies the Southwest Grove. A free, waterless, primitive campground sits at the canyon mouth.

The California fan palm, *Washingtonia filifera*, grows in scattered isolated colonies in Baja California, southwestern Arizona, and southeastern California. The trees thrive around springs in mountain canyons, forming lush oases that attract birds and animals. The park boasts twenty-five palm groves hidden in canyons. The palms reach heights of fifty feet with a trunk diameter of three feet. Dead leaves hang down from the palm's crown, forming a heavy skirt. The trees, unlike other desert plants that wait patiently for rain, need a plentiful and constant supply of water. Here in the park the palms are generally found along faults associated with the San Jacinto and Elsinore faults, two main splinters of the San Andreas Fault, where ground water is forced upward along fault lines. The Cahuilla Indians, Shoshonean speakers in the park's north section, and the Kumeyaay Indians, Yuman speakers in the south, long relied on the palm oases for food, water, and shelter. Numerous archeological sites, including bedrock mortars, potsherds, and rock art recall their life in this austere land.

A few miles up the drive a side road bumps east to Palm Spring, a state historical landmark. From Ocotillo to Scissors Crossing, the drive follows the route of the old Southern Emigrant Trail and the Butterfield Stage Line. Palm

The Anza-Borrego Desert State Park drive crosses Yaqui Pass and descends into the Borrego Valley.

Spring, with its water and shade, made an ideal stage stop between the Carrizo Station to the east and the Vallecito Station to the west. The twenty-four-day stagecoach journey began in Missouri and ran more than 2,000 miles to San Francisco. Travelers complained bitterly of bad food, searing temperatures, and motion sickness. The Southern Emigrant Trail was a popular winter route to California and its gold fields in the 1850s. Most pioneers rejoiced when they reached the cool, shaded springs of Anza-Borrego after crossing the hot, arid trail from Yuma called "Jornada del Muerto" or Journey of Death.

Juan Bautista de Anza used an historic trail corridor east of here in 1774 in search of a good land route from Sonora, Mexico, to the California settlements. At the time, the Spanish sought to reinforce their northern California outposts to stave off a growing Russian presence. Captain de Anza and his scouting party marched northward through today's park, up Coyote Canyon between the San Ysidro and Santa Rosa mountains, and into California's interior. A year later he returned with settlers, including 125 children, bound for Monterey. In upper Coyote Canyon north of Borrego Springs in the park's north section, the Anza Expedition Monument marks the spot where Salvador Ygnacio Linares was born on December 24, 1775, one of California's first non-Indian natives.

The scenic drive travels northwest up broad Carrizo Valley and reaches Agua Caliente County Park nine miles from Palm Spring. This San Diego County park land surrounds a number of warm mineral springs that gush up along the Elsinore Fault. The park offers a shady campground and a store. A pleasant 1.5-mile hike climbs up Moonlight Canyon south of the campground to a low saddle.

The drive runs four miles up a narrowing canyon carved by Vallecito Creek on the north flank of the Tierra Blanca Mountains to Vallecito Stage Station County Park. This interesting park is another California historical landmark. It protects a reconstructed replica of this famous stage stop on the Butterfield Overland Mail route. The green marshes or cienegas along Vallecito Creek here were a welcome sight to parched travelers on the emigrant trail. This shaded spot in the broad Vallecito Valley lies beneath the green forested Laguna Mountains. A sod house was first built here in 1851 to protect pioneers from marauding Indians. It was expanded a few years later to a stage station. Butterfield Stage passenger Waterman Ormsby described the area in 1858, "Vallecito, or Little Valley, is a beautiful green spot—a perfect oasis in the desert...the green bushes and grass are a most refreshing relief from the sandy sameness of the desert." The park also has a campground and picnic area.

Past the county park, the road runs across broad Vallecito Valley. After three more miles, the road climbs steeply north over low mountains onto Mason Valley, a high, dry plain. The wagon-wheel ruts of the Southern Emigrant Trail are visible to the southeast as the road climbs out of Vallecito Valley. The drive swings east into abrupt Box Canyon on the valley's east side. Rough 5,633-foot Granite Mountain looms to the north. Box Canyon Monument, a mile up the draw, offers interpretations of the history for the pioneer trails that traversed the park. Box Canyon is a significant historical site. The Mormon Battalion under the command of Lt. Colonel Philip St. George Cooke hacked a wagon trail through the rocky canyon just south of today's roadway, using only hand tools. This opened the first wagon road into southern California. Traces of two old roads can be seen from the roadside overlook—the Mormon Battalion trail above and the later Emigrant and Butterfield Mail routes below.

The drive turns north from Box Canyon and traverses the eastern slope of Granite Mountain. A turnoff leads south for a half mile to an historic marker on the Butterfield Mail Route in Blair Valley. A short hike leads from the marker up the well-preserved ruts of the old trail to Foot and Walker Pass on a rough divide that separates Blair and Earthquake valleys. Passengers on the stage line and Forty-niners on the Emigrant Trail often had to walk and push their wagons over this steep pass. Nearby is the free but primitive Blair Valley Campground.

Road S-2 runs northwest up Earthquake Valley another six miles to its intersection with California 78 at Scissors Crossing. The valley is named for the regular tremors that occur along the Elsinore Fault, a major branch of the San Andreas Fault, that runs west of the valley. Scissors Crossing, named for the scissors-shaped convergence of roads here, was long the site of Indian villages and later the San Felipe Stage Station in the 1870s. Grassy cienegas or marshes watered by the perennial flow of San Felipe Creek made the area an attractive site.

Borrego Valley spreads out below the Anza-Borrego Desert State Park drive.

Turn east from S-2 onto California 78. The highway runs east past Sentenac Cienega, a lush marshland alive with birds and green plants that look out of place in this otherwise dry country. After a mile, the drive winds down narrow Sentenac Canyon. A tangle of tamarisk, willows, and cottonwoods line the twisting creek, while rocky hillsides above are studded with agaves and cacti. After a few more miles, the canyon opens into a broad, barren valley filled with alluvium. The drive follows the creek down the valley and reaches its next intersection with Road S-3 (Yaqui Pass Road) after seven miles. Turn northeast on county road S-3.

Tamarisk Grove Campground, with twenty-seven sites shaded by towering tamarisk trees, lies a quarter-mile up S-3. This developed campground has showers, running water, and restrooms; it usually requires reservations on weekends in the busy winter and spring seasons. Two short trails loop into the desert near the campground. The mile-long Cactus Loop Trail winds across the rocky desert and offers a great introduction to the area's diverse desert plants. The Yaqui Well Trail travels 0.8-mile to a desert water hole that harbors an excellent selection of birds, including long-eared owl, Gambel's quail, ladder-backed woodpecker, canyon wren, western meadowlark, and house finch. More than 260 bird species have been identified in Anza-Borrego.

Yaqui Well, as well as other spring-fed oases, are also excellent places to spot the park's thirsty wildlife. Almost sixty mammal species, including twenty bat species and three types of kangaroo rats, inhabit the park's diverse landscape. Park mammals commonly seen are black-tailed hare, Audubon cottontail, antelope ground squirrel, skunk, raccoon, southern mule deer, and coyotes. Rarer animals are the mountain lion, bobcat, kit fox, ringtail, and the elusive Peninsular bighorn sheep. The bighorn or "borrego" ranges across the park's lofty peaks and rocky canyons. The park protects about 300 of the nation's 400 sheep. Three populations scatter across the park in the Santa Rosa Mountains, Vallecito Mountains, and Carrizo Gorge. The bighorns are often seen in fall and early winter along the park roads.

The drive climbs steeply northeast up the flank of Pinyon Ridge. After 1.5 miles, Kenyon Overlook is reached. This pull-off offers great views south to the ragged Pinyon and Vallecito mountains and east to the glimmering blue Salton Sea. Past the overlook, the road climbs over 1,750-foot Yaqui Pass and drops north down a broad bajada to Borrego Valley. Yaqui Pass primitive campground lies just east of the drive.

The drive meets Borrego Springs Road 5.5 miles north of the pass and bends left. Six miles later S-3 intersects San Diego County Road S-22 in the town of Borrego Springs. Head west on S-22. Borrego Valley was originally settled by ranchers including John McCain and the Clark Brothers. Later homesteaders planted alfalfa fields and citrus groves. Borrego Springs today is famed for its pink grapefruit and offers all services to travelers, including gas, groceries, lodging, and four golf courses.

The Anza-Borrego park headquarters and visitor center lies just west of town. The earth-bermed visitor center offers excellent displays on the park's natural history, geology, and history as well as naturalist-led programs. North of the visitor center is 117-site Borrego Palm Canyon Campground and an excellent hike up Borrego Palm Canyon to a shady palm grove. Palm Canyon Creek, which occasionally dries up in summer, shelters a lush riparian oasis. The hike is the park's most popular trail. It is filled with sound—the descending scale of a canyon wren, the rustle of palm-thatching in the wind, and the sweet song of running water.

The drive, following S-22, climbs steeply south from the visitor center up rocky mountainsides. Winding in and out of dry canyons, the road quickly gains elevation. As it ascends, the roadside vegetation begins changing from desert plants to thick chaparral that covers rounded granite hills. Great viewpoints along the road offer vistas of Borrego Valley and the Salton Sea. Eleven miles from the visitor center the drive crosses a lofty ridge crest and drops west into a broad grassy valley interrupted by dense oak groves and occasional pine trees. After the road crosses the Pacific Crest Trail, it ends at its junction with Road S-3 Continue west on S-2, San Felipe Road, down the broad valley alongside Buena Vista Creek for five miles to the drive's end at California Highway 79.

24 KELSO-CIMA ROAD/KELBAKER ROAD SCENIC DRIVE

General description: This fifty-nine-mile-long scenic drive, following two desert back roads, traverses a spectacular slice of the 1.5-million-acre East Mojave National Scenic Area past granite mountains, sand dunes, broad basins, and Joshua tree forests.

Special attractions: Cima Dome, Kelso Depot, Kelso Sand Dunes, Granite Mountains, camping, hiking, spring wildflowers, Joshua trees, wildlife, bird watching.

Location: Southeastern California in the East Mojave National Scenic Area between Interstates 15 and 40. The Kelbaker Road junction with I-40 lies seventy-nine miles east of Barstow. The Cima Road junction with I-15 is eighty-seven miles northeast of Barstow.

Drive route names: Kelbaker Road, Kelso-Cima Road, and Cima road.

Travel season: Year-round. Expect hot summers with temperatures regularly over 100 degrees. It is ten to twenty degrees cooler in the surrounding mountain ranges.

Camping: Camping is permitted anywhere on public land within the East Mojave National Scenic Area. Two established BLM campgrounds, Mid Hills Campground and Hole-in-the-Wall Campground, lie east of the scenic drive off the Black Canyon Road. Further south is a campground at Providence Mountains State Recreation Area. Good primitive camping is at Kelso Dunes.

Mountains State Recreation Area. Good primitive camping is at Kelso Dunes.
Services: No regular services are found along the drive. Be sure your gas tank is full before leaving on the drive. Complete services are found in Barstow, Needles, Baker, and Las Vegas, Nevada.

Nearby attractions: Mitchell Caverns, Providence Mountains State Recreation Area, Wild Horse Canyon Back Country Byway, Ivanpah-Lanfair Back Country Byway, Essex Road Back Country Byway, Cedar Canyon Back Country Byway, Lake Mead National Recreation Area, Joshua Tree National Park, Amboy Crater, New York Mountains, Cinder Cones National Natural Landmark, Calico Early Man Site, Lake Havasu, Las Vegas.

For more information: BLM, California Desert Information Center, 831 Barstow Road, Barstow, CA 92311, (619)256-8617. BLM, Needles Resource Area, P.O. Box 888, Needles, CA 92363, (619) 326-3896.

The drive: This scenic drive, following Kelbaker Road, Kelso-Cima Road, and Cima Road, crosses fifty-nine miles of austere desert landscapes in the 1.5-million-acre East Mojave National Scenic Area. This sprawling land is studded with sharp mountain ranges that tower above broad alluvium-filled valleys, a timeless place of distant horizons. At first glance, the desert there appears lifeless and inhospitable. But closer inspection reveals details of life—tree-lined springs that echo with bird songs; the showy colors of spring wildflowers draped across dry arroyos; and the sinuous track of a nocturnal sidewinder etched on a sand dune.

The East Mojave National Scenic Area was established in 1980. Administered by the Bureau of Land Management, this is the pristine heart of the Mojave Desert, one of North America's five great deserts. The Mojave Desert reaches from the San Gabriel and San Bernardino mountains eastward to the Colorado River and northward past Death Valley to the dry basins of southern Nevada. The desert's southern boundary is roughly marked by Interstate 10. The immense national scenic area includes twenty-six named mountain ranges, the nation's third highest dune field, water-sculpted caverns, lava flows, cinder cones, wide basins, dry lakes, and a human history that dates back 10,000 years to early paleo-hunters who camped along ancient lake shores.

Weather along the drive is generally pleasant in spring, fall, and winter. Expect warm days and cool nights. Winter highs range between forty and seventy, with occasional light rain showers or a dusting of snow. Summers are hot, with daily highs often climbing to 110 degrees in the lower valleys. Temperatures are more moderate in the mountains, including the Mid Hills and Cima Dome, and fall between 80 and 100. Summer nights rapidly cool off. The Mojave Desert averages less than eight inches of annual precipitation, much of it falling in the form of violent summer thunderstorms in July and August. Be aware of flash flooding and don't drive across any flooded section of road.

The drive begins seventy-nine miles east of Barstow on Interstate 40 at the highway interchange with Kelbaker Road. Kelbaker Road heads north,

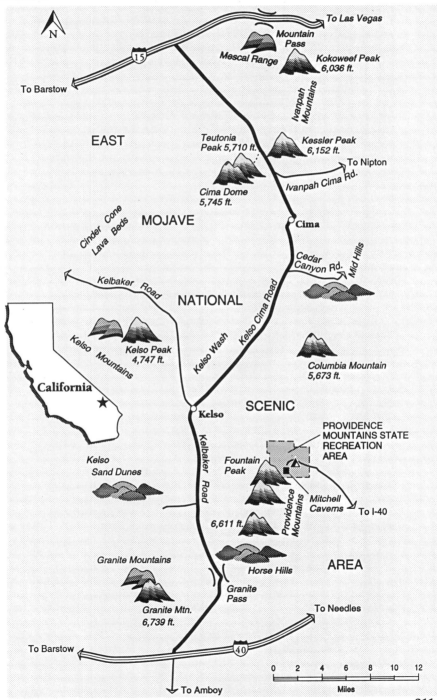

N

To Las Vegas

To Barstow

Mountain Pass

Mescal Range

Kokoweef Peak 6,036 ft.

Ivanpah Mountains

EAST

Teutonia Peak 5,710 ft.

Kessler Peak 6,152 ft.

To Nipton

Cima Dome 5,745 ft.

Ivanpah Cima Rd.

Cinder Cone Lava Beds

MOJAVE

Cima

Cedar Canyon Rd.

Mid Hills

Kelbaker Road

NATIONAL

Kelso Cima Road

Kelso Wash

Kelso Mountains

Kelso Peak 4,747 ft.

Columbia Mountain 5,673 ft.

California

Kelso

SCENIC

PROVIDENCE MOUNTAINS STATE RECREATION AREA

Kelso Sand Dunes

Fountain Peak

Kelbaker Road

Mitchell Caverns

To I-40

Providence Mountains

6,611 ft.

Granite Mountains

Horse Hills

AREA

Granite Pass

Granite Mtn. 6,739 ft.

To Needles

To Barstow

40

To Amboy

0 2 4 6 8 10 12

Miles

swinging around the east flank of the tall, rounded Granite Mountains. This rough range, studded with gleaming white granite crags, reaches its high point atop 6,753-foot-high Granite Mountain. Van Winkle Mountain, a broad mesa rimmed by an ancient lava flow, towers east of the road.

After almost six miles, the road turns to graded gravel for four miles. This dirt section allows desert bighorn sheep to travel from the Providence Mountains to the east into the Granite Mountains. The finicky sheep won't cross a hard-surfaced highway, only dirt. The diminutive desert bighorn, one of the rarest big game animals in North America, roams these high desert mountains. The sheep find "tinajas" or natural tanks filled with water from summer cloudbursts hidden in steep canyons.

The drive tops out on Granite Pass at eight miles from the Interstate at a wide saddle separating the Granite and Providence Mountains. Kelbaker Road drops arrow-straight north into a broad basin rimmed with mountains. Seven miles north of Granite Pass a dirt track bumps west three miles across a creosote-covered plain to Kelso Dunes. Creosote, "hediondilla," is called little stinker in Mexico. Creosote is a successful, drought-resistant plant that thrives in conditions that few other plants can endure. The widely spaced bushes suck up all moisture allowing little competition from other plants. Creosote are also some of the world's oldest known plants. A creosote stand, called "King Clone," lies forty miles south of Barstow (See Joshua Tree National Park Scenic Drive). This plant is the clone of a parent bush that lived some 12,000 years ago after the last ice age. Some botanists say that makes it the world's oldest living thing.

The Kelso Dunes form the third highest dune field in the United States, after Colorado's Great Sand Dunes and California's Eureka Dunes. The Kelso Dunes are one of the Mojave Desert's outstanding features. Windswept and 600-foot-high in places, the gleaming white dunes were formed by persistent westerly winds that scoured the dry Mojave River floodplain to the west, transporting loose sand to this natural trap. Other restless winds from the north and east balance the strong westerlies and keep the dune field from advancing eastward.

The dunes are a great place to explore. Park at the road's end and set off on foot. The dunes are closed to all off-road vehicle use to protect their fragile plant and animal communities. Springtime brings a tapestry of flowers to the dunes. Delicate white desert primroses creep among hollows in the dunes, sunflowers display shades of brilliant yellow, and pink sand verbena grow among the fore-dunes. Slender ricegrass stalks, laden with seed, nod in the wind. Myriad animal tracks meander across the dunes in the morning, including a lace work of beetle, lizard, mice, and kangaroo rat tracks and the S-shaped track of the sidewinder rattlesnake. Allow a couple hours to make a round-trip hike to the dune's high point. When you come down the steep faces of the dunes, listen for a low rumbling vibration caused by the sand grains rubbing against each other. These resonant chords gave the dunes the nickname "the singing dunes."

Past the dunes, the drive continues dropping into the Kelso Valley and

The abandoned Kelso Depot, an historic railroad station, lies along the Kelso-Cima scenic drive in the East Mojave National Scenic Area.

reaches the old railroad town of Kelso, which is along Kelso Wash eight miles north of the dunes turnoff. Kelso lies along the Union Pacific Railroad tracks and owes its very existence to the golden age of railroading in the early twentieth century. The town is dominated by the Kelso Depot, a Spanish-style railroad stop built in 1923. The only other remaining Union Pacific Railroad depot is now the city hall of Caliente, Nevada. Kelso's huge station served as a passenger stop and freight office, supplying overnight accommodations for both passengers and crews. The Beanery, the depot's restaurant, reportedly served the finest meals in the California desert. Deep water wells at Kelso supplied water for the steam locomotives. Kelso also housed the "helper engines" that pushed trains up the long grade to Cima. The depot closed in 1985 and now lies empty. In 1991, the Union Pacific Railroad donated the depot to the Bureau of Land Management, who along with the Kelso Depot Fund, is soliciting donations to restore this exceptional piece of western Americana for use as a visitor center for the East Mojave National

Scenic Area.

The drive turns northeast in Kelso on the Kelso-Cima Road. The Kelbaker Road continues northeast past the Devil's Playground and the Cinder Cone Lava Beds to Baker on Interstate 15. The Kelso-Cima Road parallels the railroad tracks for twenty miles to Cima. Creosote scrub dominates the roadside.

The Providence Mountains combined with the Mid Hills and the New York Mountains to the north forms a ragged range almost fifty miles long east of the drive. The highest point in the Providence Mountains is 7,171-foot Providence Peak, a sawtooth ridge of rough limestone. Bold cliffs, steep canyons, and sharp aretes characterize the entire mountain range. These desert mountains are half-buried in alluvial debris washed by quick flash floods from the peaks, leaving long, low-angle slopes or "bajadas" that drop away from the rocky mountainsides.

The seemingly sun-baked mountains teem with life. Cooler temperatures atop the 6,000-foot peaks coupled with twenty to thirty inches of rainfall allow forests of pine and white fir to cloak the upper slopes. The Cedar Canyon Road, fourteen miles from Kelso, gives access to the pinyon pine and juniper forest atop the Mid Hills. A BLM campground here can be a cool place to stop in summer. Farther south lies Mitchell Caverns with two small caves. The state-run park offers cave tours, camping, and hiking.

Joshua trees begin lining the road just before it reaches Cima. Cima is a Spanish word meaning summit. The railroad station was established here in 1907. It is another old railroad stop that is almost deserted. At Cima, the drive turns north on the Cima Road. The paved highway steadily climbs through one of California's thickest and most extensive Joshua tree forests. The Joshua tree is the most spectacular and characteristic plant of the Mojave Desert. It generally grows along the higher, moister margins of the desert. Conditions here along the drive are ideal for the Joshua tree, with plenty of water and sunshine. These Joshua trees are a slightly different species than the ones seen in Joshua Tree National Park to the south. This subspecies, named *Yucca brevifolia Jaegeriana* for the famed California desert naturalist Edmund C. Jaeger, grow larger than their southern cousins.

Joshua trees were named by early Mormon travelers for their resemblance to the prophet Joshua with up-raised arms. The trees provide a rich habitat for animals, birds, and insects. This tree-sized yucca, reaching heights of forty feet, depends on the *Pronuba* moth for fertilization of its flowers in a unique symbiotic association. The desert night lizard lives under Joshua tree debris, and more than twenty-five bird species nest in the yucca trees, including the beautiful Scott's oriole. Flickers and ladder-backed woodpeckers both dig nesting holes in Joshua trees. Look for owls and hawks perched on the branches. Fossilized dung of the extinct giant sloth indicates that as much as eighty percent of their diet was Joshua tree leaves.

After a few more miles, Cima Road passes between the long, jagged ridge of 6,512-foot Kessler Peak to the east and rounded Cima Dome. This huge, symmetrical dome is composed of quartz monzonite, a granitic rock formed when a large mass of underground magma cooled. The rounded dome is coated with Joshua trees, covers seventy-five square miles, and is ten miles in diameter. Craggy, white rock outcrops stud the dome. Teutonia Peak, at 5,755 feet, is the highest crag in the area. A two-mile-long trail leaves the drive seven miles north of Cima at a wide parking area and climbs to the peak's rocky summit. Marvelous views of the surrounding ranges and basins unfold from here. Cooler temperatures are found along this section of the drive with its 5,000 foot elevation. Good primitive campsites are also found along this road section.

The main road descends northwest from Cima Dome into the broad Shadow Valley. The lofty and roughly upturned layers of the Ivanpah Mountains dominate the eastern horizon. As the road drops, it begins to flatten. The bordering Joshua tree forest slowly thins and gives way to the creosote plant community. The drive ends on Interstate 15, just west of Mountain Pass and the Nevada border and eighty-seven miles northeast of Barstow.

Ferns and redwood sorrel in Del Norte Coast Redwoods State Park on U.S. 101, the Redwood Highway.

ABOUT THE AUTHOR

Stewart M. Green is a freelance photographer and writer living in Colorado Springs, Colorado. His photographs appear in many national publications. He is the author and photographer of *Pikes Peak Country: The Complete Guide, Colorado Parklands, Back Country Byways,* and *Scenic Driving Arizona.* He is currently working on *Scenic Driving New England.*

MAP INDEX

NOTES

NOTES

get
FALCON GUIDED

FALCON GUIDES ® are available for where-to-go hiking, mountain biking, rock climbing, walking, scenic driving, fishing, rockhounding, paddling, birding, wildlife viewing, and camping. We also have FalconGuides on essential outdoor skills and subjects and field identification. The following titles are currently available, but this list grows every year. For a free catalog with a complete list of titles, call FALCON toll-free at 1-800-582-2665.

SCENIC DRIVING GUIDES

Scenic Driving Alaska and the Yukon
Scenic Driving Arizona
Scenic Driving the Beartooth Highway
Scenic Driving California
Scenic Driving Colorado
Scenic Driving Florida
Scenic Driving Georgia
Scenic Driving Hawaii
Scenic Driving Idaho
Scenic Driving Michigan
Scenic Driving Minnesota
Scenic Driving Montana
Scenic Driving New England
Scenic Driving New Mexico
Scenic Driving North Carolina
Scenic Driving Oregon
Scenic Driving the Ozarks including the
   Ouchita Mountains
Scenic Driving Texas
Scenic Driving Utah
Scenic Driving Washington
Scenic Driving Wisconsin
Scenic Driving Wyoming
Back Country Byways
National Forest Scenic Byways
National Forest Scenic Byways II

HISTORIC TRAIL GUIDES

Traveling California's Gold Rush Country
Traveler's Guide to the Lewis & Clark Trail
Traveling the Oregon Trail
Traveler's Guide to the Pony Express Trail

WILDLIFE VIEWING GUIDES

Alaska Wildlife Viewing Guide
Arizona Wildlife Viewing Guide
California Wildlife Viewing Guide
Colorado Wildlife Viewing Guide
Florida Wildlife Viewing Guide
Idaho Wildlife Viewing Guide
Indiana Wildlife Viewing Guide
Iowa Wildlife Viewing Guide
Kentucky Wildlife Viewing Guide
Massachusetts Wildlife Viewing Guide
Montana Wildlife Viewing Guide
Nebraska Wildlife Viewing Guide
Nevada Wildlife Viewing Guide
New Hampshire Wildlife Viewing Guide
New Jersey Wildlife Viewing Guide
New Mexico Wildlife Viewing Guide
New York Wildlife Viewing Guide
North Carolina Wildlife Viewing Guide
North Dakota Wildlife Viewing Guide
Ohio Wildlife Viewing Guide
Oregon Wildlife Viewing Guide
Tennessee Wildlife Viewing Guide
Texas Wildlife Viewing Guide
Utah Wildlife Viewing Guide
Vermont Wildlife Viewing Guide
Virginia Wildlife Viewing Guide
Washington Wildlife Viewing Guide
West Virginia Wildlife Viewing Guide
Wisconsin Wildlife Viewing Guide

■ *To order any of these books, check with your local bookseller*
   *or call FALCON® at **1-800-582-2665**.*

Visit us on the world wide web at:
www.falconguide.com

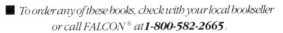

get
FALCON GUIDED

■ *To order any of these books, check with your local bookseller*
or call FALCON® at **1-800-582-2665** .

Visit us on the world wide web at:
www.falconguide.com

FALCON®

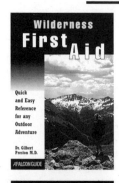
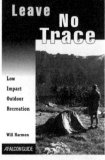